Dramas at Westminster

MANCHESTER
1824

Manchester University Press

POLITICAL ETHNOGRAPHY

The Political Ethnography series is an outlet for ethnographic research into politics and administration and builds an interdisciplinary platform for a readership interested in qualitative research in this area. Such work cuts across traditional scholarly boundaries of political science, public administration, anthropology, social policy studies and development studies and facilitates a conversation across disciplines. It will provoke a re-thinking of how researchers can understand politics and administration.

Previously published titles

Dramas at Westminster

Select committees and the quest for accountability

Marc Geddes

Manchester University Press

Copyright © Marc Geddes 2020

The right of Marc Geddes to be identified as the author of this work has been asserted by him in accordance with the Copyright, Designs and Patents Act 1988.

Published by Manchester University Press
Altrincham Street, Manchester M1 7JA, UK
www.manchesteruniversitypress.co.uk

British Library Cataloguing-in-Publication Data is available

ISBN 978 1 5261 3680 0 hardback
ISBN 978 1 5261 6042 3 paperback

First published by Manchester University Press in hardback 2020

This edition published 2021

The publisher has no responsibility for the persistence or accuracy of URLs for any external or third-party internet websites referred to in this book, and does not guarantee that any content on such websites is, or will remain, accurate or appropriate.

Typeset by Newgen Publishing UK

For my grandparents
Für meine Großeltern

Contents

Tables

Series editor's preface

Ethnography reaches the parts of politics that other methods cannot reach. It captures the lived experience of politics; the everyday life of political elites and street-level bureaucrats. It identifies what we fail to learn, and what we fail to understand, from other approaches. Specifically:

1. It is a source of data not available elsewhere.
2. It is often the only way to identify key individuals and core processes.
3. It identifies 'voices' all too often ignored.
4. By disaggregating organisations, it leads to an understanding of 'the black box', or the internal processes of groups and organisations.
5. It recovers the beliefs and practices of actors.
6. It gets below and behind the surface of official accounts by providing texture, depth and nuance, so our stories have richness as well as context.
7. It lets interviewees explain the meaning of their actions, providing an authenticity that can only come from the main characters involved in the story.
8. It allows us to frame (and reframe, and reframe) research questions in a way that recognises our understandings about how things work around here evolve during the fieldwork.
9. It admits of surprises – of moments of epiphany, serendipity and happenstance – that can open new research agendas.
10. It helps us to see and analyse the symbolic, performative aspects of political action.

Despite this distinct and distinctive contribution, ethnography's potential is rarely realised in political science and related disciplines. It is considered an endangered species or at best a minority sport. This series seeks to promote the use of ethnography in political science, public administration and public policy.

The series has two key aims:

1. To establish an outlet for ethnographic research into politics, public administration and public policy.

2. To build an interdisciplinary platform for a readership interested in qualitative research into politics and administration. We expect such work to cut across the traditional scholarly boundaries of political science, public administration, anthropology, organisation studies, social policy, and development studies.

As a student, I found the lectures on Parliament a bore. As a lecturer, I taught UK Politics 101 and dreaded the reading for those lectures. Too many books and articles were worthy but unexciting. It was like wading through sticky mud. So, a little part of me picked up Marc Geddes' manuscript on the UK House of Commons with trepidation. I sighed, put a Steven Wilson LP on the record deck, and settled in for an uninspiring couple of hours. I was so wrong. In my hands, I had the best book on the UK Parliament by a political scientist since Emma Crewe's *Lords of Parliament* (Manchester University Press 2005), and she is an anthropologist.

Marc Geddes asks three questions:

1. How can we understand the everyday lives of parliamentary actors?
2. How do political actors interpret and perform their roles?
3. In what ways do everyday practices affect accountability in parliaments?

To answer these questions, he undertook participant and non-participant observation of the select committees of the House of Commons. He worked as a research assistant to a select committee in the House of Commons for 14 weeks during the second half of the 2010 Parliament (about 600 hours). He supplemented this work with negotiated access to observe the private meetings of other committees, and 100 hours of sessions available on www.parliamentlive.tv. He supplemented observation with 46 semi-structured interviews with select committee members (23), chairs (10) and staff (13). He facilitated a focus group with eight parliamentary officials. Finally, he drew on data such as official reports, briefings and statistics. It was an exercise in partial immersion that gave him many opportunities to immerse himself in the everyday life in the House.

There are two central arguments in this book. First, the study of Parliament does not have to remain mired in a descriptive institutional approach or preoccupied with prescribing reforms of the House. We can draw on other subfields of political science to refresh our approach. In this particular instance, Marc Geddes draws on interpretive theory and the methods of ethnography to provide such refreshment. He unpacks the individual beliefs, everyday practices, webs of belief or traditions, and dilemmas faced by parliamentarians.

Second, he uses metaphors from the theatre to explore how committee members perform. He is a wandering spotlight, or Super Trooper©, beaming in on the several performing styles of members: specialists, lone wolves, constituency champions, party helpers, learners and absentees. Similarly, with the chairs, he finds they work with committee members or they act as chieftains, imposing their agenda on the committee. Committee hearings are theatre. The chair is the lead actor; the committee members are the supporting cast; the clerks act as stage directors; briefing papers are scripts; the public are the spectators; and committee rooms are the stage. In his phrase, MPs' performances build a 'web of scrutiny'.

In sum, focusing on the concepts of beliefs, practices, traditions and dilemmas offers novel ways of understanding parliamentary scrutiny. The core of this approach is telling our story about other people's stories. We recover their stories to explain what they are doing and why. The dramas in the theatre of Parliament is Marc Geddes' storyline for inscribing complex specificity in context, or writing a thick description. His book is a significant addition to the increasingly diverse literature of parliamentary studies.

Professor R. A. W. Rhodes
University of Southampton
Series editor

Acknowledgements

This book stems from a research project that owes a lot of debts – and these acknowledgements printed here will never do justice to the contribution of the people that have helped me on my journey.

It goes without saying that without the support of the House of Commons this study would not have been possible. In particular, I am thankful to Jessica Mulley, Head of the Scrutiny Unit during my fieldwork, for supporting this project. Her patience, feedback and support have been invaluable to this book. It pains me not to be able to directly mention by name and thank the select committee and its members, chair and officials for whom I worked. They know who they are, and I want to thank them for supporting me in so many large and small ways. I would also like to thank my interviewees for participating in this project. One MP, Emma Little-Pengelly, gave me permission for her photo, taken on 3 April 2019 at a particularly fraught time in the House of Commons, to become the cover of this book. To all MPs and officials that have fed into this research in one way or another: it is your candour of thought and your generosity of time that have allowed this book to come to fruition.

I am grateful to the Economic and Social Research Council for their funding in making this project possible; and to the team at Manchester University Press for helping me to turn the project into a book. I had lots of questions to which both the ESRC and MUP have been willing to provide answers and who have been patient in seeing this project finished.

It was at the Department of Politics at the University of Sheffield where the idea of this book took hold and the development of the project's research took place, and it was the academics, staff and students who were immensely supportive. In particular, Matthew Flinders and Kate Dommett have been pillars on which I have relied throughout my time in Sheffield ever since I met them in summer 2010. Matt has given me many opportunities, and his support for this project has been generous, constructive and unfailing. His detailed feedback, plentiful discussions and challenging comments have ensured that this project became a success. Kate's informal advice, meanwhile, has been crucial moral support and helped me to build my confidence as I embarked on an academic career.

Over time, I have also drawn on support from a range of further networks, groups and individuals. The Political Studies Association's Group on Parliaments has been, and continues to be, the place where I can share my ideas openly and freely, and draft ideas for this book came before the PSA Parliaments Group in many guises. Thanks also to the Study of Parliament Group, whose members have provided great insights, feedback and ideas to my research as it developed. Another important thanks must go to the School of Social and Political Science at the University of Edinburgh, where I finished this book – especially James Mitchell, Nida Alahmad, Jan Eichhorn, Meryl Kenny and Alan Convery. I am also grateful to a huge number of individual academics and researchers that have strengthened the arguments I try to make in the subsequent pages. I cannot name them all, but I would like to give particular thanks to Emma Crewe, Cristina Leston-Bandeira, Louise Thompson, Alexandra Meakin, Rod Rhodes, Daniel Gover, Alexandra Kelso, Andrew Hindmoor and Sarah Childs.

Friends have been hugely important to make this happen. Many of them are already named above, but I also wanted to add my thanks to Gemma Bird, Xavier Mathieu, Daniel Bailey, Clara Sandelind, Irene Vanini, and many more. I want to thank my housemates in Sheffield, London and Edinburgh for welcoming me and accepting my strange habits as I undertook this project. And I want to give a special mention to Louis Thomson, who courageously accepted the task of proof-reading this book at short notice. I'm grateful for his generous time and support – I'm sure he won't let me forget it anytime soon.

Finally, many thanks to my family for all their support. My family have always been there for me whenever I needed them. I cannot name them all, but especially thanks to Mama, Dad, Dom, Oma, Nan and Stan. Your love has kept me going.

Abbreviations

ACOBA	Advisory Committee on Business Appointments
ALB	Arm's-length body
APPG	All-Party Parliamentary Group
BIS	Business, Innovation and Skills
DCCS	Department for Chamber and Committee Services
ESRC	Economic and Social Research Council
FWD	Fieldwork diary
HAC	Home Affairs Committee
HI	Historical institutionalism
MP	Member of Parliament
NHS	National Health Service
PAC	Public Accounts Committee
PASC	Public Administration Select Committee
PCRC	Political and Constitutional Reform Committee
PMQs	Prime Minister's Questions
POST	Parliamentary Office for Science and Technology
PPS	Parliamentary private secretary
PSA	Political Studies Association
RCI	Rational choice institutionalism
SO	Standing Order
WM	Westminster model
WPC	Work and Pensions Committee

The quest for accountability

Situated along the river Thames in London, the Palace of Westminster evokes the grandeur and privilege of the time in which it was built: the seat of a global empire in the nineteenth century. Grand staircases and hallways are lined with statues of former prime ministers. Paintings depict famous battles fought by victorious British armies. Carved doors lead to imposing committee rooms. Intricate furnishings designed by Augustus Pugin showcase the wealth that the Empire brought to the UK. The palace symbolises power. This design is intended to impress and humble its visitors. At the same time, however, the palace's masonry is crumbling, leaks are damaging ceilings and artwork, and the building regularly catches fire. The disintegrating edifice of the UK's legislature, and the scaffolding that is swallowing many of the building's spires, symbolises a different aspect of politics in the UK: a crumbling democracy. Trust in politicians and political institutions is in long-term decline; volatile voting patterns by the public have returned surprising results at the ballot box; and established political parties are rocked by ongoing crises about their future. In that sense, the Palace of Westminster has come to epitomise nostalgia of a mythical (and misplaced) golden past, instability in established institutions and conventions, and a democracy in need of restoration and renewal.

The malaise, conflict and discontent that has gripped the UK is far from unique. Across the globe, turnout in elections has fallen to an average of 66% in the period 2011–15 (International Institute for Democracy and Electoral Assistance, 2016). Citizens are voting less often, have become more volatile in casting their vote, identify less with political parties, and are less likely to become party members (Mair, 2013). Trust in politicians and institutions has eroded. Meanwhile, anti-establishment parties and movements have proliferated. While their success has not been unambiguous, many movements have made considerable inroads into national political cultures, whether it is Podemos in Spain or the Alternative für Deutschland in Germany. It goes without saying that Donald Trump's election victory in the USA as president can be considered one of the most significant in that respect. Regardless of their success, such movements are opposed to established institutions and the existing political class, which they characterise as untrustworthy and out-of-touch in some way or another. In the UK, this has contributed to the surprise referendum result to leave the European Union in 2016. Alongside these events, trust in politicians – including their motivations, truthfulness and integrity – has markedly declined over the past 50 years (Allen, 2018; Clarke *et al.*, 2018). Parliaments, which exist to represent their respective publics and hold political elites to account, are seen as failing in their core tasks. This raises a multitude of questions about the role of politicians in their political systems. It has led some to argue that the health and legitimacy of western democracy is at stake (Foa and Mounk, 2016; cf. Inglehart, 2016).

How have politicians – and especially parliaments – responded? Many have sought to make it easier for the public to engage with them (Leston-Bandeira, 2013) and undertaken parliamentary reforms to bolster their abilities to hold government to account. Parliaments have sought to continuously reinvent themselves because they still lie at the heart of political systems. Across the world, from longstanding and established democracies to authoritarian regimes and dictatorships, legislatures are uniquely placed to represent and symbolise their political communities. In parliamentary (as opposed to presidential) systems, political authority and legitimacy is drawn directly from the legislature. It is only by maintaining the confidence of their parliament that governments survive. However, while one function of parliaments is to sustain the executive and bring the nation together, legislatures also exist to hold governments to account and to scrutinise decision-making. And despite reforms that have taken place in many legislatures to increase their policy-making capacities, publics do not believe parliaments are effective in carrying out such functions.

The UK's Parliament has not been immune from these trends. In 2013, Jeremy Paxman, former presenter of *Newsnight*, described the House of Commons as a 'remote and self-important echo chamber' (Plunkett, 2013), while a comment piece in 2016 from a former government adviser called investigative committee hearings 'grandstanding from powerless MPs' (McTernan, 2016). This was reinforced by the publication of *Why We Get the Wrong Politicians*, critiquing Parliament and politicians as dysfunctional (Hardman, 2018). The image of Parliament as distant from everyday concerns of citizens and powerless to affect government decision-making is not novel; in fact, the sentiments are widely shared by the public. The Hansard Society (2017) recently found that only 30% of respondents were satisfied with how Parliament works overall. It also found that no more than four in ten believe that Parliament has done a good job in carrying out any of its responsibilities in recent years (Hansard Society, 2017, pp. 28–9). The annual Eurobarometer has found that trust in the UK Parliament sits at 35%, which, although in line with the EU average, is also part of a declining trend (it was around 50% in the mid-1990s) and far from inspiring (European Commission, 2018, p. 43). Meanwhile, politicians languish in the polls as one of the least trusted groups of professionals, with only 19%

of the public believing that they are trustworthy (Ipsos MORI, 2018). While such trends are arguably more complex than these headline figures may suggest, it does feed into a broader narrative about politicians, political institutions and democracy more generally in crisis (Ercan and Gagnon, 2014).

It is not just journalists and the public that have a negative view of the foundational institution of the UK's political system. Academics share this view, too. Anthony King and Ivor Crewe (2013, pp. 361–2), for example, refer to the House of Commons as 'peripheral', 'totally irrelevant' and 'passive'. Another author described Parliament as 'puerile, pathetic and utterly useless' (Ward, 2004, p. 42). These views are deeply ingrained across academic disciplines and begin early in undergraduate teaching. One textbook on British politics suggests that 'the House of Commons is misunderstood if viewed as a legislator' (Moran, 2017, p. 111). Another argues that 'legislation today is substantially an executive function', and that Parliament 'legitimates rather than legislates' (Griffiths and Leach, 2018, p. 103). Research findings from the parliamentary studies community contrasts sharply with these assessments, suggesting that Parliament is now at its most powerful since at least the mid-nineteenth century (Russell and Gover, 2017; Thompson, 2015a).

The contrast between perception and reality has led Lord Norton of Louth (2017, p. 191) to conclude that 'these are the best of times, these are the worst of times' for Parliament. This has no doubt been exacerbated in recent years. Between 2010 and 2015, the UK had its first peace-time coalition in more than 70 years and, since 2017, a minority government. This has not only had repercussions for the organisation and strategies of political parties, but it also heightens the role for Parliament in adjudicating different interests while also throwing up challenges for established rules and conventions. No more is this the case than with the UK's withdrawal from the European Union. We have already seen this with, for example, the government being found in contempt of Parliament in December 2018 and losing – by a historic margin – a key vote on EU withdrawal in January 2019 (Kidd, 2019; Wright, 2018). With wider so-called 'plots' to 'seize control' over the parliamentary agenda (Shipman, 2019a), Parliament has come under the spotlight in recent times, demonstrating the accountability and law-making challenges that Parliament faces.

Although the UK Parliament faces unique challenges, these opening pages have shown that there are truly global questions about the role of legislatures in political systems, including their ability to represent the interests of citizens and respond to their concerns. It also points to widespread dissatisfaction with parliaments and the tools available to them to carry out their multifaceted roles. That said, our scholarly understanding of how parliaments employ their capacities to, among other things, hold the executive to account is still not widely understood either, nor do we necessarily know much about the everyday lives and pressures that MPs face in enacting their roles. It is in this context that this book is written. It focuses attention on how parliaments exercise their account-ability mechanisms in order to tell a broader story about politicians and their place in democratic politics. It takes the UK Parliament[1] as its starting point and case study, specifically looking at what are often described as the power engines of parliaments: committees. The book sheds new light on how the House of Commons' select committees undertake scrutiny, what this tells us about parliamentary practices and behaviour, and the role of Parliament in an ever-changing landscape of British politics that is characterised by dissatisfaction of political institutions. In order to explain this book's subject matter, this chapter will summarise the importance of committee scrutiny in the House of Commons, followed by a wider outline of the book.

Committee scrutiny in the House of Commons

Accountability is central to the relationship between government and Parliament. Broadly conceived, it refers to a formal relationship in which the government has to explain itself and to account for its decisions to the legislature. Beyond this general definition, however, the term is shrouded in ambiguity because of the wide range of issues that it includes, such as good governance, transparency, equity, democracy, efficiency, responsiveness, responsibility and integrity (Bovens, 2010; Olsen, 2013). We can distinguish between two interrelated and often used terms: 'accountability' and 'scrutiny'. Strictly speaking, 'accountability' is a formal *relationship*, while the term 'scrutiny' is used to describe the *process* (White, 2015a, p. 3). As will become clear in subsequent chapters, this book focuses closely on the latter term in order to tell a bigger story about account-ability relationships in the House of Commons.

In the UK Parliament, accountability manifests itself in many forms. Most well-known is the weekly duel between government and opposition at Prime Minister's Questions (PMQs) (Bates *et al.*, 2014; Hazarika and Hamilton, 2018). Here, the prime minister has to answer questions from randomly selected MPs without forewarning of the topic, as well as six questions from the leader of the opposition. It is a highly partisan debate that takes place in a confrontational atmosphere involving shouting, heckling and yelling from both sides of the chamber. The Speaker of the House of Commons called it 'scrutiny by screech' (Bercow, 2010). It is a spectacle in which two worldviews dramatically collide. In many ways, this makes PMQs an exceptional, rather than representative, form of scrutiny in the House of Commons. Indeed, scrutiny goes on throughout the Palace of Westminster, and its adjacent building, Portcullis House, in a range of different ways: oral and written questions in both chambers of Parliament; pursued directly between frontbench and backbench colleagues (i.e., intra-party relations); as part of activities from all-party parliamentary groups or caucuses; through debates on the floor of the main chambers or additional chambers (i.e.,

Westminster Hall); or through parliamentary committees. It is noticeable from this short and non-exhaustive list that the nature of government accountability to Parliament is not fixed or even clearly defined. This is because scrutiny is largely a process that encompasses a formal although vaguely expressed relationship. This relationship is mostly dependent on codes and conventions, i.e., non-legal understandings of how the constitution operates, rather than a codified constitutional framework (Tomkins, 2009).

Although a plethora of different scrutiny practices exist in Parliament, it is often perceived that select committees are 'the principal mechanism through which the House of Commons holds the executive to account' (Brazier and Fox, 2011, p. 354). Unlike many other parliaments, the House of Commons does not have permanent committees that combine legislative and scrutiny functions. Rather, they are separated between bill committees and select committees. Bill committees consider legislation on a line-by-line basis (Thompson, 2015b). Meanwhile, select committees are made up of a small group of cross-party MPs and exist to 'examine the expenditure, administration and policy' of government departments and their associated public bodies, as set out in House of Commons Standing Orders (SOs). In addition to departmental committees, a range of further committees exist to scrutinise government: cross-cutting select committees provide thematic, whole-of-government scrutiny; domestic or internal committees look at administrative issues within the House of Commons; joint committees with the House of Lords may be established to provide more detailed scrutiny across Parliament; and, other *ad hoc* or temporary committees may examine specific issues. Select committees examine government policy in broad terms, which is predominantly through inquiries that involves processes of taking written and oral evidence before publishing a final report (more on this below).

A brief history of select committees

When commentators and scholars talk of the present-day structure and operation of parliamentary select committees, they often refer to reforms in 1979. However, select committees have a much longer history. Examples date back to the fourteenth century, and they became increasingly used from the sixteenth century onwards. They were used frequently in the eighteenth and nineteenth centuries to inquire into important issues of the day, such as unemployment, policing, education, poverty and other social issues (Jupp, 2006, pp. 217–19). It was during the Victorian era that the Committee on Public Accounts was introduced (which had gained prominence between 2010 and 2015 under Margaret Hodge's adversarial style as chair). So, committees were widespread and a normal part of the parliamentary landscape. As the nineteenth century turned into the twentieth, however, committees of inquiry increasingly fell out of favour. This happened alongside the consolidation of the executive over parliamentary processes and procedure (Judge, 1993). For much of the twentieth century, governments used their executive dominance to prevent the development of a coherent system of committees, which would otherwise have asked irksome questions.

From the 1930s onwards, the case for a systematic committee structure developed, although it remained embryonic. In 1932, a Select Committee on Procedure was established, which recognised the declining influence of the House of Commons over government. However, it also felt that the efficient processing of the government's agenda must take precedence and therefore only made minor recommendations to expand the Estimates Committee at the time (which was created in 1912 to scrutinise government policy, and which the Procedure Committee did not believe to be effective). Furthermore, with the rise of political extremism, parliamentary observers believed in a strong government to meet the challenges of the times. Despite subsequent inquiries into the status and procedure of the House of Commons, the years that followed the Second World War increased procedural restrictions on committee activities, such as publishing evidence or providing specialist support (Hutton, 2017). This made it difficult for committees that did exist to carry out comprehensive scrutiny.

It was not until the 1960s that things began to change. During this time, academic thinking focused on the possibilities of strengthening Parliament's accountability role through committees (Crick, 1968; Walkland, 1960). Scholars were able to influence the debate through the establishment of the Study of Parliament Group in 1964 (a joint endeavour between parliamentary staff and academic researchers) and evidence sessions with the Procedure Committee in 1965. The committee, which had previously concluded against introducing select committees, came to the opposite conclusion in its 1965 report (House of Commons Procedure Committee, 1965). In 1966, following the general election, the Labour government was encouraged to experiment with committees, led formally by Richard Crossman (hence so-called Crossman reforms) and supported by the prime minister, Harold Wilson (Aylett, 2015, pp. 89–124). This included enlarging subcommittees of the Estimates Committee and the introduction of six subject-specific committees to look into agriculture, science and technology, education, race relations and immigration, overseas aid and development, and Scottish affairs. It was slightly reformed under the subsequent Conservative government in 1970s by replacing the Estimates Committee with the Expenditure Committee, which was similar but with wider terms of reference and a loosely departmental structure.

The system of committees and subcommittees that emerged in the 1960s and 1970s was diverse, and presented a considerable shift in the everyday life of parliamentarians, in which committee scrutiny became routine and arguably 'semi-permanent' (Aylett, 2015, p. 165). Indeed, while the government was free to disband critical committees in the 1960s, attitudes were changing. For example, the chief whip for the Labour government told the House in 1969 that:

I hope that the House will never abandon select committees. Indeed, I doubt whether it ever could. The idea has gripped the consciousness and general fibre of Parliament today, and Parliament would be a very much poorer institution without select committees. (HC Deb 25 Mar 1969, c1471)

Nonetheless, the system was also haphazard in its development and far from coherent (Johnson, 1988). Furthermore, the subcommittee system made scrutiny complicated, while government replies were rarely delivered in a timely fashion. Concerns regarding committees therefore led the Procedure Committee to look into the issue from 1976 onwards.

In 1978, the Procedure Committee produced its final report, in which it called for an organised system of committees to hold government to account (House of Commons Procedure Committee, 1978). The leader of the House, Michael Foot, opposed the proposals (HC Deb 20 Feb 1979, cc290–300). He had been a lifelong critic of enhancing committee scrutiny because he believed that this would take away from the primacy of the chamber. Foot echoed the general disapproval of government for the report's recommendations, despite generally supportive comments from MPs during the debate on the report, including from the opposition.

The election of 1979 returned a Conservative government that had previously committed itself to the Procedure Committee's reform proposals. Norman St John-Stevas, the new leader of the House, pressed for reform. Meanwhile, the prime minister, Margaret Thatcher, was cautious. In the end, some restraints were put in place and the proposal received Cabinet approval without arousing strong feelings (Aylett, 2015, pp. 204–10). So, on 25 June 1979, the leader of the House moved to introduce the departmental-based select committee system with which we are familiar today. At the time, St John-Stevas claimed (HC Deb 25 Jun 1979, c35):

Today is, I believe, a crucial day in the life of the House of Commons. After years of discussion and debate, we are embarking upon a series of changes that could constitute the most important parliamentary reforms of the century.

The system was well-received, both by parliamentarians themselves (House of Commons Liaison Committee, 1985) and subsequent academic research (Drewry, 1985; Ryle and Richards, 1988). However, the system also suffered a number of shortcomings: chairs were not paid (limiting incentives for an alternative parliamentary career path); committees were not given the power to force ministers to attend; the executive was not forced to accept committee recommendations; and no time was allocated for reports to be debated in the chamber (Kelso, 2009, p. 98). Arguably one of the biggest weaknesses, however, was the way that MPs would be selected for committee participation: proposed membership was made to the Committee of Selection on behalf of the party whips, effectively ensuring that political parties controlled who would make up committees and lead them. Nevertheless, the committees established themselves as independent-minded, with a positive reputation. This continued the trend that had been growing since the 1960s for a stronger committee-based system of scrutiny in the House of Commons, which was also demonstrating some, albeit mixed, ability to influence policy and hold government to account (Aylett, 2015; Hawes, 1992, 1993; Jogerst, 1993).

Between 1979 and 2010, but especially since 2000, a number of attempts were made to strengthen select committee scrutiny. The Liaison Committee, made up of all chairs of other select committees, had become increasingly vocal about the need for reform and published a series of reports on the topic (e.g., House of Commons Liaison Committee, 2000a, 2000b). These reports were informed by other groups, organisations and commissions that published recommendations for reforming Parliament (Hansard Society, 2000, 2001; Norton, 2000). Some of their calls were heeded following the appointment of a reform-minded leader of the House, Robin Cook, in 2001, including: the introduction of 'core tasks' to guide select committee activity; further powers to appoint subcommittees and joint inquiries with other committees; the creation of a Scrutiny Unit to increase select committee resources; additional payments introduced for committee chairs to incentivise an alternative career structure; and the introduction of evidence sessions between the prime minister and the Liaison Committee (Flinders, 2002, 2007; Power, 2007). While these reforms arguably strengthened committees, the continued sticking point throughout this period was the issue of nominations to select committees and the role of the whips. Hotly debated in 2001 and 2002, membership procedures nonetheless failed to change (Kelso, 2003).

In 2010, arguably the most important reforms since 1979 took place. It came at a time when Parliament faced an acute crisis of confidence following the parliamentary expenses scandal (VanHeerde-Hudson, 2014). In 2009, *The Daily Telegraph* started publishing details of MPs' expenses, showing widespread misuse of allowances or the technically correct, although morally dubious, use of public funds for private gain. It led to public outrage, decline in trust in politicians and criminal charges against certain Members of Parliament (MPs). In response to the scandal, the then prime minister, Gordon Brown, established the Committee on Reform of the House of Commons to look at ways in which the reputation of Parliament could be restored. The subsequent reform package, known as the Wright reforms (after Tony Wright, who chaired the committee), included the introduction of a Backbench Business Committee to give backbench MPs the opportunity to influence the parliamentary timetable, and changes to committee membership, shifting from selection by party whips to a process of election of members through party groups and chairs by the whole House (Russell, 2011). Although these reforms have been widely and anecdotally praised, the repercussions are not fully known to date (although see Bates, Goodwin, and McKay, 2017; O'Brien, 2012; White, 2015b).

This brief history demonstrates that select committees have been a part of the House of Commons landscape for a long time. Most importantly, however, the trend since the middle of the twentieth century has shown a clear shift in which the House of Commons has become increasingly assertive in its rights to hold the government of the day to account, and that – in line with legislatures across the world – committees have become indispensable to the effective functioning of Parliament. What does this history of committees tell us about their place in Parliament today?

Select committees today

Today, there are a range of committees to shadow departments as well as conduct whole-of-government scrutiny (the types of committees are captured in Table 1.1, and the range of committees since 2010 in Table 1.2). As noted, select committees are a small group of cross-party MPs. Specifically, they are normally made up of between nine and 18 MPs. The party balance typically reflects that of the House of Commons. So, over the 2010 parliament (the main period of study), a typical select committee of 11 members would have had five Labour Party MPs, five Conservative Party MPs and one member from a third party (often a Liberal Democrat MP). This has been replicated following the 2017

Table 1.1 Types of select committee in the House of Commons

Type	Description with example
Departmental	One committee for each ministerial department to oversee the expenditure, administration and policy of that department. For example, the Education Committee, which shadows the Department for Education.
Cross-cutting	Committees to investigate government policy on a more thematic basis, without a single department. For example, the Science and Technology Committee, which looks at science policy across central government.
Domestic	These committees look at the internal governance of the House of Commons and how it is administered. For example, the Procedure Committee, which looks at procedural matters in the House.
Legislative	Committees that undertake scrutiny of legislation in some way, but which do not examine legislation on a line-by-line basis. For example, the Statutory Instruments Committee, which examines secondary or delegated legislation in the Commons.
Joint	There are some joint committees with the House of Lords, which scrutinise certain issues either on a permanent or temporary basis. For example, the Joint Committee on Human Rights.
Other	Some committees are appointed on an *ad hoc* basis to inform the House. For example, the Reform of the House of Commons Committee considered ways to make the House more effective in 2009 (informally known as the Wright Committee).

Table 1.2 Select committees, 2010–present

Departmental committees	Cross-cutting committees
Business, Energy and Industrial Strategy Committee (formerly Business, Innovation and Skills)	Environmental Audit Committee
Defence Committee	Petitions (since 2015)
Digital, Culture, Media and Sport Committee (formerly Culture, Media and Sport)	Political and Constitutional Reform Committee (until 2015)
Education Committee	Public Accounts Committee
Energy and Climate Change Committee (until 2016)	Public Administration and Constitutional Affairs Committee (formerly Public Administration)
Environmental, Food and Rural Affairs Committee	Science and Technology Committee
Exiting the European Union Committee (since 2016)	Women and Equalities Committee (since 2015)
Foreign Affairs Committee	
Health and Social Care Committee (formerly Health)	
Home Affairs Committee	
Housing, Communities and Local Government Committee (formerly Communities and Local Government)	
International Development Committee	
International Trade Committee (since 2016)	
Justice Committee	
Northern Ireland Affairs Committee	
Scottish Affairs Committee	
Transport Committee	
Treasury Committee	
Welsh Affairs Committee	
Work and Pensions Committee	

general election, where no party has an overall majority. Similarly, chairs were allocated based on party balance. The precise balance is informally agreed by party whips but approved by the House. Since 2010, members have been elected through their party groups, while the chair is elected by the whole House, both by secret ballot (for a more detailed summary on current procedures, see Besly *et al.*, 2018).

In order to carry out scrutiny, committees usually undertake inquiries, which involves taking written and oral evidence before publishing a final report. Committees can investigate any topic of their choosing (guided by ten 'core tasks' as defined by the Liaison Committee). Increasingly, committees have also begun to hold one-off evidence sessions, undertake 'evidence checks' and scrutinise government in more innovative ways to engage with the public (House of Commons Liaison Committee, 2015). All select committees have the power to 'send for persons, papers and records' (HC SO No. 152(4a)). They are supported by a small secretariat of around six permanent members of staff that work towards the committees' inquiries full-time, as well as specialist advisers that are appointed on an *ad hoc*, part-time basis.

How effective or important are select committees? Traditionally, the UK Parliament's committees were assumed to be weak (Mattson and Strøm, 1995). There are two reasons for this. First, select committees had a poor reputation in the first half of the twentieth century among parliamentarians and were sparingly used (Hutton, 2017). Second, the creation of a coherent system of committees to hold the executive to account developed after a number of key landmark comparative studies were published and shaped the field (e.g., King, 1976; Mezey, 1979; Polsby, 1975). Consequently, the academic literature assumed that House of Commons committees were ineffective. This fed into a wider narrative of Parliament as a weak policy actor (Flinders and Kelso, 2011). However, more recent research has challenged this dominant view. Andrew Hindmoor and colleagues (2009), for example, look at the Education and Skills Committee between 1997 and 2005 in much detail, and evaluate the extent of committee influence positively (although also cautiously). They look at, first, how many committee recommendations were accepted by government and, second, interview a range of parliamentary actors to establish influence. They acknowledge that identifying broad patterns and consistent effects is difficult, although identify specific instances of (often informal) committee influence. Meghan Benton and Meg Russell (2013) have conducted a similar piece of research, but looked at seven case study committees over a longer period (1997–2010). They find that 40% of committee recommendations were accepted by government for their case study committees (including 55% of small-level, 31% of medium-level and 14% of large-level proposed changes to government policy). Not only do select committees influence government policy through scrutiny practices and publishing reports, Russell and Gover (2017, pp. 205–33) also find that committees influence the legislative process in a substantive, meaningful way. This suggests that, contrary to our assumptions about the UK Parliament, the institution exerts a significant influence on government policy, particularly with regards to 'anticipated reactions' and behind-the-scenes negotiations. Other research reinforces these findings (Bochel et al., 2014; Foster, 2015; Hazell et al., 2012), which demonstrates the value of committee-based scrutiny and accountability.

While we are coming to understand more and more about the policy impact of parliamentary committees in the UK and elsewhere, this knowledge is based on institutionalist lenses. Research that looks at the practice of how accountability operates and is practised has received far less attention (for exceptions, see Crewe, 2015; Grube, 2014; White, 2015b, 2015c). What this indicates is that the everyday behaviours and practices of parliamentarians themselves is a neglected area of research, without clear theoretical and conceptual reflection to guide them. Most importantly, it means that we still do not fully understand how the formal accountability relationships are enacted and developed along the committee corridor of the Palace of Westminster, nor what MPs and officials themselves make of the system today. This book seeks to change this by focusing directly on our conceptual understanding and practical engagement with accountability in the UK's House of Commons. It asks how everyday practices along the committee corridor shape scrutiny, and how actors interpret the wider accountability framework in which they are placed.

A drama of accountability?

This book engages directly with everyday practices as an analytical tool to better understand political phenomena and outcomes. This contributes to a wider ideational turn in political science, which has the potential to have considerable impact: *theoretically*, it asserts the relevance of interpretation in political science over positivist explanations that have dominated the second half of the twentieth century; *analytically*, it centralises the importance of ideas, beliefs, passions and desires to explain political outcomes; and *methodologically*, it broadens the opportunities to use different tools to study political phenomena that have hitherto relied on traditional methods of inquiry. Taking an interpretive approach enables us to deepen our understanding of what happens in political institutions on a day-to-day basis, and how those quotidian practices make an impact on the broader political landscape. This is the precise aim of this book. So, I ask three questions:

1. How can we understand the everyday lives of parliamentary actors?
2. How do political actors interpret and perform their roles?
3. In what ways do everyday practices affect accountability in parliaments?

These questions are answered in the subsequent seven chapters.

The following chapter focuses directly on the first research question. As a subfield, parliamentary studies has rarely been theorised (especially so in the UK). Instead, it has relied on traditional or 'old' institutionalism since the 1950s, unaffected by trends in other subfields of political science. Chapter 2 identifies the broad themes of this literature, which can be placed in four loose traditions: historical, rational choice, sociological and interpretive. The aforementioned legacy of old institutionalist lenses and legalistic approaches, however, means that a lot of studies fall outside these traditions. Although current scholarship has made significant contributions to our understanding of parliamentary democracies, this chapter argues that parliamentary studies would benefit from a more theoretically explicit and interpretive approach. To argue this, I therefore also outline such an approach by building on the work of Mark Bevir and R. A. W. Rhodes (2003, 2016). Their work has reshaped the study of governance and public administration, in which their decentred approach looks to unpack individual beliefs, everyday practices, webs of belief or traditions, and dilemmas that political actors face. I apply these core themes to parliamentary studies, focusing particularly on the analysis of everyday practices as performances (in the theatrical sense of the word) (Geddes and Rhodes, 2018). This framework is applied in the remaining chapters of the book.

The next three chapters look at how parliamentary actors interpret their accountability roles in Parliament (thereby engaging with the second research question). Chapter 3 looks at Members of Parliament, specifically exploring how individual committee members interpret and enact scrutiny. This finds a range of performance styles, including specialists, lone wolves, constituency champions, party helpers, learners and absentees. These performances are affected by other individual beliefs, practices and dilemmas that MPs face. Chapter 4 looks at committee chairs, who not only interpret scrutiny in different ways, but additionally enact a leadership role. This usually takes one of two forms: either, they seek to act as catalysts of committees, and thus seek to work with committee members; or, they seek to act as chieftains of their committees, and thereby seek to impose their agenda onto the committee. Chapter 5 turns to parliamentary staff, who have traditionally been overlooked in academic studies (but see Crewe, 2017b; Gay, 2017). Officials undertake a range of roles to support committees and so deserve scholarly attention. Their beliefs are underpinned by unparalleled service to the House, being hidden and passionate impartiality.

How do these interpretations and practices affect parliamentary accountability? I address this in the remaining chapters. Chapter 6 directly focuses on the developing drama of accountability along the committee corridor of the Palace of Westminster. It looks at back stage preparations for committee hearings as well as how scrutiny plays out on the front stage. This draws on all different performance styles covered in previous chapters and casts committee hearings as a piece of theatre: the chair becomes a lead actor alongside the witnesses; the committee members are the supporting cast; staff act as stage directors and other support; briefing papers act as loose scripts; the public become spectators; and committee rooms become a stage. This is where the book's original contribution comes into its own by illustrating the often symbolic value of representation and accountability. Chapter 7 goes on to explore how those scenes of scrutiny are mediated through evolving relationships between actors (focusing predominantly on MPs). In particular, I explore how committees sustain effective working relationships, create norms and values, and build coherence within their groups. All of these factors affect how committees undertake their inquiries and, ultimately, construct consensus. They also build what may be termed a 'web' of scrutiny.

Finally, the book returns to broader themes of accountability in its concluding chapter, Chapter 8. In this book, I argue that: first, an interpretive approach – specifically the concepts of beliefs, practices, traditions and dilemmas – offers novel ways of understanding parliamentary scrutiny; second, committee members, chairs and staff interpret scrutiny in diverse (and occasionally conflicting) ways, which allows them to use committee work in different ways; and third, that everyday practices are crucial to explaining how committees undertake scrutiny, publish reports and seek to impact government policy. This means that formal accountability involves pushing and pulling a web of scrutiny in different directions. There is, arguably, no such thing as 'systematic' accountability but, rather, only dense webs of scrutiny that rely upon parliamentary actors to identify and interpret scrutiny in such ways as to make them conducive to holding government to account.

This book offers a departure from the way that we currently understand the House of Commons, in particular, and sheds light on parliamentary democracies more generally. Indeed, the explicit attempt of this book is to push our understanding of accountability to new limits and identify new ways of studying scrutiny practices. Most importantly, this book seeks to provoke a debate about the study of parliaments. I do not propose all the answers, but instead I hope to lift the lid on everyday life along the House of Commons committee corridor. It is an attempt to open up parliamentary studies a little further and, in all honesty, pose more questions about the rightful place of Parliament in UK politics, than to give all the answers. Why does all of this matter? It matters because parliamentary democracies are facing multiple dilemmas of legitimacy. It is in this context that many parliaments have sought to introduce new ways to represent the public and hold governments to account. Our understanding of such processes remains surprisingly thin. This book begins in earnest to address this gap.

Note

1 In this book, 'Parliament' refers to the UK House of Commons (unless stated otherwise). Moreover, while 'Parliament' refers to the institution, 'parliament' refers to a specific time period or legislatures in a general sense.

2

Perspectives on Parliament

Conventionally, research on legislatures has not engaged with themes of everyday life as a hook to study politics. It is, often justifiably, associated with ordinariness. This ordinariness is pervasive: from the way we choose to organise our personal and working spaces to the way that we communicate with others both verbally and non-verbally. We do not notice the everyday as in some way politically significant or relevant for political analysis precisely because it is perceived to be typical, routine, settled – perhaps even boring, unremarkable, mundane. However, as we try to negotiate the world around us, it is important to realise that this ordinariness and this normality that we associate with the everyday is something that we have *willed* into being. That is to say, the things we consider normal or routine are the result of our interpretations about the world, and the choices that we have made (or, indeed, others have made on our behalf – willingly, unwillingly; knowingly, unknowingly). Everyday life is only ordinary or unremarkable insofar as we interpret that to be the case. This is an important point because it implies the possibility that everyday practices are political and deserve attention. While this insight has been commonly accepted in many disciplines of the social sciences, it has been underplayed by political scientists interested in parliaments – at least until recently.

In linking everyday practices with political behaviour, this book adopts a distinctive focus on understanding accountability in the UK House of Commons (and beyond). This chapter contributes to this in two ways. First, by reviewing the current scholarship's analytical and methodological principles that underpin parliamentary studies, it shows a tendency to rely on institutionalist lenses without significant theoretical reflection. This omission is unfortunate because it leaves many analytical and methodological assumptions implicit. Second, it summarises an interpretive approach for the analysis of legislatures. This alternative approach is developed by drawing on Mark Bevir and R. A. W. Rhodes' (2003, 2016) interpretive political science, among others. The broad thrust of their approach has given us novel ways to study political issues, and made a significant impact across a range of subfields in political science. The chapter concludes with an interpretive framework for analysis and a brief methodological outline. This will form the basis of subsequent empirical chapters.

Traditions in parliamentary studies

Past and current research on Parliament has made significant contributions to explaining parliamentary behaviour and executive-legislative relationships. This chapter does not critique this. However, the majority of research on Parliament in the UK has also avoided an explicit discussion of theoretical and analytical principles that underpins the outlook of this research. This has arguably constrained the analytical horizons available to legislative scholars, in the sense that the toolkit for analysis of parliamentary issues hasn't radically altered beyond institutionalist lenses despite innovations from political scientists more generally (Hay, 2002). This book addresses this by identifying four broad scholarly traditions in parliamentary studies: historical, rational choice, sociological and interpretive traditions (summarised in Table 2.1). The first three have emerged out of the shift from 'old' to 'new' institutionalism (March and Olsen, 1984), while the fourth has roots in constructivist ideas and methods. These traditions do not aim to be comprehensive, nor are distinctions between them always clear-cut by those that draw on them. Some studies overlap and borrow elements from different traditions to form hybrids; many more do not place themselves in any tradition at all (and possibly wouldn't want to be forced into one). This makes an overview of the scholarship's intellectual roots more challenging, yet all the more important because much of our analysis hangs on the assumptions we make about political behaviour and institutions.

In the first subsection, I begin by looking at the legacy of the Westminster model (WM) and modernist empiricism on the study of Parliament. This model has shaped not only policy-makers' assumptions about Parliament (as the previous chapter showed) but has also influenced many academic studies of parliaments. The second subsection turns to the impact of new institutionalisms, which have considerably widened the debate and perspectives in parliamentary studies. The third subsection identifies the emergence of a recent constructivist or interpretive turn, on which this book builds.

The legacy of the Westminster model

The study of the UK Parliament has often been placed in the wider context of the Westminster model (WM) and the ideas that surround it. Among other things, the WM is commonly associated with an appeal to the sovereignty and primacy of Parliament; the centrality of individual ministerial responsibility to Parliament; and the selection of the executive through a competitive, adversarial electoral system (Gamble, 1990). However, others also associate the model with

Table 2.1 Approaches to the study of Parliament

Tradition	Analytical focus	Contribution to parliamentary studies	Contribution to select committee research	Key examples
Old institutionalist	Formal organisation of government; powers of the legislature	Greater understanding of the way that parliaments work	Demonstrates the impact of select committees on government policy	Russell and Gover (2017)
Historical institutionalist	Role of historical context in shaping behaviour of MPs	Situates parliamentary change and reform in its historical context	Explains the broad history of select committees and how they have changed	Kelso (2009)
Rational choice institutionalist	Asserts that all institutions are goal-seeking individuals	Explains institutional behaviour in rational, utility-maximising terms	Select committees are useful for giving information to MPs, but lack formal power	Mattson and Strøm (1995)
Sociological institutionalist	Influence of rules, norms and values on MPs	Helps us to understand how MPs conceptualise and are socialised into their role	Few detailed studies	Searing (1994)
Interpretive or constructivist	Shifts focus from institutional landscapes to everyday practices	Explains parliamentary activities and practices in terms of the interpretations and practices of MPs	Few detailed studies	Crewe (2005, 2015)

single-party majoritarian government, a two-party system and a unitary state (Lijphart, 2012). For some, then, the WM is bound up with ideas that associate British politics with a strong, central and dominant executive. These ideas have been informed by a British political tradition that stresses a conservative notion of responsibility and a decisive government as the most effective, efficient and desirable form of decision-making (Hall, 2011). The multitude of debates on the WM have stretched, widened and pushed the meaning of it so far that no single-agreed definition of the model exists. Nonetheless, it often serves as a 'standard account' (Judge, 2014, pp. 1–18) in British politics in that it supposedly identifies and describes some of the core features of the UK polity. Most importantly, it is also how most politicians and officials perceive the system, regardless of the model's accuracy and even if they do not use the same academic or technical language.

Looking at British politics through the prism of the WM often involves locating Parliament in a broader constitutional framework, in which analysis focuses on institutions, rules, procedures and formal organisations of government and state. Contemporary debates typically revolve around the extent to which parliamentary government in the UK follows the central tenets of the model. This includes, for example, debates over the extent of parliamentary sovereignty in the UK (e.g., the relationship between the UK and the EU or the expanding scope of the judiciary in recent years); the extent of ministerial responsibility to Parliament and the relationship with civil servants and public bodies, especially given restructuring of the British state since 1979; or the ways in which devolution have affected the constitutional model (Flinders, 2009). These debates continue to rage, in part because of the different ways the WM is defined. Both the narratives of the Westminster model and the focus of analysis on formal organisations has had a long-lasting and profound effect on the study of legislatures in the UK.

A significant focus of legislative research has been on parliamentary reform, rooted in a literature that emerged in the 1960s (e.g., Ryle, 1965; Walkland, 1960; Wiseman, 1966). One of the most influential books at the time was Bernard Crick's *The Reform of Parliament* (1968). He arguably set the tone for parliamentary debates about reforming the House of Commons, such as his call for a structured committee system that would enable specialisation and scrutiny in Parliament. Echoes of these debates persist today, with innumerable questions about how to make Parliament more effective. Many scholars employ institutionalist lenses and formal-legal approaches to concentrate on the effect of reforms on Parliament, especially on its ability to hold government to account, and often supported by reports and studies by think tanks (such as the Hansard Society's *Audit of Political Engagement* and the Institute for Government's *Parliamentary Monitor*, both published annually). Many studies share a methodological outlook through the interpretation of documents, texts and parliamentary procedures to evaluate the nature of reforms on the efficiency (that is, streamlining parliamentary processes) and effectiveness (that is, scrutiny and policy-making capacity) of Parliament.

Besides the reformist literature on the House of Commons, a second and closely related strand focuses on the effect of reforms on the broader role of the legislature in policy-making. As noted in Chapter 1, the growing consensus among UK legislative scholars contrasts directly with perceptions of the public, commentators and indeed some corners of academic research, in which Parliament does play a significant policy-making role. For example, Philip Cowley (2002, 2005) challenges the view that MPs are nothing more than lobby fodder, instead demonstrating the increasingly independent-minded behaviour of MPs. This behaviour affects the control of government over its legislative and policy programmes. Elsewhere, scholars have shown the influence of the House of Commons' bill committees (Thompson, 2015b) and select committees (Benton and Russell, 2013; Hindmoor *et al.*, 2009). Finally, the House of Lords continues to be an understudied yet important revising chamber (Russell, 2013). Once again, what underpins these studies is a shared interest in the efficacy of parliamentary processes, the relationship between the executive and the legislature, the place of committees, and the role of political parties. Overall, it suggests that Parliament is a significant policy actor, as demonstrated in Meg Russell and Daniel Gover's (2017) far-reaching research.

What does all of this tell us? First, that the chief focus of discussion, debate and scholarly interest has been on the functional role of the legislature in British politics – whether this is the way that the legislature works, its policy-making capacity *vis-à-vis* other political institutions (most notably government), or the way that Parliament relates to the public (Kalitowski, 2009; Leston-Bandeira, 2016). Second, it tells us that the sub-discipline has shared theoretical and methodological roots. Many of these studies have made important contributions to the field. Yet, as B. Guy Peters (2011, p. 60) has pointed out:

> The study of Parliament has produced primarily ... descriptive studies of institutional dynamics ... These studies describe one or more aspects of parliaments extremely well, and fit them into broader patterns of governance in the United Kingdom, but they do not move the theoretical literature forward, nor locate the British parliament in a comparative context.

While UK political science has shifted its focus from formal political institutions to a more diverse set of approaches, methods and topics from the 1960s onwards (e.g., Hay, 2010), legislative studies has been slower to adapt. That said, the growth of new institutionalist approaches has made an impact, to which the chapter now turns directly.

From old to new institutionalisms

New institutionalism emerged as a force in the 1980s in response to questions over what constitutes a political institution and how they might shape behaviour (March and Olsen, 1984). Answers to those questions are diverse, and have spawned a range of different types of 'new' institutionalist analyses, including historical, rational choice, sociological, constructivist and feminist. It is worth summarising these to understand their analytical perspectives, which have shaped debates about legislatures, and to offer context for how I complement these approaches with an interpretive alternative.

Historical institutionalism (HI) has arguably made the most extensive inroads into studies of Westminster. This is unsurprising given the resonance between

HI and the Whig approaches that have emphasised the evolutionary nature of UK politics and history. HI is underpinned by a belief that political actors are rule-following satisfiers, interpreting dominant value systems and fitting their actions to institutional rules of the game. This means that actors' preferences are socially and politically structured by their surroundings, i.e., the institutional setting within which they operate. This assumption about actors' behaviour has consequences for political analysis. It implies that institutions and political actors generally behave in the future as they have done in the past. As a consequence, institutions are prone to 'path dependency', or 'the tendency of institutions to be self-perpetuating and static' (Armitage, 2012, p. 137). This stability is reinforced by the concept of 'sunk costs' in the form of information, trust and shared expectations that sustains the bedrock of institutions. Subsequently, future policy choices are constrained by the past. Accepted ways of doing things, either through habit, tradition or legal precedent, reduce uncertainty (and therefore potential risks) for political actors. Central to HI is that change occurs in an incremental fashion; it is evolutionary.

HI has made an important contribution to parliamentary studies, allowing scholars to explain both the stability of the British political system through path dependency, and particularly contributing to debates about parliamentary reform. For example, Alexandra Kelso (2003, 2009) proposes that the weight of history is a constraining force:

> [T]he structured institutional context of parliament has a highly significant degree of influence over those actors who operate there, and [...] parliament's path dependency substantially [constrains] the range of reform options that might be realistically contemplated. (Kelso, 2009, p. 25)

Proponents of this view (Crick, 1965; Flinders, 2002; Walkland, 1976) argue that reform originates, and is sustained by, the executive. This contrasts directly with other positions that have argued that parliamentary reform depends on the inclination of Members of Parliament (for a summary, discussion and alternative approaches to explaining change in legislatures, see Geddes and Meakin, 2018). Other examples of the use of HI include Faith Armitage's (2012) research on speakership elections or Matthew Flinders' (2004) analysis of the relationship between Parliament and public bodies. The focus of this type of research is on the structured context in which political actors operate, and the effect of those structures on the specific activities of actors. In privileging the historical fortunes of institutions as an analytical focus, it arguably limits the extent to which scholars examine actors' individual interpretations of their surroundings. In other words, some (and by no means all) studies of histories of institutions can elide the voice of individuals that act within those institutions (Schmidt, 2008; cf. Bell, 2011). As a result, these studies may overlook the unintended consequences of daily life in legislatures, and the importance of those everyday practices on broader events and traditions in parliamentary politics.

In contrast to HI, the approach that places political agency at the heart of their research is rational choice institutionalism (RCI). However, political agency is developed in a very precise fashion, presuming that human behaviour is inextricably bound up with self-interest. As Kaare Strøm (1997, p. 158) puts it: '[b]esides all their other charming idiosyncracies [*sic*], legislators are goal-seeking men or women who choose their behaviour to fit the destinations they have in mind'. Rational choice scholars are aware that re-election is a means to an end, which can be both diffuse (making the world a better place) and particular (securing a specific policy outcome). However, to achieve those ends, politicians need to maximise their power through office-seeking, utility-maximising behaviour. This assumption is extended to all political actors and parliamentary institutions, who are governed by a will to increasing their power. This forms the bedrock of rational choice approaches to political science.

RCI dominates large portions of legislative studies, and especially so in studies of the US Congress (Loewenberg, 2011) and, to a slightly lesser degree, continental European research on legislatures (Schöne, 2018). The simple framework means that it is well-suited to comparative research, often using quantitative methods. As a result, RCI scholars often find the UK House of Commons as weak or underdeveloped (Mattson and Strøm, 1995; Saalfeld, 2003). However, beyond isolated studies, RCI has not made significant inroads into research on UK debates on Parliament (but see Kam, 2009; Norton, 2001). A contributing factor may be the informal and unwritten rules on which many actors in Westminster rely, something that sits uneasily with a rational choice framework that is commonly used to analyse clearly observable behaviour for quantitative analysis. Indeed, this latter type of analysis often relies on the availability of data from publicly identifiable (and quantifiable) sources, such as formal powers of parliamentary committees or voting records of politicians. While this enables scholars to indicate broad, generalisable trends, it also sacrifices depth and nuance and overlooks informal relationships that are far more complex than rational choice scholars are willing to admit (or at least able to include in their analyses). While some scholars believe these methods ensure rigour, parsimony and objectivity, others argue that this could elide other causal mechanisms, whether the weight of history (as proposed by historical institutionalists), or norms and values, as proposed by sociological approaches, to which we now turn.

One of the most well-known sociological studies of the UK Parliament remains Donald Searing's (1994) research on roles in the House of Commons. Searing brought together elements of institutionalist and behaviouralist approaches to argue that rule-following is a powerful force but also that politicians can and do act purposefully in their own right. He does not reject self-interest as a motivation for action but, rather, argues that it is one of many reasons for actors to pursue a course of action. Searing interviewed 521 MPs during 1970–71 to explore how MPs conceive of their role. He identifies a range of roles and subcategories and, while he notes that roles are not mutually exclusive, Searing nonetheless implies that each role is fairly fixed with little role switching. This has been criticised by others that have developed more flexible role categorisations (Andeweg, 1997; Scully and Farrell, 2003; Strøm, 1997). Role theory and analysis remains a small subset of debates within legislative studies (for a discussion, see Andeweg, 2014; for recent contributions, see Blomgren and Rozenberg, 2012), complemented by other studies that explore the socialisation of MPs (Rush and Giddings, 2011).

The foundation of sociological approaches is that norms and values matter. Subsequently, the focal point of their analysis is the interaction of those norms and rules with the perceived political identities and the institutional context in which actors find themselves. This type of research is taken a little further by Sarah Childs (2004, 2014), who analyses the role of gender in the House of Commons and the extent to which women have developed alternative styles of behaving in Parliament (on feminist institutionalism more generally, see Krook and Mackay (2010)).

Research in this tradition rejects the assumption made by rational choice scholars that MPs always behave in a self-interested, utility-maximising way. Rather, they look at the claims that political actors make about their role and use interviews, surveys and other data to analyse what roles MPs adopt and/or how the institution shapes behaviour. While this approach has a range of opportunities in the sense of posing questions that other institutionalist approaches may overlook, there is little that explicitly calls itself sociological institutionalism, and no research within the tradition that has looked at accountability relationships or scrutiny practices in recent years (although for a European perspective, see Brichzin *et al.*, 2018).

An interpretive tradition?

In recent years, an emerging literature has combined traditional parliamentary research topics with innovative methods and theories drawn from anthropological and post-structuralist perspectives. Emma Crewe and Marion Müller (2006, p. 7), for example, criticise traditional political science, including studies in the sociological tradition, as too focused on institutional structures; instead, they argue that the study of politics would benefit from exploring the effects of rituals, ceremonies and symbolism in political behaviour. The edited volume from which they speak explores such topics, and shares a tradition with other scholars on the French Assemblée nationale (Abélès, 2000) and German Bundestag (Schöne, 2010). The most comprehensive analysis of the UK Parliament using anthropological perspectives comes from the innovative and insightful work of Emma Crewe. In her two volumes, she studies the House of Lords (2005) and the House of Commons (2015) to establish the broad rituals, manners, rhythms and everyday behaviour of peers and MPs. She demonstrates that politicians are far more complex than a rational choice approach would allow, and not shaped by historical context alone – although both can be important. She identifies the importance of political culture to explain how parliamentarians conduct themselves. Her research sits alongside other recent research that pushes the frontiers of legislative research (e.g., Judge and Leston-Bandeira, 2018; Leston-Bandeira, 2016). Some of this has been brought together in edited volumes (Brichzin *et al.*, 2018; Rai and Johnson, 2014; Rai and Reinelt, 2015), special issues (see *The Journal of Legislative Studies*, 2010, volume 16, issue 3) and workshops and conferences.

The insights offered by this growing interpretive (some might prefer constructivist) tradition question the way that parliamentary scholars have commonly approached the study of parliaments. They have carved out an interpretive tradition that focuses its attention on the everyday practices and/or performances of political behaviour, matched with ethnographic methods that have been sparsely adopted in parliamentary research. That said, this tradition is not without its critics (Weinberg, 2018) and remains in its infancy. I want to take this literature forward by considering, explicitly, the analytical possibilities of an interpretive approach.

Developing interpretive parliamentary studies

In the remainder of this chapter, I reflect on the theoretical foundations that guide this book, which are important to consider because they frame much of the subsequent analysis on select committees.

From anti-foundationalism to situated agency

Most interpretive approaches to political science have their roots in anti-foundationalist (or anti-naturalist) philosophy, which broadly asserts that our knowledge of the world cannot be regarded as certain (Bevir and Rhodes, 2010). Anti-foundationalism suggests that there is, as the name implies, no foundation or essence to reality. In contrast to positivists, who assert that objective meanings are 'out there' in the world waiting for us to discover or find them, anti-foundationalists take as their starting point the principle that social (and political) realities are constructed through our experiences of and engagement with what we perceive of the world. Some scholars conclude that this means reality can have no meaning apart from what is believed by any particular group and that, therefore, knowledge must be relative. However, this is a simplistic caricature. Anti-foundationalists do not argue that reality does not exist, but rather that individuals do not have pure, unmediated or objective access to it. As a consequence, an anti-foundationalist approach to knowledge is committed to a more holistic understanding of reality (or realities) by emphasising the contested nature of truth. It suggests that truths are contingent, provisional and socially negotiated through communication and everyday actions; they are temporary, fleeting and valid only until new, more convincing interpretations become accepted. This is not only true of social sciences, but the natural and physical sciences (Kuhn, 2012; Latour, 1999; Longino, 1990).

Although the above poses question marks over truth and objectivity, I argue that it remains a regulative ideal, and must be located as part of an analysis of human practices (this view is developed cogently by Mark Bevir, 1999, pp. 78–126 and Bevir and Blakeley, 2018). In contrast to positivism, anti-foundationalists argue that, as we do not have pure access to the world around us, so too it means that we cannot have access to 'pure' or 'given' facts. Instead, we must rely on 'agreed facts', which is 'a piece of evidence nearly everyone in a given community, especially any of them present as witnesses, would accept as true' (Bevir, 1999, p. 98). Furthermore, concepts and ideas we have of the world (such as 'parliamentary sovereignty', 'accountability', 'scrutiny') only make sense as part of wider webs of belief, or traditions of thought (such as the WM). We build or construct these webs through theories we have in an attempt to categorise, explain and narrate our experiences. Rival theories and webs of belief must be tested, compared and negotiated. It is through this process that objectivity becomes possible. While 'pure' objectivity is not possible, it remains an ideal based on our interactions with the world, in which we make approximations to truths. In doing so, we naturalise social realities. We *will* them to be ordinary, normal and routine because we accept them as part of our everyday life; they have become 'facts'. It is in this vein that R. A. W. Rhodes (2011, pp. 280–309) explains everyday life as 'willed ordinariness'.

This discussion of objectivity has political implications because it centralises 'interpretation'. Things could always be interpreted in different ways, but those other ideas may be beyond the horizon of what is politically acceptable, legitimate or even imaginable within a particular tradition. What makes something specifically political is the contested nature of social practices in that it describes the contest of ideas and resources with respect to how society should be ordered, preserved or changed (Mouffe, 2005). Politics is not necessarily about the resolution of a conflict, the settlement of a dispute, or the (ostensibly successful) outcome of a policy. Rather, it describes the process of contestation itself. The 'resolution' of a conflict, if accepted by a community, is merely a settled – and contingent – set of social practices that remain inherently unstable, complex and value-laden (Finlayson, 2007; Geddes, 2018b).

This has further consequences. It means that we must take seriously individuals' interpretations of the world – including their beliefs, values and interests – in order to explain their behaviour, including (for example) in parliamentary institutions. Individuals do not have given or fixed interests, as others may assume; they are constructed, learned, shared, debated. Moreover, individuals do

Table 2.2 The interpretive approach: concepts

Concept	Definition
Situated agency	Individuals are situated in wider webs of beliefs (traditions), which largely shape their beliefs, yet they keep a capacity for agency in that they respond to traditions, beliefs and dilemmas in novel ways.
Beliefs	Beliefs are the basic unit of analysis, in that they are the interpretations of individuals of their world and their surroundings.
Traditions	Traditions are 'webs of belief', and form the background of ideas in which actors find themselves. Actors will adopt beliefs from traditions as a starting point, but may amend them.
Dilemmas	A dilemma is an idea that stands in contradiction to other beliefs, posing a problem. Dilemmas are resolved by accommodating the new belief in the present web of beliefs or replacing old beliefs with new beliefs.
Practices	A set of actions that often exhibits a stable pattern across time. Practices are the ways in which beliefs and traditions manifest themselves in everyday life.

Adapted from Geddes and Rhodes (2018)

not form and act on beliefs in a vacuum. While this means rejecting the idea of an autonomous subject or self, I still distinguish this from agency. Bevir and Rhodes argue (2010, pp. 74–5), while actors cannot access experiences and reason in a 'pure' way or autonomous from their social context, actors still react to ideas and interpret beliefs in their own, novel ways based on their individual interpretations. They refer to this as *situated agency*. Through local reasoning, actors have the capacity to adopt beliefs and actions, but it is always in a particular context or social background. This indicates a symbiotic relationship between individuals' interpretations and beliefs, and the broader webs of belief in which they are situated. Beliefs inform actions and practices; and these beliefs and practices weave wider webs of belief, or traditions. It is in this way that I suggest that ideas and values become basic explanatory blocks for analysis alongside other concepts. These are summarised in Table 2.2, and explained in the next two subsections.

Traditions and dilemmas, stability and change

Webs of belief, or traditions, are the social context within which actors find themselves, or the 'situation' in situated agency. They are webs of beliefs that act as organising perspectives or ideational context for individuals, groups and other political actors. Without traditions, actors would be thrust into the world in a vacuum, something that patently does not happen. As such, Bevir (2010, p. 263) concludes that 'individuals are to a large extent what social traditions and practices make them'. Policies, beliefs and actions are naturalised as possible, legitimate and normal ways of behaving within this context. While this echoes notions of structure, paradigms or epistemes, Bevir and Rhodes (2010, p. 78) argue that traditions cannot fix or determine behaviour because actors still have a capacity to interpret traditions in novel ways. So, traditions offer 'starting points' to political actors, who are under no obligation to follow a web of beliefs (for a detailed discussion, see Bevir, 1999, pp. 174–220).

The flexibility of traditions has been a point of criticism from other scholars for at least two reasons: some argue it is too elusive (McAnulla, 2006; Smith, 2008), and some state that it is unclear why certain traditions exert greater appeal on political actors than others, or why some aspects of a web of belief might resist modification (Glynos and Howarth, 2008). While Bevir and Rhodes (2008) have responded to these criticisms by arguing that traditions need to be unpacked and analysed as beliefs (and therefore play a diverse range of roles that critics had identified), I suggest that the stability and/or volatility of traditions must be much more closely tied to the concept of dilemmas. This places the issue in a broader discussion about political change.

The concept of dilemma is rooted in Bevir's *The Logic of the History of Ideas*, in which he argues that:

> People develop, adjust, and transform traditions in response to dilemmas, where dilemmas are authoritative understandings that put into question their existing webs of belief. Dilemmas prompt changes of belief because they consist of new beliefs and any new belief necessarily poses a question of the agent's webs of belief. (Bevir,1999, pp. 221–2)

A dilemma comes about through a tension between two or more beliefs but, crucially, it depends on an actor interpreting two (or more) beliefs in this way. Given actors' capacity for agency and interpretation, dilemmas can come from anywhere: reading a book, personal moral reflection, contrasting experiences of the world, empirical evidence and/or statistics, unintended consequences, shock events, a *faux pas*, natural and/or artificial disasters, and more besides (Bevir and Rhodes, 2006, pp. 9–11). Without interpreting two beliefs as posing questions for each other, beliefs may co-exist in contradictory harmony. However, once an actor finds two beliefs in conflict, a dilemma arises and the actor needs to adjudicate between those beliefs. New beliefs could: (i) be discarded as unconvincing, (ii) be accommodated within a web of beliefs, or (iii) replace an older belief. This could lead to ripple effects as it comes into conflict with other beliefs within a wider web. This is how – incrementally, slowly and painfully – traditions and practices change over time. Alternatively, the introduction of a single new belief could rip apart the coherence of whole traditions. Dilemmas matter because they help us to understand the contingent nature of British politics and the central mechanism to explain political change in the interpretive approach. They also identify the limits of webs of belief and how everyday practices (see below) come into conflict with one another. Dilemmas also draw attention to power relations in that it is a force that mediates a rupture of contesting beliefs and traditions, making it a crucial element in the interpretive armoury. As a result of power relations, some ideas and practices are prioritised, while others are marginalised; they set boundaries for dilemmas and frame how a dilemma arises (Geddes, 2018b).

The 'drama' of everyday practices

The above discussion suggests that traditions, beliefs and dilemmas are inextricably interwoven and play out through practices. In their own words, Bevir and Rhodes define practices in the following way:

> A practice is a set of actions, often a set of actions that exhibits a pattern, perhaps even a pattern that remains relatively stable across time. Practices often give us grounds for postulating beliefs, for we can ascribe to people only in interpreting their actions. Nonetheless, practices cannot explain actions because people act for reasons of their own. People sometimes act on their beliefs about a practice, but, when they do, we still explain their action by reference to their beliefs about the practice, and, of course, these beliefs need not be accurate. (Bevir and Rhodes, 2010, p. 74)

In this quotation, it is clear that Bevir and Rhodes privilege beliefs over actions (or at least maintain a clear epistemological divide between the two). This has met with criticisms from others. Hendrik Wagenaar (2012), for example, argues that practices should be central to interpretive approaches because individuals construct meaning not only through interpretation, but through action (which can confirm, alter or discard beliefs). Bevir and Rhodes (2012, p. 201) insist that practices embody beliefs and 'cannot properly be discussed without reference to these beliefs', which, although true, does not ameliorate the criticism that beliefs are only ever partial and that actions are 'a move into an only partly known and knowable world' (Wagenaar, 2012, p. 92). Both beliefs *and* actions offer explanatory value in political science; that is to say, it is not just what people say about what they do that matters, but also requires us to closely focus on their actions, and what those actions tell us about actors' beliefs (and, by extension, the traditions on which those beliefs are based).

I offer a more condensed, bricolage conceptualisation of practices, building on Bevir and Rhodes' work. In particular, I take inspiration from the literature on dramaturgy. References to politics and drama are ubiquitous: summits between heads of government are described as taking place on the 'world stage'; discussions between political factions often take place 'off-stage'; politicians need to be able to give a good 'performance' when delivering keynote speeches; Prime Minister's Questions is often described as a piece of 'theatre' or 'drama'; the public are perceived as 'spectators' or an 'audience' (who watch politics unfold on TV, much like a soap opera or drama); and, more cynically, politicians are only 'actors', talking from 'scripts' that are handed to them by whips, political parties or lobby groups. Seeing politics as drama is intuitively appealing, too, because it draws attention to the clash of beliefs and ideas to which definitions of politics are closely related (see above). The nature of accountability in the House of Commons (as summarised in Chapter 1) often lends itself to elements of drama and confrontation between political actors (ministers, parliamentarians, civil servants and many more), whether it is the high-profile encounters between chairs of committees and powerful vested interests, or the sustained and laborious scrutiny undertaken by individual members as they analyse, question and interrogate their witnesses.

Given the fruitful link between 'practices' and 'performances', it offers one (of many) opportunities to refine the interpretive approach. The concept of 'performance' has been widely used in a range of contexts across the social sciences and humanities. For example, the anthropologist Victor Turner (1982) believed performance to be a natural form of human expression; elsewhere, Erving Goffman (1990) argued that the 'self', the 'performer' and the 'character' are enmeshed if not equated. In political terms, Maarten Hajer (2009, p. 7) argues that, through the presentation of the political self, meaning is given, roles are defined and narratives of conflict or cohesion are promoted. In order to take on these roles and perform effectively, performers need to interpret their surroundings (linking us back to situated agency, above). Performers need to interpret the social norms, values, etiquette, expectations and accepted modes of behaviour associated with that situation, which consequently requires practical judgements as well as taken-for-granted or tacit knowledge. This suggests that everyday practices as performances can have a range of elements. In this chapter, I limit my discussion to three (style, speech and space) and draw from one of the founding fathers of dramaturgy, Erving Goffman.

Style. Goffman (1990, pp. 34–5) identifies two elements of what I term a 'performance style': first, the appearance of the performer (including dress and body language), which indicates the social status of the individual; and, second, the manner adopted by the performer (gestures, tone of voice, etc.) which function to indicate the role that the performer expects to play. He describes that performers idealise their enactment by trying to remove blemishes to the contrary of their intentions, or 'conceal action which is inconsistent' with 'ideal standards' (Goffman, 1990, p. 50). Actions are stylised according to a set of informal codes or cues (of course, the performer is under no obligation to accept these codes and cues, and may choose to subvert them). Non-verbal behaviour could include, among other things, scratching heads, waving hands, knocking on desks or other furniture, clapping or shrugging shoulders. These are signs that can symbolise shock and awe, disagreement or agreement, etc. They can, consciously or unconsciously, influence the behaviour of MPs and officials (as shown by Cheryl Schonhardt-Bailey, 2017). More generally, performance styles are the ways in which actors negotiate their political space as everyday practices, which reveals much about the identities of individuals, their beliefs, and their knowledge and/or interpretation of the world.

Performances, of course, do not occur in isolation. Other actors are present as part of a cast in an enactment, which Goffman (1990, pp. 83–108) refers to as 'performance teams'. The relations within teams are vitally important. At the most basic level, a smooth performance depends on every individual remaining committed to their role and to their script. Goffman calls this a 'working consensus' among all participants, in which actors are expected to follow social codes or etiquettes, and to suppress their immediate feelings or urges of the contrary in order to allow for a temporarily acceptable social interaction (pp. 20–1, 90–1). In doing so, collective performances layer each actor into their respective role, which may of course change depending on the setting or situation of the performance, but which, in each case, determines their status in social and political terms. This reinforces earlier points about the significance of power relationships that influence everyday practices. Certain performances become naturalised and, in doing so, turn into routines and practices.

A team enacts its performance in front of an audience, although audiences behave both as spectators and 'perform' a role as audiences (Fitzgerald, 2015). For Goffman (1990, pp. 74–5, 108), a team has 'something of the character of a secret society' because each actor is 'in the know' of the performance, which the audience respects to allow the performance to take place. Too close an inspection would prevent the performance from being enacted successfully and so the audience needs to co-operate through distance between itself and the performers. In our context, it suggests that the public accept the legitimate role of politicians. If people began to question their legitimacy, the political performance would break down. It also brings to mind a distinction between insiders and outsiders, or an 'us' and 'them'. It suggests different performance roles, with some playing central parts and others supporting roles. More fundamentally, it demarcates those that should be included in a performance and those that act as an audience.

Speech. Political actors may follow a script and stage directions, whether written and formalised, or unwritten and informal. These must fall in line with the appropriate social cues or performance styles as well as the appropriate setting or stage (see below). Some voices, tones of voice or auditory rhythms are encouraged to fill spaces; others are assigned the status of hysterical, chaotic or disruptive and consequently marginalised (Puwar, 2010, p. 299); some voices can be 'cultured' or well-modulated, while others still are pejoratively labelled as 'shrill' (particularly often with respect to gender) or 'rough' (particularly often with respect to social class) (Rai, 2015). As Theodore Schmauk (1890, p. 113) put it over a century ago:

> With reference to the various properties of tone, we say a voice is rich, full, deep, piercing, sweet, rough, smooth, ringing, bird-like, flute-like, trumpet-like,

manly, womanly, child-like. As a reflection of the apparent natural mental state of the speaker, a voice is pathetic, solemn, tranquil, grave, serious, animated, gay, playful, mirthful, rollicking, melancholy, sublime, courageous, scornful, defiant, threatening, despairing, awe-stricken, alarmed, horrified, revengeful, kind, tender, hopeful, truthful.

Language, vocabulary or tone of voice are things that sharpen or blur a particular performance in a particular setting; some voices are regarded as 'fit' for certain performances, others are not. This is undoubtedly true of politics, too. We are all too aware of the public's disdain for shouting and booing in the main chamber of the House of Commons, for example. Yet, these practices persist. This is because this type of behaviour has become part of established performances within adversarial (and gendered) British political traditions. The nature of voice is therefore something that deserves further attention as part of a wider parliamentary performance and everyday practice in terms of how this affects scrutiny in select committees. While delving further into the literature on speech analysis, discourse analysis or rhetorical analysis arguably goes beyond the purview of this chapter (and perhaps the analytical framework identified here), it is sufficient to note that we must be sensitive to the voices that are attached to parliamentary performances and the spaces that they fill (Finlayson, 2007; Finlayson and Martin, 2008; Hajer, 2009).

Space. Shirin M. Rai (2015, p. 1183) argues that: 'The backdrop, the stage, the entry and exit points shape the kind of politics that is performed, the shifts and struggles that take place – who constructs, reflects, claims and polices the space of politics.' Space privileges certain types of behaviour, allowing some practices to occur, while others are seen as illegitimate, wrong or inappropriate. It follows that the way space is used or organised (whether intentionally or unintentionally) is important to regulate behaviour. Nirmal Puwar (2010), for example, has examined the way in which parliamentary spaces are gendered to segregate men from women. Elsewhere, Jean-Philippe Heurtin (2003) showed that the layout of the French parliamentary assembly changed seven times over the French revolutionary period in order to reflect different political priorities and values of its members.

In his own conceptualisation of performances, Goffman defines spatial arrangements in terms of both a 'front stage' and a 'back stage': on the front stage, performances are enacted, involving the furniture, décor, physical layout and background items that supply the scenery and provide props for actors (Goffman, 1990, pp. 32–3). At the back stage, preparations take place, illusions are constructed, props and personal items are stored or hidden, dress is adjusted and examined, rehearsals take place and, more generally, where performers can relax and 'step out of character' (pp. 114–15). Axiomatically, there is a tension or weakness in this approach because it implies that actors can step outside of their social setting or web of beliefs, which, in line with discussions above, is not the case. That said, distinguishing between a front stage and a back stage is still useful for analytical purposes because they entail different types of performances, with different expectations, social codes and cues, participants and audiences. So, in as much as a back stage exists, it remains a *stage*. This links physical space back to the ideational contexts: our interpretation, our knowledge (tacit or explicit) is fundamental to identifying appropriate stages or contexts in which we act, demonstrating the enduring connection between beliefs and practices. An example of this, discussed in later chapters, might be when select committees hold public evidence sessions (front stage) versus private deliberations to consider a draft report (back stage). Even this remains a stage, however, and so this distinction is only for analytical purposes.

I therefore use performance to refine the concept of practices as originally proposed by Bevir and Rhodes in their interpretive framework. This arguably has ripple effects for other concepts. So, with respect to beliefs, we must explore how actors produce or react to meaning-in-action; with respect to traditions, we can better understand how they are sustained through established performance styles and the power relationships they entail; and, with respect to dilemmas, we can see how contradictory beliefs and traditions are pushed and pulled in different directions and played out through everyday practices. Taken together, we can better understand how scrutiny is conducted in the House of Commons with reference to a range of concepts that guide parliamentary actors.

A framework for analysis

The interpretive approach offers a conceptually rich way by which we can inject theoretical ideas into studying the House of Commons. With respect to situated agency and traditions, we must focus analysis on the context in which parliamentary actors are placed in interpreting and enacting their roles. We already know that MPs, clerks and officials, researchers, journalists and visitors are situated into what may be termed the Westminster 'bubble' or 'village'. We also know that most official accounts of the parliamentary system formally assert the importance of the Westminster model as a tradition that guides institutional relationships in Parliament (Judge, 2014). However, is it possible to offer further nuance and depth about particular situations and traditions? With respect to this book, we can focus on and ask ourselves about the context in which committee members, chairs and staff operate as part of the scrutiny work by select committees and the accountability relationships guiding executive-legislative relations.

Turning from traditions to individual beliefs, we cannot assume that committee members, chairs and staff act with rational self-interest, as other approaches have done, but rather that actors pursue a wide range of behaviours due to a variety of interpretations about their role and the purpose of committees. Thus, we must look to their interpretations of scrutiny in order to make better

Table 2.3 A framework for analysing select committee scrutiny

Concept	Definition
Situated agency	How committee members, chairs and officials are situated in a particular context to undertake parliamentary scrutiny.
Beliefs	The ways in which parliamentary actors interpret their role on select committees and associated ideas, such as 'accountability' and 'scrutiny'.
Traditions	The wider parliamentary traditions in which committee members, chairs and officials find themselves.
Dilemmas	The problems that parliamentary actors confront based on how they have interpreted and enacted their role.
Practices	How parliamentary actors have chosen to enact the interpretations of their roles and associated ideas.

sense of their approach to their role. Of course, these interpretations are not fixed, but constantly made and re-made through clashes of beliefs and traditions in Parliament. These clashes are caused through dilemmas between interpretations of scrutiny and a multitude of other parliamentary roles and pressures that committee members, chairs and staff face in order to undertake their functions and enact their roles. Thus, when studying scrutiny by committees, this concept helps us to understand the decisions that MPs and staff make. However, this book does not undertake a diachronic analysis, which means that the following empirical chapters cannot analyse changes in belief in response to dilemmas over time. Rather, the following analysis offers a snapshot of perennial and ongoing dilemmas that actors face.

The above outlines the analysis that follows. Not all concepts can be analysed in detail (due to space, resource and time limitations). Also, the concepts are closely interwoven, which means that it will not be possible to isolate each factor and conduct a clearly demarcated analysis of only beliefs, just practices or simply dilemmas. It may well be that the conceptual clarity presented here will therefore become a little more messy as we venture into the rich detail of empirical discussion. However, the concepts are always there, either directly and explicitly to explain parliamentary behaviour, or indirectly and implicitly, to guide further discussion. To guide the reader, this is summarised in Table 2.3. However, before jumping ahead to the empirical chapters, a question remains: how are we to operationalise our analytical framework? This question turns our attention from the philosophical underpinnings to the practical questions of method, which are examined in the final section of this chapter.

Methods

Although an interpretive approach to political science rests on a philosophical analysis of action as meaningful, and therefore does not prescribe any particular method (Bevir, 2006; Bevir and Blakely, 2018), a number of influential studies tend to privilege qualitative research methods, especially through the use of observation (e.g., Crewe, 2005, 2015; Durose, 2009; Gains, 2009; Rhodes, 2011). In this book, I similarly adopt a qualitative approach, using a range of methods, including participant and non-participant observation, semi-structured interviews, a focus group, and textual analysis of written records. I summarise the key analytical focus and how it has been applied in this book. The Annex offers philosophical reflections on the approach taken; here I focus more on the analytical focus of these methods and how they have been applied.

Participant and non-participant observation

The inherent value of observation (whether as a participant or non-participant) is that it opens what is ordinarily hidden in official documents and structured interviews. It allows researchers to look at political issues from a different vantage point. While documents tend to be final products in which the process of writing has been airbrushed out, the value of observation is that the method is able to access meaning 'in the making', or as Rhodes, 't Hart and Noordegraaf (2007a, p. 2) put it:

> It is characterised by 'deep immersion' in social worlds to understand day-to-day practices, and how these practices become meaningful. Ethnographers emphasise and observe human acts and interaction in physical, economic and social context. They understand how these acts and interactions become meaningful because of bigger symbolic and interpretive structures that are the outcome of earlier acts and interactions. Ethnographers try to grasp the 'making' of meaningful social behaviour.

This quote illustrates the fundamental benefit of observation, which focuses the analytical lens on everyday practices and connects those to the beliefs of political elites. Observation allows researchers to analyse the everyday behaviour of groups and individuals because researchers have access to what Dvora Yanow (2004, p. 12) calls local knowledge: 'the very mundane, yet expert understanding of and practical reasoning about local conditions derived from lived experience'. It is a kind of non-verbal knowing that evolves from seeing and interacting with other people, places or things over time. Other research methods, such as interviews and textual analysis, would possibly miss such nuances.

Observation can be applied in a range of ways: extended periods of fieldwork and immersion; 'hit-and-run' or 'yo-yo' fieldwork; ethnographic interviewing; elite focus groups; para-ethnography and visual ethnography (Boswell et al., 2018). For this book, I worked as a research assistant to a select committee in the House of Commons for 14 weeks during the second half of the 2010 parliament (which amounted to approximately 600 working hours). Every week, I was able to observe private and public meetings of 'my' committee, attend and participate in team meetings, observe proceedings of parliamentary debates and evidence sessions, help to write briefing material for committee members and the chair, and contribute to the drafting of committee reports (as well as other duties). This was supplemented with negotiated access to observe other committees' private meetings and staff team meetings. I complemented my observations by watching and analysing more than 100 hours of evidence sessions made available online (see www.parliamentlive.tv). So, I was a full member of the committee staff team and contributed to their work, while also being able to observe the everyday lives of MPs and staff. As part of my fieldwork, I kept a fieldwork diary (FWD). This is a personal, private and confidential journal, and not accessible to anyone other than myself. I draw on the FWD in empirical work, all of which is referenced as 'FWD <paragraph number>'.

The precise details of which committee I supported, and at what precise point during the 2010 parliament, will remain confidential indefinitely. This is to protect the anonymity of my former colleagues and permits more candour in empirical sections. The research received ethics approval from the University of Sheffield (at which I was based), and both the Head of the Scrutiny Unit and I agreed to the terms of the research placement through written and verbal agreements.

Semi-structured interviews and focus groups

There are significant advantages to using interviews, in general, but particularly for this study on ideas and beliefs of political elites. As Crang and Cook (2007, p. 69) point out: 'the main aim of interviewing in ethnographic research is to allow people to reveal their own versions of events in their own words'. This is, ultimately, a central plank of the interpretive approach to political science. Interviews do not report unfiltered facts; rather, they present a particular narrative or story and, in doing so, they will undoubtedly omit certain details and emphasise others. We do not have 'pure' access to respondents' accounts and lives. However, it is precisely this which allows us insights into the beliefs of actors, and the meanings they attribute to their experiences and social worlds (Miller and Glassner, 2004). There are other benefits of interviews: you can ask individuals to explain something that you observed; interviewees can tell us which documents mattered and how they interpreted their importance (Seldon, 1996, p. 358); and interviews offer access to otherwise unrecorded or inaccessible source material (Lilleker, 2003, p. 213).

For this book, I undertook 46 semi-structured interviews, which were scheduled, one-on-one meetings with select committee members (23), chairs (10) and staff (13).[1] Almost all of these took place during my fieldwork on the parliamentary estate. In order to identify appropriate interviewees, I used a snowballing technique, where I invited individuals through email, but often followed it up with a telephone call. I began interviewing MPs from the committee for which I worked, and followed recommendations from clerks and officials. I requested an interview with almost every chair of departmental select committees and interviewed ten of those. These became 'priority' committees in that I focused on interviewing MPs that served on those committees and officials that worked for them. This has been useful, but of course wasn't fool-proof: not all my invitations were accepted. Those that agreed to an interview clearly had an interest in select committees and believe their role was important as part of scrutiny processes. Although this could skew the empirical findings about how MPs interpret their scrutiny role, I was predominantly interested in precisely why MPs *did* serve on committees. All interviewees signed an informed consent form and were recorded using a recording device (with two exceptions).

Finally, I draw on a focus group with eight parliamentary officials undertaken for a project on evidence use in the UK Parliament (Geddes et al., 2018), which provided interesting insights into the work of select committees.

Supplementary data: reports, briefings, statistics

Observation and interviews are the main forms of data on which I draw in my empirical sections, which are used to also corroborate one another where possible. However, and although written records are not the foundational method in this book, documents are a key part of the House of Commons. Parliament produces hundreds of pages of documents every single day, both internal and external, and they play a role throughout the everyday lives of all political actors involved. Documents keep Parliament running through routine tasks of recording, filing, archiving and retrieving information. Indeed, given the emphasis of past research on committee outputs, many would regard select committee reports as the most important output from scrutiny. Therefore, I used texts to supplement my analysis, including a range of committee reports, email exchanges, copies of speeches, magazine and newspaper articles (online and in print), press cuttings, the Official Report (Hansard), guidelines and instruction manuals, evidence sub-mitted to committees, briefings for MPs, correspondence between committees and ministerial departments, and more. Indeed, I was partly responsible for pro-ducing texts as part of my participant-observer role, which added great insights into the production of written records (see the Annex). Finally, I also draw on some descriptive statistics from sessional returns (e.g., attendance records, gender breakdown of committees, etc.).

Taken together, these wide-ranging sources of data offer an overarching interpretive methodology. Each method makes a distinctive contribution to this book, and it is their combination that allows us to triangulate for robustness. Every methodology has its limitations, including this one: it cannot offer a comprehensive picture of how all MPs interpret their role, nor is it possible to evaluate the role of ideas and beliefs against standards of what makes an 'effective' select committee system. Nonetheless, fieldwork conducted for this book produced a swathe of information, which required detailed analysis. In line with the analytical framework, I used an open form of coding, by which I read through material to develop various themes associated with individual beliefs, everyday practices and parliamentary traditions. This analysis established categories and codes, which became hooks on which the following empirical chapters are based.

Concluding remarks

This chapter began by providing an overview of current trends in research on parliaments, and sought to clarify what could otherwise be perceived to be an unreflexive scholarship. In doing so, I identified four dominant traditions that pervade the scholarship, underpinned more broadly by the legacy of the Westminster model. Crucially, I identified a small but growing interpretive tradition, to which this book is squarely committed. So, the second half of the chapter charted the ontological and epistemological roots that underpin this book, and the analytical framework that shapes the subsequent empirical chapters. Specifically, it has identified a pivotal role to be played by political actors' individual beliefs, the traditions in which they behave and act, the dilemmas they face in adjudicating conflicting ideas, and how their lives play out through everyday practices. In doing so, this chapter has built on previous theoretical work in the field of interpretive political science. It offers us a philosophically rigorous and conceptually consistent way to study scrutiny in the House of Commons, and it is this framework for analysis that underpins the empirical sections that follow.

Note

1 This excludes countless informal conversations I had during my fieldwork in the House of Commons. I spoke to people as we rushed to and from meetings, on my way to the office, in the cafeteria, in our committee office, over the phone, in emails, at bus stops, in the Westminster Gym, and in the Palace's numerous bars – among other places.

3

Performing scrutiny

Reaching the House of Commons after an exhausting campaign to become a Member of Parliament is undoubtedly both an exciting and also daunting moment. Not only will you have to master the complex rules and procedures of the House, but also set up a new office and deal with a huge mailbag of constituency letters. But it is also exhilarating: you've won against your opponents, you can finally address the needs of your constituency, serve your country and make the UK a better place. How? There is no job description for being an MP. You can interpret your role as you wish, and consequently focus your energy on things that you deem important. According to survey research conducted by the Hansard Society, MPs say they spend 49% of their time on constituency activities, 21% in the House of Commons chamber, 14% working for committees, 10% campaigning locally and 6% of their time on national campaigns (Korris, 2011, p. 6). So, after getting into the House, you are required to make a choice about what kind of MP you want to be. There is no right answer. But that hasn't stopped countless commentators and academics spilling ink on the topic (e.g., Flynn, 2012; Hardman, 2018; Wright, 2010). Michael Rush (2001, pp. 167–211) argues that the role can be split into three interlinked themes: representing constituents (constituency role), supporting the political party (partisan role) and holding the government to account (scrutiny role). All of these fulfil fundamental functions of parliaments across the world – what will you choose?

In this chapter, I look at what it means to be an MP today, but I focus particularly on those kinds of MPs that want to hold the government to account. In other words, the 'scrutinisers' of Parliament. I present a simple argument: MPs are thrust into a chaotic and unstructured world and, subsequently, make choices about how to interpret both their general role as elected representatives and the specific concept of scrutiny to survive in Westminster. MPs create different parliamentary habits, routines and practices, which push and pull scrutiny in different directions. To make this argument, the chapter is split into three sections. First, I go into a little more detail about all the different functions that an MP can perform, before then examining their scrutiny role in organisational context; i.e., what it meant to sit on scrutiny committees. Second, I identify different ways in which MPs interpret their role. I argue that committee members adopt different performance styles to enact their committee role, including the following: specialists, lone wolves, constituency champions, party helpers, learners and absentees. These roles are not exhaustive, nor do they form a fixed typology of roles (as, for example, in the work of Donald Searing, 1994). Rather, the aim is to demonstrate that committees are a site for a diverse range of ideas and interpretations that push and pull committees in different directions. Third and finally, the chapter discusses how we can explain MPs' choices. I explore the dilemmas that MPs face in terms of the need to build expertise and professional competence, competing time commitments, multiple (and sometimes conflicting) loyalties that MPs negotiate, and the complexities of being an MP. Select committees offer an anchor to deepen their knowledge and understanding of policy-making, and additionally offer a way to reconcile the different aspects of enacting the role of elected representative.

Being an MP

MPs have total freedom to interpret their role as elected representatives in any way they wish; there is, as noted above, no job description for the position of 'Member of Parliament'. To take forward the analogy of theatre developed in the previous chapter, it means that MPs have lots of 'parts' or 'characters' that they can choose to play on the stage of the House of Commons. However, while the stage and scene might be set, there is also no fixed plot nor script. It is an improvisation – with a helpful 'crew' of clerks and officials, contradictory stage directors in the form of whips, competing protagonists vying for the limelight and a waiting audience. So, thrust on the stage after an election victory, how do MPs decide what role to play?

Choosing a role?

The parliamentary estate makes up much more than the chambers of the Houses of Parliament. There are a disorienting set of corridors leading to hundreds of committee rooms, offices and meeting spaces, and yet many more corridors leading to restaurants, bars, a gym, a hairdresser, a nursery, post offices and more. It is easy to get lost, as I did (FWD 6.2.27, FWD 6.2.28, FWD 16.4.19, FWD 19.5.4). In one corner, with a broken lamp and discarded furniture, you may find yourself awkwardly walking past three backbench MPs planning a rebellion against their government. On stairs and escalators, you could bump into the leader of the opposition in deep conversation with the shadow home secretary on their way to the main chamber (FWD 48.11.18). In Portcullis House, you might gossip with colleagues or journalists (or both) over lunch. One thing is very clear: it is a place bursting with activity. The pace is fast. The sense of urgency is constant. A crisis is always around the corner.

MPs are keenly aware of this activity. Demands on their time are relentless and come from many places. They are asked to not only vote in the division lobbies, but debate proposed legislation (and review existing statutes); speak in the interests of their constituents on the floor of the House; address the concerns of individual constituents; support the Speaker by chairing committees or debates; co-ordinate campaigns and lobby frontbench colleagues on issues that the individual MP feels strongly about; meet with stakeholders to discuss policy issues; serve on and actively contribute to a range of committees; ask probing or supporting questions of ministers in the chamber, depending on which side of the House they sit; meet with journalists to build a profile; and so on. The list is ever-growing. To carry out these things, MPs have resources (their own offices and researchers as well as help from parliamentary officials), but need to also learn how to carry out their functions by understanding the rituals, practices and procedures of the House of Commons. All of this can, quite easily, be intimidating. And although Parliament has become much better at induction processes in recent years, they are still not comprehensive. So, many MPs rely on other informal means or look elsewhere to understand the Westminster village that they've joined: from other colleagues, instructions from the whips, training programmes from political parties, and so on (Coghill et al., 2012; Dickinson, 2018; Rush and Giddings, 2011).

Given this vast array of tasks in a bewildering workplace, how do some MPs end up on select committees? That is the essential question of this chapter. One of Parliament's overarching functions is to scrutinise the executive, so part of the answer comes from the fact that select committees are often regarded as 'the principal mechanism through which the House of Commons holds the executive to account' (Brazier and Fox, 2011, p. 354). However, Isabel Hardman (2018) argues that there are many incentives that prevent MPs from taking scrutiny seriously, such as the pressure from whips to support their party to rise through the ranks, or many media opportunities to build a better local and national profile. Such pressures make it yet more interesting to understand why some MPs do serve on committees, which is the focus of this chapter (for legislative scrutiny, see Thompson, 2015b and Russell and Gover, 2017).

Who are the scrutinisers?

Over the course of the 2010 parliament, 396 MPs (60.9%) served on the select committees I studied (see Table 1.2), a figure that rises even higher if domestic committees, temporary committees and joint scrutiny committees are included (analysis of sessional returns, 2010–15). So, we can say that select committee service is something that most MPs experience over the course of their parliamentary careers, including MPs that went on to serve on the frontbench and – in one case – became prime minister (David Cameron served on the Home Affairs Committee and the Modernisation Committee between 2001 and 2004).

During the 2010–15 period, MPs served on committees for just over two and a half years (32 months), although turnover is highly variable between committees. On average, each committee had 21 MPs between 2010 and 2015. Of the total number of MPs that served on committees, 27% were women, which is slightly higher than the 22% of women elected to the House of Commons in 2010 (for analysis of the gendered nature of select committee membership, see research by Mark Goodwin and colleagues, 2019).

The average attendance rate for MPs was 68.9% in Session 2010–12, which declines to 63.6% in Session 2014–15 (the average for the whole 2010 parliament: 65.9%). However, there is wide variety in this, with some committees experiencing more than 80% average attendance and others dipping as low as 43%. Despite the well-established trend towards greater constituency activity (Campbell and Lovenduski, 2015; Norris, 1997), select committee work takes up a considerable amount of MPs' time. Over the course of the 2010 parliament alone, 24 departmental and cross-cutting committees (excluding the Liaison Committee) held 4,555 formal meetings and published 1,349 reports This suggests that parliamentary committees play an important role simply by virtue of the demand they place on an MP's time and the range of meetings that an MP can attend.

In order to scrutinise activities of government, select committee members undertake inquiries that involve (i) deciding on a topic (agenda-setting), (ii) calling for written evidence and participating in committee hearings (evidence-gathering), and (iii) agreeing to and publishing committee findings through a final report. Axiomatically, committee activity ranges significantly from this crude simplification (as detailed in Chapter 7), but it is clear that committees rely on the active participation of members through attending meetings, asking questions in oral evidence to gather information and/or hold witnesses to account, and evaluating an inquiry's findings in advance of publishing a report.

Until 2010 (and as summarised in Chapter 1), committee members were selected by their party whips to serve. Many MPs resented this, such as this one:

> *Getting on a select committee in the first place was very difficult for me because, being on the left, the Blair machine … didn't want anybody who was going to stir up trouble. So they deliberately stuffed it full of, you know, sycophants, Blair babes, loyalists, whatever you call them, Blairites, and kept anybody who was trouble out of the serious select committees.* (Interview with MP 8)

Another MP said that she had to '*serve an apprenticeship*' before gaining membership of her preferred committee. This required '*having to prove a track record as well as not being difficult for the government*'. After 2010, this was no longer necessary and there's '*no difference between someone who's been a Member for 15 years or someone who's just joined*' (Interview with MP 20). According to Hannah White (2015c, p. 6), 58% of committee seats went to first-term members, which would have been unlikely under the old system. For White, this may have increased a willingness among committees to be more innovative and independent-minded. My interviewees have also argued that there has been a shift towards a more independent form of scrutiny, which has also been noted by the media (D'Arcy, 2011; Fisher, 2015), think tanks (Hagelund and Goddard, 2015) and the Speaker of the House of Commons (Bercow, 2015). So, what do MPs do once they are there?

How do committee members interpret their role?

In interviews, most MPs interpreted 'scrutiny' in a broad way; it was a catch-all term to describe the detailed examination of government policy and to hold the executive to account by getting it to explain its actions. And while MPs have different opportunities to do this, as summarised in the opening pages of this book, most interviewees distinguished between committee scrutiny from debates on the floor of the main chamber:

> In the House of Commons you can get one or two questions, intervention in a debate, but in a select committee you can pursue a pretty clear line of questioning ... and you've got a much better chance and opportunity of both finding out what's going on, finding out what the department is doing is consistent with the policy ... and also finding out if the policy makes sense. (Interview with MP 21)

> I think select committees are absolutely vital for the whole working of Parliament because for every government department there is a select committee which is there to ... hold it to account in a detailed way. Yes, we have Questions on the floor of the House, but they are quick fire and it's all over in 30 minutes. Whereas I spent ten years or so on the [XX] Committee. We did some very detailed inquiries into [XX]. (Interview with MP 15)

Other MPs noted that committee scrutiny provides 'a different perspective to the ... theatre of accountability in the chamber' (Interview with MP 1), and another said (although adding this is not always the case): 'You're away from the Punch and Judy crudities of the chamber where the opposition are always wrong, and your side is always right. I mean ... we're veering onto intelligent conversation on committees' (Interview with MP 2). These quotes, which acknowledge the importance attached to committee work, are hardly surprising. However, specific nuances and different emphases placed on interpretations of scrutiny are critical because they affect MPs' approaches to their role, both in terms of the questioning and conduct of inquiries, as well as the focus and aims of inquiries. The above quotes, for example, indicate that scrutiny by select committees is about explanation and information-gathering, rather than forcing government to change policy (see Christina Boswell's analysis of the Home Affairs Committee for a detailed example of this; Boswell, 2018, pp. 98–120). Some MPs believed that 'value for money' was a key factor in good scrutiny (e.g., Interview with Chair 1, Interview with Chair 8, Interview with MP 15), while others were keen on the implementation of policy and the extent to which it lived up to its promises (e.g., Interview with MP 20, Interview with MP 21).

The interpretation of one MP, who served on two committees, is a good example to illustrate the effect of individual beliefs on scrutiny practices. Although this particular MP was more interested in one policy area over another, it is arguably her interpretation of the focus of scrutiny that served as a real dividing line between her two committees (as there is some potential overlap on the two committees). While one committee was praised as working as a team, and focusing on what is happening and why in policy implementation terms, the other committee is, '*all about the theory and not about what actually happens to people*' (Interview with MP 10). She later added that the committee ignores the '*nuts and bolts*' and the '*real questions*':

> *There are times that we had* [XX] *in and you're asking them practical things about, 'Why haven't you hit this target?', 'What's the matter?', 'You don't look at the staff survey that says that all staff are working there, what's going on?', 'What are you doing about* [XX] *and* [XX]*?' And all those real questions that actually matter, it actually involves a bit of research and a bit of work. Whereas they* [the other committee] *can just go, 'Well, what do you think* [XX] *is going to be this time next year?' It's easy, innit? … just pondering, really, what they're doing.*

The underlying difference between these two committees lies in two things. First, the focus of the 'other' committee's work was a problem (and in her opinion, '*run for the benefit of the chair, not the committee*' – see Chapter 4). Second, her interpretation of scrutiny:

> *It's in the implementation that it matters and it's only by scrutinising, you know, whether what was intended is actually happening or there's unintended consequences. So I think you can dream of great ideas but it's in practice that you change people's lives, so I think you need to scrutinise the implementation and development of policies.*

Although just one detailed example, it is instructive of other MPs and their approaches. Another committee member, with a background in marketing and business, related her assessments to how events or policies would be made in the business world. In a discussion about the lack of timely responses from the government to a report by her committee, she comments:

> *It's not a way to do business. You see, it wouldn't happen in the commercial world and I don't see why you shouldn't translate the commercial world across. … If there's a criticism from a group of consumers – the company would respond.* (Interview with MP 4)

To take a final example, another MP, who used to be a school inspector in which he focused on '*evaluation and quality*', used this approach to scrutiny, i.e., focusing on '*self-evaluation*' of government (e.g., '*how do various ministers who've been with us, how do they evaluate their own performance?*') (Interview with MP 14).

Table 3.1 Styles of scrutiny

Specialists	Usually adopted by 'core' members of a committee that regularly attend meetings, in this performance MPs seek to analyse the evidence pursue policy interests.
Lone wolves	Longstanding and personal interests are pursued in meetings, perhaps at the expense of a committee's inquiry that is focused on other issues.
Constituency champions	In this style of scrutiny enactment, committee members represent their constituents in the topics they pursue or the questions they ask.
Party helpers or safety nets	A performance in which a committee member may ask questions to witnesses for party political reasons, either to make a partisan attack or protect the witness.
Learners	In this role, committee members attempt to learn about a policy area or to find out more about government activity, rather than holding it to account.
Absentees	A committee member who is conspicuous by their absence, or who has made a minimal contribution, perhaps by 'dipping in and out' of the meeting.

The broad point of this discussion is to demonstrate that scrutiny, although it has easily identifiable principles, is still interpreted in different ways that affect the way in which MPs approach their work. In the above reflections from MPs, for example, each approach leads to different lines of questioning in committee hearings. This is important because it means that committees cannot function purely based on abstract principles of accountability; they are dependent on MPs' interpretations. The variety of roles is impossible to quantify because, as Anthony King (1974, p. 74) put it, there are 'as many ways of being an MP as there are MPs'. Nonetheless, over the course of my fieldwork and following interviews and discussions with clerks, members and chairs of committees, I believe that it is possible to identify commonly adopted performance styles. This is not an attempt to create a fixed typology of scrutiny roles, nor is it an attempt to stipulate guidelines for ideal-types of MP or to generalise across all legislatures. Any such endeavour would be hopelessly rigid and inflexible, as discussion in Chapter 2 sought to show (see also Andeweg, 2014). Rather, there are different styles or dispositions that MPs can choose to adopt, which might change depending on inquiry, witness, other committee members, the broader political or news agenda of the day, etc. Each are examined in detailed here and summarised in Table 3.1.

Specialists

One of the fundamental arguments for greater committee work in the House of Commons was to allow MPs to specialise (House of Commons Procedure Committee, 1978, paras 5.45–5.50). This indeed came about, with many MPs explaining that their committee had particular experts for different areas of policy. This usually stems from members' policy interest and/or previous professional background. It is these individuals who arguably drive forward committee work and assist chairs as their most vocal supporting 'cast' (to extend the performance metaphor). This is also, arguably, the most common type of performance we see in committee meetings (public and private).

As this MP explained (with reference to his party), specialisation means that members can divide tasks between them:

> *Within my party, there's a recognition that anything to do with the First World War, that's* [XX]*'s subject, you know, because he's always rambling on about it. And there'll be other, I mean, I'm hopeless on finance, and I don't know anybody on finance, but we've got people who are brilliant on finance. So as in, as with a select committee, you all know that which members will have a specific interest.* (Interview with MP 15)

He went on to describe some of the committee-related interests of some of the members. Another MP:

> [MP A]*, who's on the committee, … she did research. So she's really, she's really read a lot of stuff about what the data means. …* [MP B] *has done a big piece of work on people who* [XX]*. So I will know that she will do that better than me.* [MP C]*, a Conservative, he's got an accountancy background, so he will want to know about the numbers.* (Interview with MP 10)

This division of expertise has wider repercussions for the development of committee norms and values or performance teams (see Chapter 7), which is significant because it indicates that effective committees work to each other's strengths. To make the most of members' talents, the chair's skills matter. One chair, for instance, prefers to allocate themes for inquiries to members who then use this theme for each witness throughout an inquiry (Interview with Chair 5). Another chair gave two examples of MPs whose advice he would seek because they are experts in two areas of the committee's remit (Interview with Chair 9).

A good indication of a specialist is the extent to which they use their expertise in other activities outside of committee work. To take just one example: Paul Blomfield, before his election victory to represent Sheffield Central in 2010, was general manager of the University of Sheffield's Students' Union. His work in Parliament until 2017 (when he joined Labour's frontbench) reflects this background. For the vast majority of this period, he served on the Business, Innovation and Skills (BIS) Committee, with an average attendance rate of 83.2%. MPs (in separate interviews) on the committee have noted his expertise and passion for higher and further education policy. However, he has also been involved in campaigns outside the BIS Committee, attending conferences, meetings and events in relation to education, speaking at debates on these issues regularly in Parliament, and participating in campaigns relating to student issues – such as vocational skills (HC Deb 24 Mar 2014, c13) and financial support for students (HC Deb 5 Dec 2013, cc1084–5). During the 2010 parliament, he was also chair of the All-Party Parliamentary Group (APPG) on Students, vice-chair of the APPG on Apprenticeships, and secretary of the APPG on Universities.

Committees rely on specialists because they play a fundamentally important role in pushing forward scrutiny. The Defence Committee grasped the importance of this and introduced new practices in the 2010 parliament to help scrutinise the Ministry of Defence by appointing members as rapporteurs to take the lead on specific inquiries. This allowed members to focus and thereby adopt a more specialist role. According to White (2015c, p. 12), this enabled the committee to grow its capacity for scrutiny.

Lone wolves

Some MPs take their policy interest and research further, and could become an extreme version of this by adopting styles of a 'lone wolf'. They zealously promote particular issues that they are interested in. However, while a specialist will provide expertise on particular areas for a committee's inquiry as part of a team, a lone wolf is not usually a team player. They are often persistent and go 'off-script'. As this clerk describes:

> It'll vary from inquiry to inquiry, but somebody will always ask about X, and we always know they're going to ask about that. On [XX], they used to be that, they asked that, even if it wasn't terribly relevant to the inquiry you were dealing with. (Interview with Official 3)

To act as a lone wolf is to follow an issue or interest irrespective of the inquiry or, indeed, irrespective of the remit of the committee on which they are serving. One interviewee cited the following example: '*I mean, one of my, of the Conservative colleagues on the committee is a passionate … Eurosceptic. Consequently, you know, at every turn, there is a, let's get [XX] in, let's get [XX] in, … whatever*' (Interview with MP 6). During my fieldwork, my committee had an MP who would often operate as a lone wolf. The potential problem with such a character is that the approach could disorientate witnesses, who could be asked about things on which they had no expertise or knowledge. When this happened on my committee, it turned into an argument with the chair, while witnesses refused to engage and flicked through their paperwork (FWD 19.5.24). While the clerk noted that the session was '*weird but fine*' (FWD 19.5.30), it disrupted the flow of the hearing. More generally, and as in this case, lone wolves can be combative and/or confrontational as they can collide with the general will of the committee (and the chair in particular). In my committee, this was often the case and – if it damages the long-term relations developed on the committee – could cause divisions in reports and a breakdown in consensual working (FWD 3.1.13, FWD 10.3.25, FWD 47.11.10).

Why do they do it? Sometimes lone wolves' passions for certain subjects are too great and/or certain witnesses can rile MPs. But it must also be remembered that MPs are political animals with strong views on many subjects. So, one MP explained that he adopted this role at times in order to put on record his own opinions:

> When we interview people, from my view you're not just finding out what they think, I'm trying to get across what I think. So the staff have a view and so sometimes the chair pulls me up and says, you know, but I want to be a witness rather than an interviewer and I do one way or another get my view across. (Interview with MP 8)

Precisely how this improves the conduct of scrutiny is unclear because it limits the ability of a committee to investigate issues and also to build effective working relationships. It also gives committees less time to hear evidence if committee members are presenting their views.

Although lone wolves might be seen to cause problems for scrutiny, some interviewees praised them because they have, as one chair put it, 'a skill of getting to the heart of the issue' (Interview with Chair 5). Another interviewee suggested that this made an impact with the frontbench: 'ministers are quite scared of us, and that's quite good' (Interview with MP 10). An example of a lone wolf is David Tredinnick, MP for Bosworth since 1987. He is known for his strong interest in and support for homeopathy and astrology as alternatives to mainstream healthcare (e.g., HC Deb 14 Oct 2009 cc412–4; HC Deb 22 Jul 2014 cc1300–1302), which has influenced some of his lines of questioning while serving on the Health Committee and Science and Technology Committee. Another example might be Paul Flynn, MP for Newport West between 1987 and 2019. He was an anti-war campaigner and a strong advocate of the legalisation of cannabis for medicinal purposes, going so far as introducing a Private Member's Bill in 2017 (HC Deb 10 Oct 2017 cc206–7) and served on the Home Affairs Committee and Public Administration Select Committee.

Constituency champions

Although there were some interviewees who believed that their constituency work was separate from their select committee commitments, many others made some sort of link between them. It is possible that most did so because they are used to relating their everyday activity to constituency work anyway. For example, the following comment from one MP who sat on the Business, Innovation and Skills Committee is arguably applicable to most other constituencies: 'and I have quite an enterprising constituency with a lot of small businesses and SMEs' (Interview with MP 18). Other interviewees noted that scrutiny work is enhanced by bringing 'constituency colour' into proceedings, sentiments with which most MPs could arguably identify (Interview with MP 19). Even if this link is often superficial, it is still telling because it shows the importance of electioneering that pervades an MP's thinking (Wright, 2010) and the significance of the casework that MPs receive (Crewe, 2015; Young Legal Aid Lawyers, 2012). That said, some representatives really do take this much further and view their constituency as a prism through which to conduct other parliamentary work. One MP puts this most starkly: '*There is really no point being on a committee if ... it's not relevant to your constituents*' (Interview with MP 17). He went on to explain that a two-hour committee meeting needed to be justified to his constituents, and that if his constituents are not writing to him on a particular topic related to a committee inquiry, then he would not spend a lot of time reading or preparing for sessions about that particular topic. In taking such a view, MPs will add constituency views to their work in almost every conceivable way: public evidence sessions, in draft report consideration, linking reports to constituencies, press releases, and so on (FWD 52.12.3). One chair noted someone with a constituency focus on her committee:

> [MP X], *who is one of my backbench members, she does it, everything she relates back to her constituency and I don't. I tend to look at the issue and if there's a constituency link I'll use it. I think she looks at the constituency and sees how she can feed that into her work. So I do it the other way around.* (Interview with Chair 8)

This quote demonstrates the pervasive importance of the constituency link. Although it is something taken further by particular representatives in their service on select committees, almost all MPs (including chairs) will have the constituency at the back of their mind as noted above. While this is not a new finding in and of itself – Michael Jogerst (1993, pp. 158–62) also found a constituency link in his study – the tension between local matters and national scrutiny is exacerbated by the growth of constituency work in recent years (Gay, 2005). For example, James Gray, Conservative MP for North Wiltshire since 1997, believes that too many MPs privilege constituency casework at the expense of scrutinising government policy (Gray, 2015). A former and very senior clerk similarly explained to me that '*there used to be a very strong convention that you didn't raise constituency matters in a select committee*'. He suggested that '*it's politically tempting because you get the great and the good and the grand in front of you and you can ask the Comptroller and Auditor General, or whoever it might be, but by the same token, using that opportunity for some local issue is really an abuse of the opportunity*' because the government is not receiving the scrutiny it deserves (Interview with Official 13).

A specific example of this approach can be seen by Greg Mulholland, Liberal Democrat MP for Leeds North West between 2005 and 2017 and member of the Public Administration Select Committee. In 2014, the committee was looking at the accountability of arm's-length bodies (ALBs). In a particular session in June, Simon Stevens, the director of NHS England, was asked to give his views on the changing nature of accountability. However, Mulholland used this committee hearing to call on Stevens to apologise for the 'kneejerk decision' that resulted in the closure of a children's heart surgery unit in Leeds (House of Commons Public Administration

Select Committee, 2014a, Q303–5, Q319–24). It was left to the chair to tease out the wider issues relevant for the committee's inquiry, while Mulholland used the exchange as part of his constituency campaigning activities (e.g., Mulholland, 2014), with minimal interest in the committee's inquiry otherwise.

Party helpers and safety nets

In one interview, a clerk referred to a *'government help person'*:

> *Someone who … if the government's sort of getting in trouble, will maybe step in a little bit. … I wouldn't call them stooges, not the right word, but they feel, you know, the government shouldn't get such a kicking.* (Interview with Official 3)

An MP similarly noted this type of behaviour, including the opposition:

> *There have been times when we've had people on the committee who've wanted to just push the … government line – and you're not there to do that. You're elected by Parliament, by the other parliamentarians, to do a job. You're not there to do the government or the opposition's job.* (Interview with MP 10)

This indicates that there are behaviours by some committee members to try to help their political parties. This type of performance style is generally not common in the committee corridor because it is unlikely to receive widespread support from colleagues, including one's own party, as it damages the ability of a committee to build consensus. However, and perhaps unsurprisingly, this mode of behaviour is more recurrent at 'set-piece' events, such as committee hearings with a secretary of state or minister.

To adopt this kind of position is to try to use the committee as a *'political tool'*, as another MP put it (Interview with MP 22). For example, on one particular issue, a committee member said:

> *There was a mood coming mainly from government, mainly from* [the minister], *that we were going to shift, move away from* [the previous policy] *… and four out of the five interviewees said* [XX] *and they took my view. And so I deliberately gave them lots of easy conversation and the one who was against* [the previous policy] *was intellectually less good.* (Interview with MP 8)

As noted with other performance styles, this has an effect on scrutiny by skewing the questioning in a way that is not necessarily productive to traditional interpretations of accountability.

Newer members of committees (and newer MPs more generally) are possibly more partisan in their activities on committees than longer-serving members (Interview with MP 7). An MP noted that there is a *'cooling off'* period for representatives who had previously served on the frontbench (or supported it as parliamentary private secretaries, PPSs), and would be discouraged by their colleagues to join a committee until they had sufficiently *'cooled off'* (Interview with MP 11).[1] Indeed, a newly appointed Conservative MP on my committee occasionally took a view on some matters that gave the government the benefit of the doubt, even though no one else agreed (FWD 52.12.3). This indicates the importance of socialisation processes – often imperceptibly informal – to ensure that MPs maintain a sense of cross-party working for their scrutiny work. This isn't easy: politicians are elected on a partisan basis, after all, and so the adversarial atmosphere still pervades parliamentary work.

Learners

Related to the previous point about socialisation, above, is a character that might be referred to as the *learner*. This can be adopted in two ways. First, newly appointed MPs may take this position in private meetings. Here, they may ask more questions that are factual in order to familiarise themselves with committee work. By contrast, in public meetings, they might not want to be particularly vocal. A recently appointed MP remarked:

> *I don't know how [XX] was going to chair it, and I'd said to him earlier on, I just want to hold back in it, so I didn't take part in the beginning part and waited until a bit further … you don't know what the dynamics were.* (Interview with MP 4)

A second way in which an MP adopts the role of learner is through inquisitive engagement more generally with committee work. One clerk believed that this a common way that MPs approach scrutiny:

> *I think too many members see the committee meetings as an opportunity for a pleasant hour or so listening to some people talk and learning about things which they previously didn't know much about and they don't really see it as a really effective scrutiny opportunity. … We've had a number of sessions recently where the chair took probably 80% of the questions because everybody else sits back and listens. And, you know, they enjoy it, it's very interesting and all the rest of it, but they're not really scrutinising.* (Interview with Official 5)

I have observed some committees (including the one mentioned by the clerk, above) where MPs attend but then do not ask questions in committee hearings. For example, on my committee, one member had thoroughly prepared for a private seminar and listened (seemingly attentively) throughout, but only asked one question of the speakers (FWD 57.13.7).

Alternatively, learners may ask questions, but their approach may not be fully developed or thought-out, as this clerk describes:

> *The sessions are not courtroom, they're schoolroom for a lot of them, and they're finding out about the topic. So therefore, whereas I've read – not all the stuff – but I've read the brief and I know what it's about, whereas quite often they haven't and they're finding out for the first time.* (Interview with Official 3)

This indicates that even high attendance at committee meetings is no guarantee of effective scrutiny – or any form of scrutiny at all. To give another example, I had observed a committee session to hold a minister to account, but a newly appointed member asked confusing and arguably minor questions of the minister. Afterwards, the clerk mentioned to me that the member could be a bit of a '*loose cannon*', while the minister remained '*slippery*' (FWD 58.13.18). This has quite obvious consequences, including giving more room for a dominant chair to push through their ideas unhindered or prevent critical and analytical oversight of a policy problem, for example.

Absentee

As the name implies, an absentee MP is attached to a committee but does not participate. It includes those committee members that appear briefly, or only for a small part of an evidence session, and who are more interested in boosting their attendance rate. They are likely to go through the motion of asking a question: they do not listen to the answer, ask few if any follow-up questions and, in essence, do not undertake any form of meaningful scrutiny. Absentee members are not thought to make much of an impact on committee work because they are not there to discuss proposals for inquiries, question witnesses or offer their views in the consideration of draft reports. However, it is not merely the absence of scrutiny; it could lead to the detriment of committee work because it reduces the number of opportunities to use the MP's expertise to inform committee work and might even cause problems to gain enough cross-party support more generally. Consequently, some committees could push inquiries forward with a particular skew in party balance.

Regular absentees were largely unreachable and, axiomatically, they were difficult to observe in committee meetings. Thus, they remain elusive. The only exception came in the form of an unfocused 20-minute interview with an MP who attended well below half of all committee meetings (Interview with MP 12). He described his committee work as a '*marginal pastime*' and '*not particularly onerous*'. He said that, although he believed MPs should spend 80% of their time on scrutiny committees, he only spent 1% or 2% on them because of the demands placed on him by his constituents (which, he believed, did occupy 80% of his time). It is not clear how this MP arrived at his figures. But, in any case, it suggests that one reason for low committee attendance is explained through competing pressures placed on them and the fact that they have prioritised other aspects of their role (to which I return in the next section).

These roles – specialists, lone wolves, constituency champions, party helpers, learners and absentees – do not exhaust the possibilities of how MPs may interpret committee work, although they are the most common ones that I have witnessed during my time in the Committee Office. My committee, in particular, had many sessions where these performance styles were on display (and clashed). However, not all of the time. This is a key point. A performer may change their style depending on circumstance: an MP will not be a specialist for every area of policy, and so while another fills that gap, the aforementioned MP may be placed in a learning role. Another time, she may not attend the session, and the following one she will be perceived as a lone wolf because she did not hear previous oral evidence but wanted to interrogate witnesses on her preferred topic. The role may also change depending on the constituency, the balance of power between government and opposition, the performance and style of the chair, relationships with other committee members, the political agenda of the day, and so on. Furthermore, these roles must be distinguished from individual questioning techniques and styles. No single type of behaviour noted above necessarily leads to particularly combative or conciliatory questions (on question techniques in political settings, see research by Peter Bull, 2003).

So, performance styles are not mutually exclusive or fixed. However, they are important ways of grounding the focus of analysis for approaching scrutiny and demonstrates the variety of ways in which scrutiny happens along the committee corridor. It demonstrates that different conceptualisations of scrutiny and their enactment directly affects the way in which scrutiny processes play against one another and affect various stages of the inquiry process. While these issues are covered in later chapters (particularly Chapter 6 and 7), we now turn to how these interpretations and approaches to scrutiny are affected by wider pressures of the role of MP in the twenty-first century.

Negotiating dilemmas

In order to better understand the roles that MPs adopt in select committee work, four everyday dilemmas deserve detailed attention: building expertise, time commitment, multiple or competing loyalties, and the formation of a 'willed ordinariness' to tame the storm of being an MP. Although these are dilemmas that MPs do not strictly face through select committee work, they do make an impact on committee work, and so each deserves detailed attention.

Building expertise

Policy interest is an obvious underpinning that explains why MPs serve on committees. As one MP put it: '*it was a way of really immersing myself in an area that I was interested in*' (Interview with MP 4). In some cases, this stems from professional experience before becoming an MP (as noted in various interviews). This is quite common on, for example, the Communities and Local Government Committee, which has a number of former councillors serving on it (including its chair, Clive Betts). Elsewhere, the chair of the Health and Social Care Committee, Dr Sarah Wollaston, has a medical background, as do other committee members. Related to this, some noted the importance not only of policy interest, but policy influence. One MP, for example, remarked that it is the ability to set the agenda through a good report that is most rewarding for her: '*wanting to try and make sure we're not just commenting in a vague* [way] *but trying to actually say something that might actually, genuinely make an improvement*' (Interview with MP 18). These sentiments were echoed by others (and reinforces previous research: Jogerst, 1993; Kellermann, 2014).

Interest in policy issues is often linked to wider abilities to build expertise and skills of an MP. One MP said that consistent involvement in her committee meant that she could be better prepared than a newly appointed minister before their appearance in front of the respective committee, for example (Interview with MP 10). This feeds into a broader point about professional development and continued learning. One MP, for instance, explained the move from a territorial committee to a departmental committee in order '*to do something more stretching*' (Interview with MP 9).

Importantly, therefore, committees are not only used to gain knowledge of policy or content, but also to develop their skills. Using committees as a way to improve their policy knowledge and skills is especially important in the absence of systematic induction processes for MPs, even if this has been changing (Coghill *et al.*, 2012). During fieldwork, it was noticeable that some MPs were practising points that they would make later, in the chamber or elsewhere. In one private meeting, for example, a member raised a point, prompting the chair to ask him, '*Can you not practise your questions now?*', only for the MP to continue to make his point (the MP spoke in the chamber later that day: FWD 52.12.3). This may explain why some committee members adopt a more partisan role (to test the weaknesses of their perceived opponents or arguments that they don't like) or a learning or constituency role (to understand a policy area for other parliamentary work, including addressing constituents' grievances).

In recent years, select committees have given training to their committee members, usually by experienced QCs or journalists (Interview with Official 8). This seems to indicate a growing awareness of the need for further professional training for MPs. MPs, on the whole, did not phrase committee service in terms of fulfilling a training or rehearsal space. However, it arguably does happen, which would reinforce other arguments that committee service socialises MPs into parliamentary roles more generally (Norton, 1998; Rush and Giddings, 2011). This does raise a wider question as to whether select committees are the best place for training, however, because, as shown in the previous section, it means that committee work arguably becomes equated with learning, rather than scrutiny.

Time commitment

The variety of roles that MPs perform are shaped in part by their priorities as representatives as a whole, which, consequently, means that the commitment to committee work varies greatly between MPs. Committees usually rely on a 'core' band of members (in addition to the chair) to participate and drive forward committee work (Interview with MP 1). At a private meeting of my committee, for instance, this numbered five MPs who were involved in discussions with the chair about all issues regarding the committee, while the remaining four members (that attended) chipped in only on occasion (FWD 57.13.7). Staff have pointed this out too:

> *I think committees always, you know, rely on a sort of central core of members who are the most engaged, the most knowledgeable and you always have, in my experience, a few who don't turn up that much or, you know, turn up but don't engage or whatever.*
> (Interview with Official 11)

As pointed out earlier, the average attendance rate for MPs was 65.9% over the 2010 parliament. For some committees, the average attendance fell far below the minimum attendance rate of 60%. However, 'core' members tend to have an attendance rate that typically exceeds 75%, of which there are usually four to five. Other than this broad-brush attendance figure, quantification of the level of commitment for committee work is very difficult, for at least two reasons. First, attendance at meetings does not indicate commitment to scrutiny, and therefore represents only a coarse proxy for commitment. It does not, for instance, tell us how long an MP attended a meeting or how many questions they asked (and fieldwork observations indicate that MPs drop in and out of meetings rather frequently) or if they understand the topic; moreover, some MPs may well be in attendance at meetings but not enjoy their time there, using that time to answer emails (FWD 47.11.8, FWD 47.11.10), to inspect the paintings around them rather than listening to the witnesses (FWD 58.13.17) or, as in the infamous case of Nigel Mills MP, to play Candy Crush on their tablet (BBC News, 2014b).

A second factor, and in contrast to the above, is that attending meetings is not the only way that MPs contribute to committee scrutiny. An MP may raise committee-related issues through Parliamentary Questions (oral and written) (Kellermann, 2014) or conduct meetings with stakeholders to understand a policy area a little better. Indeed, a number of MPs said that they find it difficult to isolate their select committee work from their other (scrutiny) activities (Interview with MP 6, Interview with MP 10). One MP serving on the Defence Committee:

> *I probably spend about 80% of my time looking at defence issues and engage with defence. At lots of different levels, whether it's going to meetings ... going over to Chatham House, meeting people who are coming to speak in Parliament about defence issues and defence-related issues. Probably about 80% of my time.*

When I asked how the constituency could fit into the remaining 20%, the MP responded:

> *I'll go into schools and they'll ask me about climate change and I'll talk about defence, and the importance of climate change from looking at the defence of the UK, the importance of being able to generate our own electricity and that's why wind is important, that's why waves are important ... going to have to look at whether or not fracking is feasible.* (Interview with MP 9)

This tells us, more than anything, that the many different roles that MPs play are intertwined and exceptionally difficult to separate. It also tells us that MPs' interpretations of what is important makes an impact. And those that take committee work seriously are often also likely to develop far more expertise into a policy area.

Multiple loyalties

Irrespective of the proportion of time that MPs say they devote to committee (and other) work, and contrary to popular belief and wilful media misconceptions, the House of Commons is underpinned by a culture of long hours, as evidenced by fieldwork observations, interviews and pre-existing research (Weinberg, 2015; Weinberg and Cooper, 2003). One MP said, for instance, that she would occasionally be forced to read committee papers at 1.00am (Interview with MP 19); another admitted to having done parliamentary work in hospital (Interview with MP 4). During fieldwork, one MP mentioned in passing that he stayed overnight in the Palace to attend the day's committee meeting because the previous evening's debate finished too late for him to return home (FWD 10.3.3). It was not much of a surprise to hear from one committee member that he wished for a 30-hour day to help fit everything in (Interview with MP 22). Were MPs saying this to impress me, a researcher interested in hearing from MPs and their commitment to the conduct of scrutiny? To a degree, certainly; but these issues were also raised in passing as we discussed other issues.

A culture of long hours (and associated stress that may result) is driven by the competing pressures of or multiple loyalties placed on MPs, who face a daily dilemma in how they choose to enact their representative role – as noted in the opening section of this chapter. The competing demands and the fluidity of the role explains, in part, the variable attendance of some committee members. It is not that MPs are not doing work, but rather that they are enacted in different ways. It is therefore not surprising to see that some MPs try to reduce their workload by combining elements of their role – such as using select committee work to support constituency interests.

As a consequence of multiple loyalties, MPs tend to get involved in only particular inquiries of their committees and not all of them. For example, one MP noted that if it is an inquiry that he had suggested or helped to develop, then it would not be uncommon for him to speak to the committee's clerk about it, help with its general focus and direction, arrive early to discuss questioning and so on. In contrast: *'if it's an inquiry I'm not particularly bothered about, I just arrive and, you know, pitch with whatever. And I think that's the approach that most people adopt'* (Interview with MP 1). Indeed, this was echoed in other interviews, such as: *'sometimes one* [inquiry] *comes through … actually, I'm not that interested in this, I'm not that fussed – then I probably won't do very much of any of that'* (Interview with MP 5). Some MPs admitted that they sometimes did not have the time to prepare for meetings and at other times it will happen at the last minute (Interview with MP 17, Interview with MP 23). This explains why some MPs adopt a specialist role in select committees – to focus on 'their' preferred issue or type of inquiry/theme. Others take this further, becoming lone wolves.

A further factor that may explain certain committee behaviour – and that is often overlooked – concerns the personal and social lives of MPs, which are frequently perceived to bear little on decision-making (for an exception, see Hardman, 2018 and Norton, 2018). The families of MPs matter, and so some MPs will prioritise taking their children to school on some days, or want to look after their small child but are therefore unable to travel with a committee on field visits – both of which happened over fieldwork (FWD 12.3.20; see also Interview with MP 18). The effect of this in terms of stress and strain has been documented elsewhere (Weinberg, 2014), yet deserves a comment here because it is a further (and gendered) pressure that MPs face in terms of how and with whom they spend their time. In addition to family bonds are the social ones between friends, who MPs are likely to want to support in Parliament. Some MPs joined a committee in part because they are friends with other serving committee members (Interview with MP 10; Interview with MP 12). In another case, an MP was willing to see past a colleague's frustrating behaviour at meetings because of the bond of friendship between them (Interview with MP 8). Indeed, some noted that friendships and personal relationships are what makes committee work rewarding:

> *The committees can be a lot of fun, you know? The work is very serious, but in terms of the personal relationships and the banter, it can be quite fun. And it's the characters. You get to know people in greater depth. This place can be a very lonely place. And the people you're on committee with, because you've gone away together, you've done things together.* (Interview with MP 9)

A committee chair, similarly, noted friendships that he has made out of the process (Interview with Chair 4). These personal and social factors are important because they, too, affect representatives' choices, something to which I return in Chapter 7 (but, for a general discussion of parliamentary friendships, see Childs, 2014 and Crewe, 2015, pp. 64–72). More generally, this dilemma of social relationships and navigating personal issues feeds into a broader point about the culture of the House of Commons and parliamentary life more generally, returning us to the opening themes of this chapter.

Willed ordinariness: being an MP in the twenty-first century

The choices that MPs make over their commitment to scrutiny is made more difficult because, as one MP explained, parliamentary timetables are increasingly '*crashing into one another*' (Interview with MP 7). One member explained that, because of these difficulties, she left one committee and joined a different one (Interview with MP 3). Given executive control of the parliamentary timetable, MPs' everyday behaviour and their commitments are governed by factors outside their control that can make their workplace unpredictable at times. This dilemma was noticeable during fieldwork, where a range of MPs changed interview time and location with me, sometimes on more than one occasion and only with very little notice (FWD 36.9.6, FWD 31.8.5, FWD 51.12.11, FWD 56.13.9). Others were rushed or busy throughout the interview. On one occasion, I bumped into a committee chair a few days after my interview and wanted to briefly speak with him – only to realise that he had no idea who I was (FWD 53.12.5).

One chair noted that regular committee meetings are a '*constant*' on an otherwise fragmented parliamentary agenda (Interview with Chair 2). Another chair commented:

> *As an MP you are subject to a blizzard of information, questions, interactions, of every sort and the, being on a select committee allows you to … focus on an area of policy and within that area of policy on specific strands for a sustained period in-depth and, so, there's a certain joy in being able to do something which isn't passing and … is in fact, you know, allows for a sort of deep reflection and continued learning. So, from a personal point of view, being on a select committee offers a real opportunity to feel that you're getting to grips with some of the big issues in an area and, by dint of the position we hold, influence policy.* (Interview with Chair 6)

This quote demonstrates a theme of not only gratification, policy interest and building expertise, but the fact that it is part of a long-term routine and helps to manage some of the many demands placed on you as MP. Other MPs have pointed towards something similar. For instance: '*for me, select committee stuff provides a kind of structure of parliamentary life*' (Interview with MP 1), and, '*the vast bulk of my work is through the* [XX] *Committee and things that flow from that*' (Interview with MP 6). Both MPs have a strong interest in their respective policy areas, and use committee work as a basis to carry out some of their functions as MPs. This goes on to feed into other work that they conduct, both of which are also woven into their professional experiences before becoming MPs. Another former committee member contrasted his role with PPS work:

The main difference, I would say, between the two is that the select committee work was a bit more structured. You knew when the meetings were coming up, or the trips, and you knew the process of ... we always [met] on a Monday. So you would get the papers for the following meeting normally on the Thursday before it. So I knew I had the week-end to read through it and, you know, edit draft reports ... the PPS role is, you know, more variable and less structured than the select committee. (Interview with MP 22)

Other MPs alluded to loneliness in the vast Palace of corridors, meeting rooms and unknown adversaries, and that committee meetings offer a way to combat this. Why is this important? It suggests that committee work has a completely overlooked additional benefit for MPs: to weather the so-called blizzard of information, questions and interactions that MPs face. It is, to put it into the language of Chapter 2, a way to 'willed ordinariness'.

This factor – alongside the dilemmas explored above of building expertise, time commitment and multiple loyalties – shows the fluidity of being a representative in the House of Commons. There are many more dilemmas that MPs face that have not been covered here, including: the effectiveness of politicians (Hardman, 2018); how to deal with rising distrust, harassment and abuse (Clarke *et al.*, 2018; Flinders, 2012; James *et al.*, 2016); or how to maintain mental wellbeing (Flinders *et al.*, 2018). In making choices about how best to enact the role of MP, some committee members emphasise their constituency role, others may be more likely to adopt more specialist roles. The key point is that these are everyday or perennial dilemmas that each individual MP needs to navigate within the contours of wider parliamentary cultures and traditions. Being an active member of a select committee is only one of many ways to enact their scrutiny role, and in any case makes up only one element of the wider role in Parliament.

Being an MP is complex and contested, with no right answer. One MP summarised the role through the metaphor of a jigsaw, which is worth quoting in full:

The role of a Member of Parliament is like a jigsaw. Okay? And there are many pieces of the jigsaw and ... now, is the [XX] Committee, is it the corner of the jigsaw? Is it the edge of the jigsaw? Is it the heart of the jigsaw? I don't know, because everything is jumbled up. ... They are pieces of the jigsaw, of the totality of being a Member of Parliament on a select committee, constituency MP, a parliamentarian, that ... the great joy of this job is that it's not a factory production line where 9 o'clock on Mondays is the same as 2 o'clock on Mondays is the same as 9 o'clock on Tuesday, et cetera, et cetera. (Interview with MP 15)

This quote encapsulates many themes of what it means to be an MP in the twenty-first century. It takes us back to the very opening comments of this chapter, which started by setting the scene of an MP's broader role and the many different functions that they must fulfil and the innumerable tasks that come with doing so. It is precisely because of these many demands and the dilemmas that they cause for scrutiny that we can explain why certain MPs adopt different positions when sitting on select committees and scrutinising the government.

Concluding remarks

This chapter shows that being a Member of Parliament is a complex business, and that their diverse individual beliefs push and pull committees in different directions. Crucially, select committees are not single-purpose institutional entities that allow the House of Commons to scrutinise the activities of the executive. The role of committees is far broader and they can act as: rehearsal spaces for party politics in the main chamber; tools to build expertise, learn about policy areas and gather information for individual MPs and the House of Commons generally; mechanisms to represent and serve the interests of constituents; a way by which MPs escape the tumult of adversarial politics; and, indeed, ways to hold ministers, civil servants and public figures to account. Even this last aspect may be influenced by different strategies, such as the decision by committees to either shape public debate or to focus on unexposed policy areas. This chapter has concentrated on the diversity of committee work and MPs to show that they affect how scrutiny is enacted. Those interpretations lead to different performance styles that, while not being fixed or totalising, are often recurring and recognisable dispositions. The performer and the performance may differ from session to session (or from stage to stage), but the elements seem frequently present on many occasions in committee rooms. It is likely that MPs adapt these styles and tailor them, perhaps even enmeshing different styles together or forming completely different ones not covered here.

The chapter shows that 'scrutiny' and 'accountability' are much broader terms in practice than academic or abstract definitions that we might ordinarily associate with these terms. We can explain why MPs adopt different positions on scrutiny based on the multiple stressors and strains that MPs face in twenty-first-century democracy, particularly at a time of distrust. This chapter focused especially on how MPs can build professional competence, tension about time commitments, multiple and conflicting loyalties MPs must negotiate, and a desire to tame an unstructured life in the Palace of Westminster. And while we can be sympathetic to those issues, this chapter also raises serious questions over what it means for a committee to be 'effective', how some positions adopted by MPs add meaningful scrutiny to government, and ways in which MPs' engagement with select committee work can be improved. For some MPs, the scrutiny role is the centre-piece for their work in Parliament, and there is no doubt that committee effectiveness and influence depends on these MPs. For others, committee work is a route to achieve other things. In order to be effective, I would suggest that committees need to think hard about how those other aims can be combined with effective scrutiny. There are some positives that may come from the different approaches, such as bringing a diversity of ideas and perspectives to the scrutiny process. It is about how to bring this together, and this often falls to chairs of committees. Chairs are actively involved in all aspects of committee work, prepare for every meeting, ask questions in every committee hearing, and so on. They often see themselves as the star of the show; the protagonist in the quest for greater accountability. It is to that role that I turn in the next chapter.

Note

1 Parliamentary private secretaries should 'withdraw from any involvement with inquiries into their appointing Minister's department, and they should avoid associating themselves with recommendations critical of or embarrassing to the Government' (Cabinet Office, 2015, p. 7). This means that PPSs may serve on select committees, so long as the committee does not shadow the PPS's department.

4

Catalysts versus chieftains

Unimpressed, the chair of the Public Accounts Committee (PAC), Margaret Hodge, interrupted the hearing. For 30 minutes, the civil servant and lawyer for HM Revenue and Customs, Anthony Inglese, was not providing sufficiently detailed answers for PAC's members. Hodge had become increasingly frustrated as the committee hearing went on, and, in the end, concluded that 'we are going to examine you on Oath – that is a power we have'. Inglese asked for a minute's 'time out', provoking an angry refusal from another member of the committee, Richard Bacon. After a long pause, Inglese swore the oath. Questioning continued; a tense atmosphere remained. The committee hearing made multiple headlines for the confrontation between Hodge and the civil servant, and sent ripples of anger throughout Whitehall. It was part of the committee's inquiry into tax deals negotiated by HMRC with private companies that had led to tax disputes, media and public outcries, and – ultimately – lost revenue for HMRC at a time of public expenditure cuts (House of Commons Public Accounts Committee, 2011). This inquiry was one of many where Hodge built a strong reputation as a high-profile inquisitor, taking politicians, civil servants and others to task for their actions. She is not alone in this. Other chairs of committees have raised their public profiles in recent years, including the chair of the Health and Social Care Committee, Dr Sarah Wollaston, or the two recent chairs of the Home Affairs Committee, Keith Vaz and Yvette Cooper. Many have attributed this trend to the 2010 Wright reforms, which introduced elections to chairs of committees by the House of Commons. However, and despite high-profile media performances and speeches, chairs have arguably remained somewhat understudied, with only anecdotal references to their importance in conducting scrutiny (exceptions are Kelso, 2016; White, 2015b, 2015c).

In an attempt to shed further light on the role of what is often perceived to be the most important role on select committees, this chapter turns directly to the position of chair and asks how chairs interpret their role and what this means for accountability. To do so, this chapter is split into three sections. First, I explore the institutional and historical context (or situated agency) of chairs. I focus on the development of the position and how chairs have themselves assessed recent changes to their role, which reveals a renewed sense of authority through the introduction of elections. For some MPs, this has strengthened the belief in an alternative career in the House of Commons away from a traditional ministerial route, although the invitation to join the executive remains formidably strong (since the introduction of elected chairs, and at time of publication, five MPs have voluntarily given up their posts for junior ministerial roles, all since 2015: Rory Stewart, Jesse Norman, Nicola Blackwood, Andrew Murrison and Nicky Morgan). Second, I turn to the different ways by which chairs interpret their role. Here, I identify two performance styles at opposing ends of a spectrum along which chairs enact their role: committee-orientated catalysts and leadership-orientated chieftains (in practice, most chairs adopt elements of both styles). In order to examine how these performance styles have come about, I explore how chairs negotiate their beliefs about their role in the third section. I focus on three particular dilemmas: (i) chairs' approaches to leading committees; (ii) their role in building norms and values (or performance 'teams'); and (iii) the choices that chairs make to represent their committee beyond the committee corridor. In negotiating these issues, chairs make choices about the kinds of leaders they want to be. While committee members push and pull their committees in different (and perhaps divergent) directions as a result of their interpretations of scrutiny, it falls to chairs to bring coherence to members' approaches and questioning.

From selection to election

One of the aims of creating a more coherent system of select committees was not simply to enhance scrutiny of government, but to broadly emphasise the differences between legislature and executive by introducing a greater range of parliamentary roles in British politics and, ultimately, allow for alternative parliamentary careers. The Procedure Committee's report of 1978 acknowledged that some MPs regard select committee work as an alternative career structure and that 'our structural proposals, if implemented, are likely to further that tendency'. The committee went on to argue that chairs should therefore be given a 'modest additional salary', as well as an independent method of appointing chair (House of Commons Procedure Committee, 1978, para 6.33). Neither of these proposals were implemented, which – although it made the introduction of departmental committees more palatable to the government (and reinforces the broader political tradition of executive dominance; Kelso, 2009) – meant that the incentives for an alternative career path were watered down quite considerably. Nevil Johnson (1988, pp. 181–2), for example, concluded that chairs 'have not generally become dominating figures in Parliament, shadow ministers, or anything like that'. This may, at least in part, be due to the weakness in how chairs were selected. As Chapter 1 summarised, this was arranged through the whips, who were not afraid to remove critics from chairing committees (e.g., after the

1992 general election, the Conservative Party prevented an independent-minded MP from continuing to chair the Health Committee; Davies, 1992).

Pressure to reform select committees had increased since the 1990s, but especially after New Labour's election victory in 1997, who had pledged and introduced a range of political and constitutional reforms. This grew yet further after MPs believed that the whips were overreaching themselves, such as when they attempted to prevent two vocal critics of government from chairing committees in 2001 (Kelso, 2003). In May 2002, an additional salary for chairs was finally agreed and implemented for the 2003–4 session. By April 2019, this amounted to a 20% increase in an MP's income, or £15,928 in addition to the basic salary of £79,468 (Independent Parliamentary Standards Authority, 2019). This, in addition to other changes – introduction of core tasks and Liaison Committee evidence sessions with the prime minister, for example – arguably strengthened the select committee system (Flinders, 2007). However, these changes were not universally welcomed by some MPs, including some chairs of committees. Gwyneth Dunwoody (chair of the Transport Committee between 1997 and 2008), for instance, feared that an increased salary would make chairships another 'office of patronage' given that whips still appointed committee members (HC Deb 14 May 2002, c662). This changed in 2010, when the House of Commons introduced direct elections for select committee chairs by the whole House through the Wright reforms.

Trends in electing chairs

The process of directly electing chairs in 2010 was conducted swiftly. Chairs were allocated to parties on 23 May, two and a half weeks after the general election (this allocation is informally decided by the usual channels but approved by the House (HC SO No. 122B(2)-(5)). Nominations closed two weeks later, on 8 June with voting taking place the next day. This arguably limited opportunities for debate between candidates or to conduct committee-specific hustings (which changed in 2015 and 2017). The results were announced on 10 June 2010.

Out of 23 positions, seven were uncontested.[1] Propensity to stand for election is reduced by an incumbency factor: of these seven cases, more than half of the nominations came from a chair seeking re-election. One interviewee told me that he did not stand for election as chair of the Defence Committee in 2010 because James Arbuthnot (chair since 2005) was '*entitled*' to a second term and '*I didn't feel it would be justified in my opposing him*' (Interview with Chair 4). Elections in 2015 and 2017 reinforce this view, with the majority of uncontested posts being sought by incumbents (nine incumbents sought re-election in 2015, of which only three had competitors, while in 2017 there were 18 incumbents, of which only four faced competitors). Since 2010, challengers to incumbents have increased: two in 2010 (both saw off their challengers); three in 2015 (with one, Adrian Bailey, losing the Business, Innovation and Skills Committee to

Iain Wright); and four in 2017 (one, Crispin Blunt, lost his chairship of the Foreign Affairs Committee to Tom Tugendhat). Although Diana O'Brien (2012) found that experience is correlated with winning the election, and that women are more likely to win their elections than their male counterparts, there are other indicators to show the dominance of men: in 2017, for example, more than half of the elections were contested only by men (including the Education Committee, which had six male candidates) (for further analysis of gender in committees, see Goodwin and colleagues, 2019).

If we take a wider view, at least 50 MPs stand for election for these chairships, with an average of three candidates per post. In 2015 and 2017, the average number of candidates increased to 3.5, indicating that these posts are becoming more competitive. Indeed, there are various other indications that these elections have become important. First, by-elections receive significant attention. In 2014, for example, eight candidates stood for the Defence Committee chairship while five candidates put themselves forward for the Health Committee (with further by-elections taking place in 2015 and 2016). Candidates conducted hustings and *The House*, Parliament's in-house magazine, published statements and profiles of candidates. Second, in 2015 and 2017, there was at least a week between nominations closing and election day, which allowed candidates to gather support, campaign among their colleagues and circulate election literature (Richards, 2017). Although unsuccessful in his bid, Barry Gardiner provided the most memorable leaflet, who circulated tree leaves with 'Leave Environmental Audit For Barry Gardiner' written on them (Walker, 2017). Both of these factors, and the statistics above, show that these are sought-after positions that carry respect and influence among MPs and possibly the media (e.g., White, 2016; Williams, 2018). In order to assess this, it is worth reflecting on chairs' own assessments of these processes.

The impact of electing chairs

Every chair that I interviewed welcomed the Wright reforms, particularly with regards to their election. One interviewee, who had been chair of a departmental select committee both before and after the Wright reforms noted that it has *'raised the status of committees very significantly and given them more autonomy and independence'* (Interview with Chair 1). This was echoed by another chair, who described the change as *'huge'* (Interview with Chair 4).[2] Indeed, wider assessments by the Institute for Government (White, 2015b, 2015c), the Political and Constitutional Reform Committee (2013), and the Liaison Committee (2012a) conclude that elections to committees have had an important impact in this respect (but see analysis by Stephen Bates and colleagues, 2017). In particular, the election of chairs seems to have increased respect and prestige not only among fellow backbench MPs, but also among government ministers and, perhaps most important, outside Parliament through increased media coverage (Dunleavy and Muir, 2013). This perception of greater independence is important because it means that stakeholder groups take them more seriously and respond to them. In other words, the beliefs of actors have changed and those beliefs inform their actions and behaviour.

These perceptions are important because they have also affected relationships within committees. Before 2010, chairs were selected from among those that gained a place on the committee, which meant that chairs were directly account-able to their committee members. After 2010, this has changed. Now, chairs are in theory if not in practice accountable to their colleagues from across the whole House who elected them – and not their fellow committee members. Even if a committee did not like its chair and sought to remove them through a vote of no confidence, this would arguably override the legitimacy of the House (although this has not yet been put to the test) (Interview with Official 5). While this does not necessarily reduce the accountability of the chair to the committee, it does change its nature (this is particularly the case for opposition chairs, who do not have a majority on their committee but who do have the endorsement of the House). Ultimately, this changed relationship means that committee chairs are more likely to '*follow their own agenda without much reference back to the commit-tee*' (Interview with Official 4; FWD 36.9.9), and see themselves as '*independent operators*' (Interview with Official 12) or '*free agents*' (Interview with Official 13). This change of perceptions allows chairs to take the initiative, such as calling for evidence or inquiries without necessarily getting approval from the committee. This became especially obvious after the 2017 general election because potential committee members were elected to their positions a great deal of time after chairs had already been elected. As a result, a number of them had announced, or even started, investigations and inquiries, including Frank Field (Work and Pensions Committee) in August 2017 about university pension schemes (Cumbo, 2017), Yvette Cooper (Home Affairs Committee) about wrongful deportation of EU nationals (Bennett, 2017) and Nicky Morgan (Treasury Committee) on the Bank of England's readiness for the UK's departure from the European Union (Treanor, 2017). This has arguably allowed chairs far more control over a committee than in the past (Interview with Official 12), sparking the Procedure Committee to launch an inquiry into the issue in 2018.

In one important respect, the Wright Committee did not succeed in changing the balance of power: the allocation of chairs. This remains in the hands of the whips. Some MPs noted that this is something that still needs to be addressed (Interview with MP 2). One chair believed that if the whips did not like a par-ticular MP chairing a committee, then they could offer this to the opposing parties (Interview with Chair 6). This could have significant consequences. Paul Flynn, who had been MP for Newport West in Wales, explained that this affected the chairship elections of the Welsh Affairs Committee, in which 32 of 40 Welsh representatives were denied the chance to lead the committee because it was allocated to the Conservative Party (Flynn, 2012, p. 34). While I gossiped with interviewees about whips, it was ultimately just that – gossip. None of us knew the secrets of how whips allocated chairs or how to fairly resolve the issue.[3]

This section began with the Procedure Committee's report of 1978, arguing that the 'tendency' of an alternative career structure could be strengthened by improving the role of chairs. This has undoubtedly happened through the modest salary increase for chairs and the direct elections introduced in 2010. That said, the pull factor for ministerial office remains strong, with four MPs (at time of writing) giving up their posts to chair committees since 2015 in order to enter government. Nonetheless, chairs have become respected figures in the House, and the chapter now turns to exploring how they interpret their role and work.

How do chairs interpret their role?

Positive sentiments about scrutiny are widely shared among chairs: it is broadly about making sure that *'the government is getting it right'* (Interview with Chair 5) and that *'the country is better governed if effective scrutiny takes place'* (Interview with Chair 1). However, our knowledge beyond this, and understanding precisely how chairs contribute to 'good' or 'effective' scrutiny, is less well-known. Here, I ask why chairs stood for election and what the role means to them.

Becoming chair

Most chairs – similarly to committee members – were extremely interested in their policy area, which sparked their involvement in committee work: *'I've always loved select committee work because I think you can really get your teeth into something'* (Interview with Chair 5). Policy interest, and the added hope of making a policy difference, drove MPs to aim for a chairship. One chair commented:

> *Well, I've been interested, obviously, in [XX] policy for the best part of a quarter of a century now, so … I knew that in the parliament that was going to be elected in 2010, I wanted to be active outside the Commons as well as inside it. So, I wasn't likely to be … so I wasn't wanting to be a minister. But I wanted to play a part in policy development and the select committee chair provided an opportunity to do that.* (Interview with Chair 10)

Another said:

> *As soon as I saw the Coalition chose not to go for [XX Committee], whoosh, I'm in and made it, nominated myself. There was no, you know, dream job for me. Thoroughly enjoyed it.* (Interview with Chair 3)

Both quotes reveal not only policy interest, but also allude to a lingering effect of the usual channels in allocating chairs. Two chairs (one Labour and one Conservative) noted this explicitly:

> I've never really particularly been interested in being a minister and I, you know, as I said, I loved the select committee work and I've really enjoyed it and I had dropped a hint to the whips in previous parliaments and – because it was in the gift of the whips. So when it wasn't in the gift of the whips and even before the [general] election as I knew it was going to be elected [the position of chair], well, if I get through, then that's what I want to do. And I was lucky enough to win. … So, yeah, taken out of the hands of the whips, I suspect I might not have got it … had it not been for the open election. (Interview with Chair 5)

> Well, if I was the whips, I wouldn't have made me chair. … More because they have their own, they might have done it for the fairest reasons, but more likely, they would have chosen someone who had served in shadow ministerial office and they felt, you know, deserved something. (Interview with Chair 6)

Taken together with the previous section, this indicates that, for some independent-minded MPs, becoming chair offers an alternative route to a ministerial career (echoed in other interviews). This is reinforced by changes in party politics, with new leaders in 2015 for the Labour Party and 2016 and 2019 for the Conservative Party promoting different teams to their frontbenches and leaving previous career politicians to pursue backbench leadership roles through committee work (e.g., Yvette Cooper, Hilary Benn, Nicky Morgan, etc.).

Once elected as chair, MPs have the opportunity to fashion their role as they wish, which has a considerable impact on the committee's work, as discussed below, but also on the MP's workload and priorities. One high-profile chair remarked:

> It's my role in Parliament. It's completely my role in Parliament. Sadly. I mean the thing I miss is I don't have time to spend in the chamber and where I would like. (Interview with Chair 8)

Another chair echoed that he spent far less time in the chamber because of the amount of work that chairs have to do (Interview with Chair 3). A further chair put it like this:

> Today I've had a select committee meeting. I've had lunch with [a] journalist talking about the select committee. I've got you talking about the select committee. I've got somebody coming in from [a charity] talking about the select committee, and I've got something else on, after that. I've got Liaison Committee, which I'm only on because I'm chair of the select committee. (Interview with Chair 5)

She accepted that this had an impact on her other roles: 'something's had to give and I don't do nearly as much in the constituency because I, you know, even at weekends I've got so much reading to do' (Interview with Chair 5; echoed in Interview with Chair 2). Other chairs played down the extent to which the role affected constituency work. Some acknowledged the impact of their role but noted the trade-off was with other Westminster-based activity (Interview with Chair 7; Interview with Chair 9).

As a consequence of the demands on chairs, questions about resources are not far away, especially with the more significant profile that accompanies election (Interview with Chair 1). My committee's chair was frustrated by this on a number of occasions in meetings, and wished to see the role of the committee expand further to allow it to commission and undertake its own primary research and work more closely with think tanks and professional groups (FWD 21.5.8). Another clerk noted that his chair wanted to be able to consult a panel of experts on a range of issues relevant to his policy area (rather than a single specialist adviser assigned to a committee) (Interview with Official 3). Not only was this echoed in other interviews with chairs, but the issue of resources was also acknowledged by the Liaison Committee (2012a). This suggests two closely related things: first, for most MPs, they interpret their own role as something that encapsulates their wider engagement with Parliament; and second, it suggests a wider shift in attitudes and profile of chairs by Parliament more generally, which has taken the decision to resource chairs directly as leadership positions. This still leaves questions, however, as to what chairs *do* with their role.

Identifying performance styles: catalysts and chieftains

With the exception of best practice guidelines published by the Liaison Committee (2012a, paras 94–100), there is no job specification for the role of chair, nor any written set of criteria that chairs should exhibit. One chair explained that he learnt about his role by reflecting on how other chairs, particularly his predecessor, behaved. He saw what worked and what did not work for them, and changed his role accordingly (Interview with Chair 9; post-interview conversation, FWD 53.12.14).

Similar to the previous chapter, I weave together individual beliefs and everyday practices to identify performance styles that chairs adopt. However, different to the previous chapter, I do not identify a number of discrete styles but argue that there is a spectrum along which chairs choose to sit, ranging from committee-orientated *catalysts* to leadership-orientated *chieftains* (summarised in Table 4.1).

Turning first to committee-orientated interpretations, one chair explained the role as a '*catalyst*' (Interview with Chair 10). By this, he meant that he was to act as a facilitator for discussion within the committee and to steer the committee to find cross-party agreement. This interpretation arguably maintains a traditional, committee-orientated view of the role of chair, in which they approach their role in tandem with the wider interests of the committee and make sure that

Table 4.1 Catalysts and chieftains

	Catalysts	Chieftains
Leading inquiries	Ideas about inquiries nestled within an agenda that is more likely to be driven by MPs	Strong ideas about inquiries and is likely to fit MPs' views within strategic priorities of chair
	More likely to allow members to develop lines of questioning	More likely to be interested in leading questions put to witnesses
	More likely to foster cross-party consensus throughout all stages of an inquiry	More likely to seek trade-offs within and between inquiries to ensure consensus
Norms and values	Committee-orientated view	Leadership-orientated view
Representing Parliament	More likely to seek to develop the policy-influencing role of the committee	More likely to seek to develop the media-influencing role of the committee
Possible examples	Adrian Bailey (BIS), Anne Begg (WPC), Stephen Dorrell (Health)	Keith Vaz (HAC), Bernard Jenkin (PASC), Graham Allen (PCRC)

other members of the committee play a key role in scrutinising the government. One chair, for instance, said that it is part of her role to '*spot the different skills that people have and allow them to flourish*' (Interview with Chair 5). Thus, chairs lead inquiries by allowing committee members to develop lines of questioning and fostering a group ethos throughout various stages of an investigation. This gives committee members a sense of ownership over the committee's agenda and hearings. Based on interviews and fieldwork observation, this type of performance was often the style adopted by the then-chairs of the Business, Innovation and Skills Committee (Adrian Bailey), Work and Pensions Committee (Dame Anne Begg), and the Health Committee (Stephen Dorrell).

On the other side of the spectrum, other chairs adopt a more leadership-orientated approach to their role. The following MP couched this in a very polite manner:

> *I see myself as in a guardianship role on behalf of the committee as a whole and on behalf of Parliament, and it's very important that what I do is on behalf of the whole committee and on behalf of Parliament and can be, and I'm accountable to them. Within that, however, it's,* there is a strong leadership role to be a source of ideas and to stimulate thinking about what the committee's programme should be ... *and within that framework, it is occasionally right for the select committee chairman* [sic] *to use that position to say, you know, to ... raise the profile of a particular issue or events as part of the accountability process.* (Interview with Chair 4, emphasis added)

These are – to caricature – select committee chieftains, in that they believe more strongly in their own strategic priorities, as the above quote implies. A strong leadership-orientated chair does not necessarily lead to a less inclusive committee or more divisions over committee reports. This was noticeable on my committee, for example, where the chair and some members – who have very particular but fundamental disagreements – were able to carry on working with each other (humour acted as a crucial social lubricant), even though the chair often exhibited symptoms of a chieftain. Chieftains are more interested in setting the committee's agenda, leading evidence sessions and ensuring their perspective in committee reports is central. Contra catalysts, they do not give members the same sense of ownership; instead, they emphasise input to the agenda instead. This type of performance was arguably often adopted by the then-chairs of the Home Affairs Committee (Keith Vaz), Public Administration Select Committee (Bernard Jenkin), and Political and Constitutional Reform Committee (Graham Allen). Some interviewees have suggested that the legacy of the Wright reforms has made the chieftain approach to chairing more likely (Interview with Official 12).

These two performance styles are not fixed, monolithic or even ideal types. Given that each chair has their own individual beliefs and ways of working, and attempts to stamp that onto their role, it is impossible to reduce all chairs to these overarching approaches. The distinction between catalysts and chieftains serves as a crude heuristic device in order to render explicit some of the ways in which chairs can interpret their role along a broader spectrum. They may do so for the duration of a parliament, or may operate as chieftain for one inquiry but as a catalyst for another. Neither choice is right nor wrong, although they do have consequences for the focus of scrutiny. This reinforces a central argument of this book that scrutiny is fragile and dependent on the everyday behaviours of MPs and other parliamentary actors. It also indicates that chairs face a number of choices in enacting their role. In adjudicating between these distinct set of dilemmas, chairs exhibit patterns that lead them towards either a style of catalyst or chieftain.

Negotiating dilemmas of leadership

The previous section has alluded to choices that chairs make about their leadership style, something that puts the leadership role in tension with promoting the interests of individual committee members. This manifests itself in different ways, and I limit my discussion here to three issues: the way in which chairs lead their inquiries, which forms the bulk of committee day-to-day work (what one clerk called the '*bread and butter*' of committees; FWD 45.10.3); the role of the chair in building the norms and values, or approach, of the committee (see also Chapter 7); and the wider representative role of chairs of committees in Parliament and beyond. Each of these themes requires choices about the types of inquiries that committees pursue, the way questions are allocated the nature of the committee ethos, and so on. In negotiating these issues, chairs develop dispositions about the kind of styles they adopt more broadly to their role and the reputation they attain.

Leading inquiries

Few chairs would admit that they are controlling or dominating but, unavoidably, the attitude of chairs is a key deciding factor in the focus of inquiries. Chairs are in daily contact with the policy area associated with their role, which means that they are more likely to be knowledgeable about it and are instinctively able to see the strategic and political implications of the key issues within it. While committee members will have specific interests that they wish to pursue, chairs keep an eye on the overall picture (with the help of clerks). For example, weekly agenda items for meetings will be drafted by clerks in consultation with the chair and only minimal involvement from committee members.

One clerk said that, while MPs can dip in and out of committee work depending on their interests, '*it's only the chair that is interested in everything we do*' (Interview with Official 2). This highlights the importance of staff, who are committed to their policy area, but also the relationship between the chair and staff. On my committee, staff would get a steer from the chair informally about the aims and objectives for inquiries before asking the committee more widely at a formal meeting (FWD 2.1.16). We can also see this steering role in other ways where chairs and staff interact. They are in email or telephone contact daily (e.g., Interview with Official 11; FWD 6.2.23; FWD 12.2.7), so much so that I made a note one day in my diary when my chair did not call the office (FWD 23.6.13). This may go beyond specific inquiries. On my committee, the chair would ask for advice on how to handle certain witnesses (FWD 54.12.7), Freedom of Information requests (FWD 39.9.15), and potential committee visits (FWD 9.3.10). While small examples, they are a flavour of the wider interest that the chair will have in the committee's work. Sometimes, this can go too far. On my committee, the chair would be so enthusiastic that he ended up micro-managing staff (FWD 20.5.27, FWD 59.13.2), something that a senior clerk believed to be a '*nightmare*' for officials (Interview with Official 13).

Not only do chairs become immersed in their policy area, but they are also the first port of call for staff. The extent to which chairs dominate committee agendas varies greatly, however, and here we must return to catalysts and chieftains. While a catalyst is likely to seek a wide discussion about possible inquiries, chieftains are more likely to, at best, place members' ideas in wider context of the chair's priorities or, at worst, drop the idea unceremoniously (FWD 10.3.9). This brings us to the conduct of chairs in meetings. Indeed, beyond the committee's agenda, the approach of the chair in meetings – often most visibly associated with chairs – plays a significant role. Chairs will frame committee hearings with witnesses in ways to place the event in a larger context of the inquiry. During this 'backstage' planning period in the form of a private committee meeting, the chair will establish the strategic priorities for the committee. My chair would often begin by saying '*What I want to establish from these witnesses...*' (or variations thereupon) (FWD 19.5.20; FWD 42.10.6). The private meeting will also allow chairs to allocate themes for questioning witnesses, which can be done in a variety of ways (e.g., distributing questions according to themes; allocating each member a certain amount of time; or giving members total freedom to jump in without structure). I observed one committee meeting where the chair allocated themes and then added: '*I can just chip in and do whatever ... 'cos I'm chairman'*, followed by a light chuckle from another member. It may well have been a joke, but there was more than a hint of truth that lay behind it (FWD 10.3.15).

Irrespective of how chairs allocate questions, they play a vital role in keeping the performance coherent throughout the public session. One chair explained that: '*I prepare for every hearing. They* [committee members] *prepare for some. I get my brain round everything just in case because I feel as chair I've got to*' (Interview with Chair 8). This often gives chairs the ability to press witnesses further when individual members are finished with their questioning. One clerk explained that occasionally an MP may ask a question with an interesting reply or an evasive answer from a witness, but will do nothing to follow things up (Interview with Official 3). Chairs can and will intervene. This arguably raises a dilemma because, if the chair intervenes too often and even with the best of intentions, this could alienate members (Interview with Official 3).

Chairs not only lead during committee hearings but also bring the subsequent evidence together in the hope of building cross-party support (see also Chapter 7). A number of interviewees have pointed out that split reports have far less impact or resonance with the House of Commons, with one chair identifying it as part of his duties:

The ... added value of a select committee, really, is its cross-party nature. And so, there's not much point in seeking to align a committee for a point of view that leads to a split or an argument within the committee. The whole point of being chair of a committee is to try to ... steer the committee in a way that you as chair think is right but reflects a cross-party view within the committee. (Interview with Chair 10)

This indicates, once again, the balancing role of chair, who will have to both promote their own value but also ensure cross-party support.

What do these insights reveal about the nature of catalysts and chieftains of committees? First, it suggests that catalysts emphasise committee members' ownership over the agenda, while chieftains are more likely to give members input into it. Second, catalysts proactively involve members when it comes to evidence-gathering, while chieftains, as one MP put it, act as '*the star with a few supporters*'

(Interview with MP 6). Third, the style of chairs affects the final outcomes of inquiries. While I return to this in more detail in Chapter 7, it is worth noting here that catalysts tend to build consensus over the course of inquiries while chieftains broker compromises towards the end. This last factor is often shaped by the wider committee norms and values, or the sense of a group ethos or 'performance team' (to use Goffman's language) that is established within a committee. The chair will be crucial in this, and it is the second theme that I want to explore.

Developing norms and values

Most interviewees agreed that the chair's individual approach to committee work is a crucial ingredient not only for inquiries (as above), but for setting the tone of a committee:

> *I think the ethos kind of reflects, you know, the ethos of these committees kind of reflects now, for better or for worse, it reflects the chair's method of working.* (Interview with Official 4)

> *I think the chair sets the tone and that's true of most committees.* (Interview with Official 11)

One MP who has served on the same select committee for three parliaments noted the wide-ranging impact of chairs:

> *Well,* [Chair A] *as chair was a very aggressive, theatrical person and we ended up, I think, choosing more controversial areas because* [Chair A] *liked controversy. Whereas* [Chair B] *is a kind of technocrat. ... She'd hate me for saying that because that's unfair, but there isn't, if you wanted to separate out why they were different, that would be ... So it, that's what's difficult to convey, really, about committees.* (Interview with MP 21)

This quote makes three important points: first, it links the chair's approach and style to the priorities of a committee's inquiry; second, it illustrates that the style and tone of committees is shaped by chairs; and, third, that these styles cannot be easily pinned down. Chairs are particularly important in developing these styles or ways of working because they are the most permanent actor on a select committee. While chairs are usually in post for the duration of a parliament (and often longer), staff move to different positions for career development reasons and, as pointed out in Chapter 3, the commitment of members varies. The general stability of the chair thereby means their style of working is most likely to become instilled over time through the committee's everyday behaviour and forms the biggest influence in sustaining a committee's webs of beliefs.

While the chair is only one of a range of actors involved in select committee scrutiny, interviewees regarded the effectiveness of committee relationships as the chair's responsibility (e.g., Interview with MP 16). Indeed, when I asked one chair about her role, this is one of the first things she mentioned:

[Being chair] *means taking a leadership role in respect of committee members and for me that means helping to actually build an inclusive committee, one where we look at things in an informed, non-tribal basis, where every member's able to be, or feel fully part of the scrutiny process that we're doing.* (Interview with Chair 2)

Another chair explained that relationships matter because this will enable the committee to '*hunt as a pack*', and therefore strengthen the ability of the committee to scrutinise government (Interview with Chair 5). These sentiments are widely shared among chairs. However, the extent to which chairs are able to foster this depends on the disposition of chairs. On my committee, this occasionally caused a clash between the chair – in chieftain mode – and committee members, particularly ones that adopted a lone wolf performance during questions with witnesses.

The significant point to take from this discussion is that select committees are strongly influenced by personalities, and this often throws up a dilemma for chairs in how they enact their role and, more widely, how their own personalities affect the conduct of scrutiny. This is arguably acknowledged only rarely in academic research. With scrutiny of government affected by this factor, it indicates that there is potential for volatility in the effectiveness of scrutiny and undertaking inquiries.

Representing Parliament

Increasingly, chairs conceive of themselves as playing a 'House role'. One clerk noted:

The chair, if he's giving a talk to outside groups, will start with, 'The big change in 2010 was: I am elected by the whole House, I represent the whole House…'. They all do this. (Interview with Official 3)

This was reinforced through interviews with chairs. One chair stated:

I just get the sense that all of the elected committee chairs have been empowered by that [being elected]. *That they feel they've got a House role. That they've been endorsed by people across the House, not just from their own side. And I think that's given us greater licence to speak up and out.* (Interview with Chair 5)

This was echoed by another chair who said that being elected by peers means that it '*enhances their status in Parliament*' (Interview with Chair 8). Taken together with the previous two subsections, it suggests that chairs have a unique position of parliamentary leadership.

The wider leadership role for chairs means that they are increasingly in demand beyond the committee corridor by stakeholders, professional groups and the media. One chair named this the '*representative role*', in which he has '*a relentless round of meetings*' with charities, trade unions, relevant consumer groups and public bodies, as well as a perceived duty to attend public engagement events and conferences (Interview with Chair 6). Another chair stated: '*what I discovered when I became chair is, everybody and their dog want to meet you. So every organisation that's within your sphere of influence*' (Interview with Chair 5). This was similarly noticeable during fieldwork, in which my chair would be in touch with a range of interested bodies to discuss issues relevant to the committee, whether it was advice to stakeholders (FWD 9.3.10); writing an essay for a think tank (FWD 16.4.13); commenting on a report published by an executive agency to the media (FWD 11.3.10); or giving speeches to stakeholders (FWD 15.4.21, FWD 39.9.7). Given this wide-ranging interest from policy communities and the media, it raises a question: what do chairs prioritise?

In terms of a media role, one chair noted that: '*in the eyes of the media, you're … a media expert and "go-to" person of everything that happens in this* [policy] *area*' (Interview with Chair 9). Chairs are usually in control of press notices or press releases (working closely with parliamentary staff), allowing them to stamp their perspective on an issue within the committee's remit. Some MPs have voiced their unhappiness with this (Interview with MP 2), but others pointed out the difficulties of trying to manage a media strategy by committee (Interview with Official 5). This is becoming increasingly important because of the growing demand placed on chairs to respond quickly to issues as they arise on a more frequent basis (Interview with Chair 3). Particularly since 2010, journalists have taken a greater interest in the work of select committees, as Patrick Dunleavy and Dominic Muir (2013) have pointed out in their research (see also Kubala, 2011). Hannah White (2015b, pp. 14–22), in her study of select committees, points out that the chair of the Home Affairs Committee, Keith Vaz, was especially keen to build a wide media profile. MPs believed that government would not be influenced by the committee's work unless pressure was exerted by media coverage. They also believed that it was the committee's duty to make the public aware of its inquiries.

While not every committee adopts an explicit strategy to influence the media, as the Home Affairs Committee has done, the importance of a media role is an interesting issue. Other committees have used this strategy to put pressure on reluctant witnesses to appear before them, such as Mike Ashley's eventual appearance before the Business, Innovation and Skills Committee on working practices in 2016, or the Digital, Culture, Media and Sport Committee's inquiry into fake news in 2018 (with – to date – no success in getting Facebook's chief executive officer, Mark Zuckerberg, to appear before it). Meanwhile, with the growth of social media, other chairs have begun to make extensive use of clips of their exchanges with witnesses on platforms such as Twitter. For example, Yvette Cooper has shortened hearings with ministers and civil servants from the Home Office into two-minute clips that have been widely shared online (Cooper, 2018). It seems to have become received wisdom that greater media coverage is axiomatically a good thing to ensure that a committee exerts pressure on the policy process. However, some clerks have suggested that chairs with a high media profile can also make it difficult to persuade policy experts to give oral evidence because of their often adversarial and politicised style of questioning in committee hearings (e.g., Interview with Official 4).

By contrast, other chairs shun the media limelight and think of the representative role in a different way, namely through building and maintaining policy connections that situate the committee in a wider policy network. The reputation of the chair is crucial in this. On my committee, a new network in the policy area had overlooked involving the chair because they did not think of him as influential (FWD 19.5.3). Elsewhere, an MP commented that his chair had an extensive and *excellent network* in the relevant policy area, which allowed the committee to undertake more high-profile evidence sessions with witnesses that would otherwise have been difficult to persuade to appear in front of the select committee (Interview with MP 11). Although difficult to establish a direct or tangible link, the activity of the chair in relation to the policy communities may have an effect on who gives evidence to a committee, who might assist the committee as specialist adviser, or, indeed, who might read the final report (David Monk (2010), for example, suggests that committee effectiveness should be related to how it is received by others). One committee member noted that the approach to influencing policy communities is equally effective, if not more so, than a media-focused approach (Interview with MP 1). Although it tends to be chieftains that focus on building a media profile (because these types of chairs see themselves as the important actors) while catalysts tend to focus on policy communities, this is not clear-cut. For example, some chieftains (such as Andrew Tyrie) adopt that role precisely because of their knowledge and involvement in policy and therefore have the confidence to stamp their agenda onto committee inquiries.

These three dilemmas, once negotiated, indicate that chairs are pervasive actors in many processes of select committee work, but crucially also develop dispositions as to a committee-orientated approach or a leadership-orientated approach. Catalysts are more likely to lead committees by trying to involve the committee, fostering a group ethos, and making policy influence a priority; chieftains, meanwhile, are more interested in their strategic priorities, inculcate a more compromise-based ethos among members, and believe media influence to be more important.

Concluding remarks

This chapter has given a general overview of the role of chair and identifies styles of leadership that have otherwise been curiously absent from the literature on select committees (with some exceptions noted above). It has used insights from interviews and fieldwork to explore the beliefs, practices and dilemmas of chairs in building a role as backbench parliamentary leaders within the House of Commons. The first section demonstrated that the idea of select committee service may be viewed as an alternative career route with growing prestige, while the second section has then explored how chairs make sense of their role once elected. This was brought to the fore by exploring the dilemmas that chairs face in interpreting their role. By navigating their ever-changing worlds, chairs develop dispositions as catalysts or chieftains (although in practice take elements from both).

At its broadest level, this chapter opens a wider debate about leadership within the House of Commons, and select committees in particular. This is important because the literature on committees has generally not focused on the input side of committee work (with exceptions examined in previous chapters). This chapter has not been revolutionary in the sense of comprehensively assessing the rising backbench stars of committees. Rather it has *opened* novel ways to conceive of chairs' roles and the many fruitful avenues of research that need to be explored yet further. For example, what leadership skills can we expect from chairs? To what extent would professional development and training make a difference to the role? Where do the majority of chairs of committees sit along the catalyst-chieftain dimension? Are there alternative styles of leadership not examined here? If so, how many chairs use their new position in new and creative ways? It is arguably difficult to pin down the role of chair because each MP interprets their role differently and also plays a role in almost all chapters across this book. Indeed, this is arguably the simplest yet most important conclusion: the process and conduct of scrutiny relies heavily on the chairing MP of a select committee.

Notes

1 Twenty-four chairs were elected on 10 June 2010, but the focus of this book excludes domestic and internal committees (i.e., the chairs of the Procedure Committee and, since 2015, Standards Committee and Backbench Business Committee). The chair of the European Scrutiny Committee is not elected by the House, and the chair of the Liaison Committee is chosen after these elections take place.
2 Another interviewee said that 'huge' was a bit of an overstatement, however (Interview with Chair 10).
3 For one recent and interesting exception, see Albrow (2018).

5

Hidden servants

The clerk excitedly recounted: '*He banged his fist on the table three times!*' She went on to explain that the meeting with the chair had not gone terribly well because he was upset over the lack of press coverage about the committee's latest report. The clerk and her colleagues spent the meeting trying to assuage him. The chair had an opportunity to make a speech about the report in the chamber, for example, an idea which he took up. Unfortunately for the clerk, this meant that her entire morning's work plan was derailed. The chair needed her to stay behind to listen to his drafted statement, amend it with him, proof-read it, and listen to his rehearsal a further time (FWD 4.1.19). Later that day, the committee team huddled around an iPad to watch the speech and its responses (while we were having lunch). They noted that he spoke well, answered all the questions and had support from other committee members in the chamber. They were happy and relieved (FWD 4.1.25).

One of many examples, the above vignette shows the commitment of clerks to supporting their elected rulers. At the table in the chamber, in the parliamentary libraries or at any committee meeting, staff are at the service of MPs. They exist across every legislature in different shapes and sizes, although they are also generally understudied and barely noticed by the public. This is true in the UK, too, where few studies of this elusive group of servants exist (e.g., Crewe, 2017b; Ryle, 1981). This is despite the House of Commons Service considerably outnumbering MPs, with approximately 2,700 staff (House of Commons Commission, 2018, p. 16), and headlines in recent years (Coates, 2014; Shipman, 2019b).

Parliamentary officials exist to serve MPs in all kinds of tasks: from writing briefing notes and debate packs for MPs to suggesting witnesses for committee inquiries; from outlining how to table amendments to giving advice on parliamentary procedure.[1] One group of staff, numbering around 200 in the Committee Office, provides permanent support to committees. They help to identify and invite witnesses for committee inquiries, they are present at every committee hearing and private meeting to take notes and analyse information, and they write briefing material and draft reports for members and chairs of committees. Clerks deserve our attention, and so this chapter looks at how staff interpret their role and how this affects accountability in the House of Commons. This is borne out in three parts. First, the chapter situates committee staff in their administrative setting (i.e., the Committee Office). Beset with a string of reforms and reviews, it reveals a sense of organisational complexity and a persistence of silos – something that the Service has sought to address since 2014–15 (i.e., after fieldwork was undertaken). Second, the chapter turns to how staff interpret their role by turning to their individual beliefs and everyday practices. There are three predominant themes: (i) a desire to offer unparalleled service to Parliament; (ii) a sense of being hidden; and (iii) a commitment to passionate impartiality. These weave together to what may be termed a performance style of 'clerkliness', which, although ephemeral and difficult to pin down, explains the behaviour of staff in committees and their relationships to MPs. In the third section, the chapter explores how officials' beliefs interact with the procedures and practices along the committee corridor. Staff undertake the majority of inquiry work but, in doing so, they face a number of challenges. First, staff resources are limited, so clerks cannot offer unlimited support. Second, committee members and chairs want frank and candid advice, while clerks have to be tactful and act politically impartial. And third, staff seek to ensure that MPs build effective relationships with one another and between MPs and officials. However, staff are occasionally seen as *'the chair's creature'* (Interview with Official 3), which can create wider tensions with committee members.

The everyday challenges that staff encounter can be couched within a larger and ongoing dilemma. Throughout my fieldwork, it became clear to me that parliamentary officials are incredibly proud of their workplace, regarding themselves as servants of democracy, as one official put it to me (FWD 33.8.9). However, as Dame Laura Cox concluded in a recent high-profile and critical report, the sense of pride, affection and loyalty of officials has been 'tested to breaking point by a culture, cascading from the top down, of deference, subservience, acquiescence and silence, in which bullying, harassment and sexual harassment have been able to thrive and have long been tolerated and concealed' (Cox, 2018, p. 4). This report, and reaction to it, strongly indicates a range of deep-seated challenges that the House of Commons administration faces. While some of these issues go far beyond what this book can offer in terms of its analysis of scrutiny practices, it highlights an uneasy and ongoing dilemma for officials about their place in Parliament, and how to ensure that they offer the best possible service to demanding MPs of every sort, on the one hand, while serving the institution and traditions of Parliament as a whole, on the other hand. This dilemma runs throughout the chapter.

Situating staff: the House of Commons administration

The House of Commons Commission is at the centre of the administration, responsible for the House's finances and its principal employer. It was established in 1978, following a review from the Comptroller and Auditor General, Sir Edmund Compton, and a report from a committee of MPs under the chairship of Sir Arthur Bottomley (Ryle, 1981, pp. 508–9). The Commission is made up of the Speaker, leader of the House, shadow leader of the House (or another MP appointed by the official opposition), four backbench MPs, two officials (the clerk and the director general of the House), and two external members. Although they are formally in control of the House of Commons Service, delivery has been delegated in large part to an Executive Committee (replacing a Management Board in 2015), which is made up of permanent parliamentary staff.

Collectively, the Service ensures that the House of Commons functions effectively on a daily basis. This includes: research and information for MPs (e.g., the Parliamentary Office of Science and Technology, the House of Commons Library); chamber and committee services (e.g., the Public Bill Office, the Official Report (Hansard), the Committee Office); participation (e.g., the Education Service, Public Outreach and Engagement); in-house services such as catering, accommodation or cleaning; security; corporate services estates; media and communications teams; and a digital team (some of these services are shared with the House of Lords). The organisation is complex and diverse to cater to complex and diverse elected rulers. The way that services have been delivered has been subject to considerable reforms over time. This is worth exploring because of its ripple effects on the day-to-day life of staff.

Reforming the House of Commons Service

Governance of the House of Commons has generally not been a topic of concern for MPs. As one MP put it, 'no one came to Parliament to spend a lot of time considering the price of a bottle of Coke [on the estate]' (Nigel Mills MP giving evidence to the Governance Committee, 2014b, Q303). Instead, periodic reforms were carried out based on recommendations from external consultants in 1990 (Sir Robin Ibbs), 1999 (Michael Braithwaite), 2007 (Sir Kevin Tebbit), and 2010 (Alex Jablonowski). These initiatives repeatedly identified, and tried to deal with, problems of strategic leadership and a lack of transparency. None of the reforms adequately addressed underlying issues despite continuous reorganisations (for a full overview, see analysis by Ben Yong, 2018). Further reforms, however, were back on the agenda in recent times: first, as a result of the resignation of the clerk of the House in 2014; and, second, following allegations of bullying and harassment, especially from 2017 onwards.

Until 2014–15, the clerk of the House was both the chief procedural adviser to the Speaker and the House, and also the chief executive of the House of Commons administration. Following the resignation of the then clerk, Sir Robert Rogers (now Lord Lisvane), in 2014, the appointment process for a new clerk and chief executive was anything but smooth. The transparency of the process was questioned, as was the suitability of a newly announced candidate, an Australian parliamentary official with little procedural experience. This ultimately led to a much wider debate over the governance of the House of Commons, something which was investigated in detail by the formation of an *ad hoc* select committee, the Governance Committee. It concluded that the responsibilities of procedural advice and management for the House administration should be divided into two roles, which was implemented in 2015. Two candidates took on the roles, with David Natzler as clerk and Ian Ailles as the inaugural director general of the House of Commons (for a full discussion and debate, see Geddes and Meakin, 2018).

The Governance Committee's remit was broader than the issue of clerk, and considered the culture of the organisation, key challenges to House governance, and proposals for reform. Many of these issues were taken forward by the new DG, who undertook a further review following his appointment and instituted reforms to streamline the administration (Executive Committee, 2016). At the time of writing, these reforms continue to be implemented (e.g., in March 2017, a new Centre of Excellence in Procedural Practice was established, while the Parliamentary Digital Service continues its roll-out of new online resources and services). And the House of Commons administration remains – understandably – complex. It serves a vast variety of different purposes from looking after a UNESCO World Heritage site (not an easy task, as Alexandra Meakin (2019) has pointed out) to supporting 650 MPs, all with different interests, priorities and objectives; or from engaging the public of all ages in parliamentary work to supporting the effective conduct of Parliament in scrutinising and passing legislation. Indeed, one senior official points out that:

> *Parliament is not, cannot and never will be a well-run organisation with a single, overarching purpose to which its resources can be bent. … it is a chaotic, conflicted, pulling in many different directions at once, inconsistent body. That's what it's there for.*
> (Interview with Official 12)

It is clear that with organisational complexity comes a degree of ambiguity in the relations between key actors. This is exacerbated further by opaque working methods (especially with respect to the House of Commons Commission) in a high-pressure and highly political environment. Unfortunately, this has had a number of negative effects on the culture of Parliament as a workplace, with a number of allegations of bullying and harassment that have come to light in

2017. The conclusions from the independent inquiry that came as a result (see Cox, 2018) demonstrates that the House of Commons has much further to go to address its own working practices (at the time of writing, the impact of the report is not yet clear). Although it may seem that the everyday practices of committee clerks and other parliamentary officials might be removed from the tensions in how the administration works, I believe that there are clear ripple effects from how the House of Commons Service is structured and governed on the individual beliefs and everyday practices of officials. It is to those that I now wish to turn.[2]

The Committee Office

The Committee Office (or sometimes the Committee Directorate) lies within the Department for Chamber and Committee Services (DCCS), and 'provides secretariat, advice, research and administrative services for each of the House's Departmental Select Committees and most other Select Committees' (House of Commons Management Board, 2014). To fulfil those functions, small teams of parliamentary staff serve specific select committees (with further pooled resources in a Scrutiny Unit and a Web and Publications Unit). These staff teams usually include: a clerk of the committee, who is responsible for the committee overall; a second clerk, who will lead on some inquiries and provide support to the leading clerk; one or two specialists, who manage particular inquiries and who are usually subject-specific experts; one or two committee assistants to provide administrative support; and a media officer (usually shared between three or four committees). This is a typical structure that can be found across most committees, although there are some variations or additions. For example, the Justice Committee usually has one or more legal specialists, and the Treasury Committee has senior economists and a range of secondees from other economic or financial organisations (Tyrie, 2015). Additionally, committees can appoint specialist advisers from outside the House of Commons (e.g., academics or lawyers) to provide expertise and advice to committees on an *ad hoc* basis. These advisers matter because they can have a significant bearing on the direction of an inquiry and the sorts of witnesses that are invited to give evidence. For example, when I was stuck with my inquiry briefings, I would ask the appointed adviser for suggestions or to look over a draft document. My clerk told me that they are very useful in terms of getting ideas (FWD 56.13.6), but clerks generally also noted that they can be powerful gatekeepers and care needs to be taken to ensure that a committee's report is not the mouthpiece for a specialist adviser's view (Interview with Official 13). Such influence is often dependent on the wider policy network that surrounds the parliamentary committee, however, and the relationships that develop between the adviser and the committee (particularly the chair).

At the time of fieldwork, committee teams were grouped together as part of 'colour groups' or units to co-ordinate and share practices between committees, which in turn are governed through the DCCS. Working for a particular select committee, however, can feel far removed from these overarching governance structures for some officials (especially less senior ones). Although colour group meetings offer an opportunity for feedback through regular meetings and monthly summary reports, they did not break down the impression among staff that each committee is its own independent (and possibly remote) island, particularly because participation in these meetings is limited to first and second clerks. Consequently, committees were perceived to work in a siloed atmosphere. For example, a new member of staff was disappointed that she had not been introduced to staff in neighbouring offices; I sympathised because this was also the case for me (FWD 41.10.4). Interviews also corroborated this feeling, with one interviewee lamenting that committees '*don't really talk*' (Interview with Official 2).

The consequences of a '*siloed mentality*' is that it can prevent a sharing of resources and expertise necessary for the day-to-day operation of committees. One clerk acknowledged that there is a wide range of expertise across the House of Commons Service, but that this is not often utilised (Interview with Official 10). Aforementioned governance reforms have attempted to address this. The most visible has been the introduction of 'co-location' of office space between committees and Library staff, completed in August 2015. This meant that parliamentary officials from different services and committees sat in open-plan offices to encourage further sharing of ideas between them. It demonstrated that the House of Commons Service was aware of the importance of everyday practices and of 'rubbing shoulders' (see Chapter 7) in order to deliver services to MPs effectively (Interview with Official 13). Although the extent to which this has worked has not been evaluated, some have suggested that co-location may explain the rise of joint parliamentary inquiries by select committees since 2015 (Interview with Official 13; personal communication with former official, December 2018). In addition to these challenges, officials need to adjudicate between competing beliefs and interpretations of scrutiny. All committees are run by their members, and particularly the chairing MP, which often means that there are not only 24 chairs with 24 different views on how to run their committees, but also a plethora of interpretations from committee members. One clerk argued that this diversity is a good thing because '*you want a thousand flowers to bloom*', especially as the basic principles of the administrative system are in place for all committees (Interview with Official 9). Irrespective of the normative value of such diversity, it certainly has an effect in terms of the support that staff can offer because it, once again, indicates a need to juggle competing views.

This section shows that the 'situated agency' of officials has a direct impact on their everyday work, and consequently on scrutiny. In drawing out this wider administrative setting, it reinforces the role of ideas and beliefs at a micro-level, affected by a number of dilemmas. In order to tease out some of these underlying issues, the remainder of this chapter considers how staff interpret their role by looking at their individual beliefs and how they have sought to enact those beliefs in practices and routine, everyday behaviour.

How do staff interpret their role?

In a guide to MPs that serve on select committees, it is described that the clerk of a committee is 'to make committees as effective as they can be in performing the tasks given to committees by the House' (Department for Chamber and Committee Services, 2015, p. 3). The DCCS guide goes on to summarise the responsibilities of a clerk: organise oral evidence sessions; provide briefing and suggested questions; issue calls for written evidence; draft final inquiry reports; draft amendments where desired; draft press notices; maintain the committee's webpages; and make travel and accommodation arrangements. In this section, I want to suggest that this is only the tip of the iceberg. While previous chapters have demonstrated the variety of styles available for MPs to perform their role, this is limited for officials. Undoubtedly staff have a variety of interpretations, but they have also been given a far clearer role specification (unlike committee members and chairs) and inherit a strong public service ethos. So, unlike members and chairs, clerks behave through a predominant performance style that I term 'clerkliness'. It is made up of three aspects that are explored in turn: unparalleled service, being hidden and passionate impartiality.

Unparalleled service

After a particularly difficult day, where the chair had made a complete *volte face* and decided that an inquiry should argue the opposite from what he had suggested before, the clerk sighed and said: '*We live to serve*' (FWD 37.9.6). The timetable needed to be redrawn, new witness lists drawn up and other work put on hold. In many ways, this example shows the commitment of clerks to their jobs and what it means to be in their position in the House. To ensure that members remain in the driving seat of inquiries, clerks need to be willing to accept that they are at the mercy of their elected rulers, who are prone to change their minds on a frequent basis. One clerk accepted that when MPs '*change their minds and muck about*', it is staff who will '*take some of the brunt if things go wrong*' (Interview with Official 3). Clerks have got used to volatile behaviour. For example, during another interview, a clerk noted that the meeting may be cut short because the chair had emailed earlier that day to request a meeting at the '*splendidly un-specific time*' of '*mid-morning*' (Interview with Official 7).

Officials' working environments are unpredictable, yet they try to be as responsive to the wishes of MPs as they can. One MP called it a '*largely unspoken*' symbiotic relationship, in that she felt clerks picked up the norms, values, ways of working, approaches and nuances of members without needing to be told about them (Interview with MP 23). In that sense, the support that clerks offer goes beyond administrative or procedural advice. It is about, '*making members feel like they're getting what they wanted and making them understand the services that are available to them and the value that we can add*' (Interview with Official 10). Fieldwork offered many examples of this, from administrative preferences to writing styles (FWD 21.5.35, FWD 51.12.13). One MP explained that her committee's briefing papers were completely restructured following a discussion between members and staff (Interview with MP 10).

One member of staff, who recently moved from one committee to another, explained that she had to learn to write draft reports in the '*chair's voice*':

> *I've got to get used to a new chair's voice … you slip into their voice in a way. … it's not … what you hear, it's just you are supposed to, you're writing a chair's draft, so you are supposed to write in their voice.* (Interview with Official 8)

The attentiveness to members is found in other examples: staff will note appearances of 'their' MPs on the floor of debates (FWD 58.13.17), and remember their views in those debates; they are there at committee-sponsored debates, assiduously taking notes and helping the chair with their closing remarks (FWD 49.11.18, FWD 49.11.33); or they will watch 'their' Question Time to flag up any issues raised in the chamber that are relevant for the committee (FWD 11.3.6). Without such levels of commitment, the member-driven process in select committees would not be maintained. That said, one of the reasons that this symbiotic or largely unspoken relationship remains precisely unspoken has practical causes: there is simply a lack of contact with committee members, often due to their competing diary pressures. This is additionally compounded by the fact that membership of committees, and attendance at meetings, can be sporadic. Even though the role of chair is pivotal to ensure the committee stays strategic and stable in the face of these challenges, the role of staff in providing a sense of continuity and, consequently, an institutional memory for their committee cannot be understated.

The persistence of the public service ethos (despite its perceived decline in the civil service generally; Interview with Official 12) can be illustrated in another way, namely through career development. Axiomatically, clerks wish to develop their own careers, but this is part of a wider tradition in which officials frequently adapt to different subjects and build up a knowledge base fairly quickly (Interview with Official 7; Interview with Official 11). For example, clerks on my committee would specifically ask to write certain briefing material for members or lead certain inquiries in part to develop their own expertise or knowledge in a particular area (FWD 19.5.30). Staff were regularly involved in other parts of the House of Commons Service, too: working for the Library, clerking Westminster Hall debates, going on 'division duty' (counting votes in the division lobbies when the House is sitting), or through secondments with other organisations. Although all this is part of the job of clerk (indeed, a possible motivation to become clerk in the first place), this needs to be placed in a wider generalist culture. Through a 'policy of circulation', clerks shift in their job every four to five years in order to experience all aspects of their work in Parliament. In this way, clerks become sources of an institutional memory of Parliament as a whole, sustaining many of its traditions, and enabling clerks to share procedural knowledge.

This is embedded further through things like a regular and voluntary 'Monday seminar', in which early- and mid-career clerks get together to share best practices in handling certain types of events or situations, find out about different topics (e.g., clerking at the Table Office or the effect of the Wright reforms), and test one another on their procedural knowledge (FWD 1.1.12, FWD 18.5.21, FWD 36.9.9, FWD 41.10.6). Some clerks also attend conferences and lectures (for example, the UK's Study of Parliament Group is a joint academic-practitioner endeavour with an annual two-day conference; or participation in the global network of clerks through the Society of Clerks-at-the-Table in Commonwealth Parliaments and its journal, *The Table*). In few other professions can something similar be found. Initially, this makes it all the more surprising to hear some officials speaking of a siloed mentality as noted earlier. However, there is a subtle difference here between these aspects of procedural knowledge and culture, and the operational, day-to-day work of committee scrutiny (Interview with Official 10).

Overall, officials aim to build a generalist knowledge of Parliament and serve it in a variety of capacities. This is sustained by a belief in loyalty to the institution of Parliament. One member of staff, for example, commented that she could not work for the government or the state (i.e., as civil servant) because she loved the impartiality of her current job (FWD 33.8.9) allowing her to serve democracy more generally. These were also sentiments noted by the Cox Report (2018) and the Governance Committee (2014a).

Being hidden

The cautious or guarded culture in the House of Commons administration was striking from the beginning of fieldwork and noticeable throughout my research placement. This was made clear to me by the careful type of access given to me, and the cautious approach necessary to draw on my observations (both of which are fully justified, as discussed below). To work in Parliament, every member of staff must sign a confidentiality agreement, which immediately establishes the importance attached to privacy in the Palace of Westminster. It is perhaps for this reason that so little has been written about the administration of the House of Commons, as one respondent pointed out at the end of his interview:

> *I've always thought there's a lot of scope for people to look on the inside and try and think about what's going on. We obviously don't like to lift the lid very often, but you know … the cat's out of the bag!* (Interview with Official 5)

Another time, after I had commented on the lack of research on staff in the Commons, one clerk replied that, *'that's as it should be. … we're not the main show'*. He went on:

> *Even if we do the heavy lifting behind the scenes, there is that sense that this is a member-led endeavour, not one that is driven by the staff and so it's only right that when you ask that question, the staff are not visible. There'd be something wrong if we were visible.* (Interview with Official 10)

Both comments refer to a wider tradition in the Committee Office – and House of Commons Service more widely – of being hidden. All interviewees demonstrated this commitment to hiddenness by the mere fact that they insisted on anonymity in their interview responses. Almost all other informal conversations with clerks were off-the-record and not to be cited; or, if cited, needed written consent.

This culture is not something that is unique to Parliament's relationship to outsiders, but something that characterises everyday life for everyone inside the Palace of Westminster (and, indeed, beyond; Vincent, 1999). With regards to clerks' relationship to MPs in committees, this manifests itself in a range of ways. The most discernible sign of their invisibility is physically in committee meetings. At this front-stage performance of scrutiny, the leading clerk assigned to a particular inquiry will usually sit to the left of the chair in meetings in order to provide administrative support and procedural advice during private meetings or public hearings. But other staff will sit at the sides of the room, almost out of view. They are, literally, at the edges of a select committee performance. Additionally, clerks do not often have microphones in these large committee spaces, nor name cards to identify them (each MP, meanwhile, has one for their seat). Although there are clear reasons for this when public sessions are underway (clerks are forbidden to speak), it is curious that in private meetings members can be heard through microphones, but clerks face a greater difficulty (FWD 38.9.12).

The most interesting facet of being hidden, however, is the way in which clerks enact their role to ensure that their own preconceptions or beliefs do not become visible. One official explained that *'you should always leave them* [MPs] *with a faint but reassuring sense that if only you could speak your mind, you would agree with everything they said'* (Interview with Official 12). Some clerks in the Committee Office referred to this as their *'clerkly poker face'* (FWD 10.3.36). It is noticeable whenever a clerk is in the presence of an MP: in meetings with the chair, for instance, political assessments are met with polite smiles or neutral looks (FWD 49.11.11). On one occasion, a clerk described to me how, after briefing a new member of her committee, she sat through the MP giving her political opinions on a range of matters about which the clerk couldn't do any-thing but nod politely (even though she privately agreed with a number of those assessments) (FWD 26.6.3). Clerks joked when they accidentally dropped their clerkly poker face (FWD 14.4.37), which often made me feel guilty as I dropped my clerkly poker face on a regular basis (e.g., FWD 38.9.10).

This does not mean, of course, that clerks are some sort of empty vessels without their own assessments of situations. Their views are more frank 'back stage', in the privacy of the staff office. Indeed, this space is crucial. Staff are able to relieve their frustrations from a highly pressured and fast-paced working environment, whether this is a committee member not submitting amendments in advance of considering a draft report (FWD 2.1.29) or the chair asking for advice on matters that had nothing to do with the committee's remit (FWD 33.8.12). The office is also a place where, as Erving Goffman (1990, pp. 114–15) pointed out, performances are rehearsed. In the case of the Committee Office, this meant that weekly team meetings allowed clerks to touch base and discuss issues concerning the committee in frank and open terms. It would give clerks an opportunity to debrief after an evidence session: What worked? What do committee members think? In what direction is an inquiry going? In this way, although committee offices are still a particular kind of stage and therefore offer a particular kind of performance, the stage is of a very different kind in which clerks use their office as a setting to rehearse their performances away from MPs and as an opportunity for improvement.

The key point of this discussion is to demonstrate that there are multiple stages for clerks, as there are for other actors. Importantly, clerks adopt different types of performances according to those settings. This is characterised by a sense of ambiguity or privacy through their clerkly poker face within a wider trad-ition of hiddenness. Being hidden is important for clerks because even a minor discrepancy in their performance, especially when in the company of MPs (but more generally on the front stage), could damage their equitable and impartial service that the House of Commons administration seeks to provide. Clerks rely on being trusted by MPs, and giving overt political opinions would damage their credibility. Thus, this facet of the clerkly tradition, and its enactment through everyday practices, is pivotal in order to explain how the scrutiny process in the House of Commons remains largely member-driven – despite the extensive involvement of staff throughout the process.

Passionate impartiality

The two subsections above are closely interwoven and may come into tension with one another, which arguably plays out in this third aspect of clerkliness: a passionate sense of impartiality (linking unparalleled service to being hidden).

This is not about neutrality or indifferent service, but a conscious attempt to sustain the member-driven process (by acting, for example, as amplifiers for MPs' interests) and to ensure that parliamentary scrutiny of the executive is as effective as possible. For example, during fieldwork, one clerk was worried about the limited direction of an inquiry, but acknowledged that the chair is not concerned by this and therefore the inquiry must be made as effective as possible within the narrow remit that the chair had set (FWD 8.2.3). Amplifying MPs' work is not necessarily specific to select committee work: a clerk at the Table Office joked that supporting backbench MPs is the *'most entertaining bit'* of being a clerk, especially if it causes a debate or discussion in the main chamber (FWD 1.1.18). Among parliamentary staff, there is a sense of trying to create a level playing field. In interviews, clerks would appeal to a sense of fairness in adjudicating competing ideas and interests of members:

> *I think you've got to have a good sense of fairness between the different members, so that the minority get their say as well as the majority … judgement and balance. I mean you've got to be very, all fair to all sides and appear not to be too partisan.* (Interview with Official 9)

> *There can be occasions when … political inclinations of members of the committee can conflict with principles of trying to give everybody a fair hearing. … and that can apply to all members of the committee across the political spectrum.* (Interview with Official 4)

> *I think … managing* [the] *provision of information in a way that is fair to all sides of the argument is a key role.* (Interview with Official 12)

This sense of fairness is very important for clerks because it helps to build cordial and effective working relationships with members (see also Chapter 7). As noted in earlier chapters, during fieldwork, one member would disagree with the chair on a frequent basis (often passionately). Usually, disagreements were in private, but occasionally this would spill over into public committee hearings, which worried clerks because it breached a *'fundamental principle'* not to disagree in public where avoidable. This had consequences for the committee's ability to work effectively, and clerks suggested that the chair work harder to rebuild bridges (FWD 14.47–14.4.10, FWD 16.4.5, FWD 2.1.16). It is important for clerks that MPs work well together because it helps to ensure that there is ample opportunity for consensus to develop, something that clerks believe is key to ensure effective parliamentary scrutiny (e.g., Interview with Official 4; Interview with Official 5; Interview with Official 7). In that sense, clerks are not indifferent about what happens in Parliament; they are passionate defenders of the institution. They believe that they play a role in scrutinising the executive by offering equitable and fair service to all committee members irrespective of the political views that MPs wish to push forward. This point is crucial because staff retain the confidence and trust of elected MPs through this impartial service; trust is a clerk's highest form of currency in dealing with MPs.

It is rare that the impartiality of clerks is questioned. When it does happen, it is met with dismay on their part. On one occasion, for example, an MP was frustrated that his questions in a public evidence session were not publicised using the committee's Twitter account; other MPs' questions had been explicitly referenced. The MP said to the clerk that this seemed to be happening frequently (glossing over the fact that his own approach to questioning had little to do with the policy focus of the committee hearing). The clerk was horrified. She had done so because she didn't know what to tweet at the time given the constituency and party-political nature of the MP's interventions. It led to a re-evaluation of how staff manage their committee's Twitter account (FWD 47.11.12, FWD 47.11.21).

Being hidden, unparalleled service and passionate impartiality are crucial beliefs that underpin clerks' behaviour and, when taken together, indicate the existence of a wider performance style of clerkliness within the Committee Office. MPs need to be able to trust clerks to offer high-quality and impartial support, which is only made possible through this approach of clerkliness. This matters because it indicates that staff and MPs, although they have similar aims in furthering the scrutiny capacity of Parliament, do so in contrasting ways. These point towards a tension that is at the heart of what it means to be a clerk: they are asked to passionately serve MPs while simultaneously acting impartially in accordance with parliamentary procedure to ensure service to the House of Commons and the wider traditions of the UK Parliament. This tension is a recurring theme in this chapter, and it is played out in the Palace on a daily basis.

Beliefs in action; dilemmas in practice

When asked what he considered the most important part of his role, a clerk said that it is '*nebulous*' but broadly identified it with '*meeting the requirements of the committee and balancing, keeping the members happy, doing what they want*' (Interview with Official 3). This echoes multiple themes from the previous section, but immediately also suggests a sense of flexibility for staff. So what exactly does it mean to do what MPs want? This section looks at three examples in order to explore how clerks have attempted to enact their role and negotiate dilemmas that occasionally flare up: offering adequate inquiry support; giving committee members and chairs advice that is impartial; and, managing relationships between MPs.

Supporting inquiries

Clerks are placed in a position of leadership because they are in charge of a small team of permanent staff to help support a select committee. Most interviewees acknowledged this. One clerk identified two key parts in his interpretation of his role:

> *I think … managing the team is extremely important, and carrying out the wishes of the committee and trying to make sure that the briefing of the reports that are produced reflect their wishes is the second main part of the job.* (Interview with Official 4)

Another clerk believed the management role was as important, if not more so, than the advisory role (see next subsection, below) commonly associated with House of Commons staff:

> *I think it's essentially manager of the staff team and it's the primary, the official role is the primary procedural adviser to the committee but that, I think, understates it to a large extent. It's the manager of the team and the sort of prime interface between the team and the committee so the prime mediator between* [what] *the committee wants and the team is able to provide.* (Interview with Official 6)

He went on to say that this means managing the demands placed on the team, and the nature of their work. This is essential as to manage expectations as to what the committee can and can't do, revealing a potentially difficult balancing act. It means that responsibility for committee support rests with the clerk:

> *I was the, you know, ultimately, on the staff side, the buck stops with the clerk. … Nothing should happen in the committee that the clerk isn't aware of, hasn't authorised in some way or isn't part of, even if you're not directly responsible for it. There should be nothing happening which you haven't had sight of or thought about or done yourself.* (Interview with Official 5)

For instance, during fieldwork, there was an occasion where briefing material in advance of a committee hearing was labelled too sparse by the chair. It was the clerk that took responsibility, even though a different member of staff had written the brief; it was part of the clerk's role to make sure that everything was of a consistently high quality (FWD 47.11.20). The clerk plays a *'quality assurance role'* (Interview with Official 11). For example, clerks would read briefing material and comment on suggested lines for questioning, often with a view of cutting these down because otherwise, *'staff will want to bring everything in'*, which might affect committee members' ability to question (Interview with Official 3). This is a proactive attempt to make sure that the process of questioning remains member-driven, not staff-driven.

On a daily basis, members of the team would discuss their progress with the clerk to make sure they were on track. Discussions that began, '*Where are we with…?*' would close with '*Going forward…*', both of which were frequent phrases (FWD 18.5.6). They are quotidian, but also important, because they helped to wrestle back control of the unpredictability of everyday life in the Committee Office; it was a coping mechanism.

This management role has consequences for the quality of a committee's inquiries. One clerk argued:

> *I think that provision of leadership to the team and helping to shape and helping to draw out of the team what the issues are and what the narrative around an inquiry is is really quite important.* (Interview with Official 10)

Of course, responsibility for inquiries rests with members that populate committees, not supporting officials. However, as detailed in other chapters, the multiple pressures that MPs face on a daily basis means that they become somewhat reliant on staff to ensure that committees are on top of policy and news developments (Interview with Official 13), and that the specific details in scoping notes, witnesses lists and briefing material are appropriate for MPs. MPs need to place significant trust in clerks, which they can only do due to their good reputation (Interview with Official 6).

Regardless of MPs' commitments to their scrutiny role, they all take briefing material seriously and generally praise them. No interviewee distrusted parliamentary briefings or their appeal, even if they veered off the suggested themes in evidence sessions. One MP said that he will always cover his section of the brief before '*doing my own thing*' because '*clearly the clerks put a lot of effort into figuring out how we're going to get a report that covers the areas that are needed*' (Interview with MP 17; echoed in Interview with Chair 6). Mistakes in briefings are rare, but when they do happen, MPs have called these '*absolutely unforgivable*' (Interview with MP 23).

Beyond briefing material, clerks also offer crucial inquiry support through drafting of reports. They will need to consider the evidence brought before them, and additionally consider a possible way in which the report will get consensus among members. This requires '*political antennae and feelers that equip you to keep, help the chair keep a committee together*' (Interview with Official 13). As one MP noted:

> *I mean a good committee clerk will also understand the politics in the team and will, in the drafting of reports, need to know what the committee is likely to find acceptable in a way that it's working and … not seek to introduce elements in there which might upset the chair or might be okay to the chair but upset members and get them to turn on the chair. So a degree of political sensitivity is necessary.* (Interview with Chair 9)

This discussion shows that clerks offer foundational support for select committees, and they themselves acknowledge that they do the vast majority of work towards inquiries. They provide MPs with oral and written briefings to allow elected representatives to fulfil their work as scrutiny actors, identify and invite witnesses to give evidence, and act as team leaders for inquiries. To some degree, this means that clerks play a gate-keeping or agenda-setting role. One senior official notes that '*a clerk who didn't do this wouldn't be doing his or her job properly*' (Interview with Official 13). However, the extent to which a clerk's veto-playing role could develop is limited because MPs would ignore briefing material in questioning witnesses and may not agree to a report or ask for significant redrafting. So, it is better to think of officials as political amplifiers of MPs' interests, rather than agenda-setters, in the sense that staff will bring things to the attention of committees without '*imposing on the committee*' (Interview with Official 13) or '*pushing a line*' (Interview with Official 12). This also requires the development of political antennae that staff cultivate through interactions with MPs and the types of advice that they give them.

Advisory role of clerks

The clerk of a committee acts as its principal adviser on procedure, something that most clerks mentioned in their interpretation of the role either explicitly or implicitly. Clerks are not subject specialists (with some exceptions), but typically get appointed to committees for four to five years. This makes them generalists on policy, but specialists in procedure and process. As a result, their advice predominantly focuses on procedural matters or more general matters to help the smooth running of the committee. As one clerk put it, '*you are the guardian of process*' (Interview with Official 12). To take a few examples from fieldwork, advice ranged from how to make a formal amendment in considering a draft report (FWD 53.12.5), to whether a secretary of state behaved unconstitutionally (and what the committee could do as a result) (FWD 52.12.3), to discussing the central conclusion of an inquiry's report (FWD 49.11.11), and making a point of order in the main chamber regarding the committee's work (FWD 19.5.30). This makes the advisory role quite broad and arguably difficult to pin down. As one clerk put it:

> *I will be the committee's chief adviser on what they could and couldn't do and what they should and shouldn't do. I was the chair's chief, sort of, go-to person for anything that she wanted done.* (Interview with Official 5)

However, he also noted that he is not '*there just to facilitate any sort of conduct*', in the sense that there are rules of the House that should not be contravened. This demonstrates that there are limits to the advice that clerks are prepared to give, creating a '*tricky*' balancing act. This tension is implicit in the following quote, where a clerk summarises his role:

> *The job of the clerks of all select committees is essentially similar. It is to try to carry out the wishes of the committee in terms* of the work that it wants to undertake *within the committee's terms of reference and* in accordance with the procedures and practices of the House. (Interview with Official 4, emphasis added)

Does this mean that clerks consequently saw themselves as stewards of a committee rather than servants? The quoted clerk, above, accepted the distinction *could* be made in the abstract, but did not believe that it was applicable in practice:

> *We can think of ourselves, I suppose, as stewards of the continuing or Platonic ideal of each committee but in fact, in practice, we are largely the servants of committees, of actual committees as they are operating on a day-to-day basis.* (Interview with Official 4)

Because of this, giving advice is far from easy, which is felt most acutely on an everyday level. On one occasion, this was borne out on my committee. It came in the form of social media (specifically, Twitter). A committee member had tweeted that his committee would be agreeing a report later that day. Although seemingly harmless, the clerks alerted the chair that this disclosed private business, something that breached the principle that deliberations among committee members should remain private. When the chair brought up this contravention of procedure at an otherwise uneventful meeting, the member in question refused to accept that he had breached any rules, looking directly at the clerk. Staff remained silent – it was not their place to confront or respond to the MP. The chair followed the MP's line of sight, and realised that the member was confronting the clerk, not the chair. He quickly intervened, saying that '*it is the duty of the clerks to remind us of the rules*' and that it is an '*absolute requirement*' to follow them. The MP reneged, but noted that he would ask the Speaker to look into the matter (FWD 2.1.9). Later that day, at a staff meeting, clerks concluded that a guidance note about the use of Twitter was needed (FWD 2.1.19).

This particular case shows that the role of staff is advisory only – they could not enforce the rule by reprimanding the committee member or imposing sanctions. They looked to the chair to speak to and deal with the matter, and to defend clerks and the rules; officials themselves did not get involved. A wider observation is that, in committee meetings, clerks try not to get involved when MPs are in discussion; they limit themselves to outlining possible options that the committee could follow, in line with procedure (FWD 52.12.3). This echoes the earlier theme of being hidden, and reinforces the member-driven nature of the select committee system.

In a similar vein, clerks rarely give political advice, unless it directly impacts on the work of the committee. On a few occasions, my chair would go on a tangent in team meetings with staff to give his view of a political situation. I interpret this behaviour as part of his sense-making process (he was rehearsing his ideas on the 'back stage'). However, it was understandably met with a cautious response from officials, who would direct him back to the agenda (FWD 49.11.11). Although just one example (of many more), it reveals the extent to which a tension between loyalty to the House and to MPs is played out in the everyday life of the Commons. In general, MPs accept that clerks' loyalty is to the House (e.g., Interview with MP 9). They also accept and follow their advice on most occasions, but this does not guarantee that they will always do so (Interview with Official 5). This creates a difficult balancing act for clerks, who need to act as a buckle between MPs' wishes, on the one hand, and parliamentary procedure, on the other.

Because of the effect of everyday events, one clerk found it difficult to summarise her role. She noted: '*A lot of the time it feels like I am dealing with stuff as it happens*', and went on to say that, '*there's an awful lot of spontaneous stuff that you can't plan for that seem to make up large chunks of your day*' (Interview with Official 7). This unpredictability manifests itself in many ways. The chair could ask for advice at a moment's notice, which consequently would require staff to drop everything else they had planned to get the advice to the chair in time (as the opening of this chapter showed). This feeds into a wider point about the unpredictability of the role of clerk and that staff are frequently at the mercy of their elected rulers. This is also reflected more generally in considering the relationship between clerks and MPs.

Managing relationships

It will have become clear by this point that disentangling the role of clerks and their everyday practices from their relationship to and demands placed on them by MPs is difficult, but has important consequences for committee scrutiny. One senior and long-serving official, for example, said that he couldn't think of a single effective committee where there wasn't also a good clerk-chair relationship (Interview with Official 13). One clerk noted that he met with a chair every week without fail, irrespective of how long or short the agenda; when placed with another committee, the chair did not wish to meet with the clerk at all (the clerk had to guess what the chair wanted on the agenda) (Interview with Official 10). On my committee, meetings were held on a weekly basis. They served the important purpose of touching base and understanding the wishes of the chair, and as an attempt to manage unpredictability. He would indicate these in general terms, and staff would go on to implement those where possible. So, it was not uncommon for the chair to close meetings by commenting things like, '*you've got the gist*' (FWD 9.3.10), or, '*can you flesh out what we've discussed?*' (FWD 16.4.18). Chairs set out the general direction and leave it to clerks to implement their wishes. Meetings are therefore a vital opportunity for clerks, who will be able to ask him about the direction of a report (FWD 34.8.7), the central themes that they noticed in oral evidence sessions (FWD 39.9.3–39.9.17), or to give advice on handling certain witnesses (FWD 54.12.7). Even if clerks and chairs did not meet formally, all clerks I spoke to mentioned that they were in contact with the chair – through email, telephone calls or text messages – most days a week (including out-of-hours).

One chair commented:

> *The ability of the clerks to develop a strong and personable relationship with the chair-man* [sic] *is absolutely vital. The relationship is so much more productive if it's enjoy-able, open, trusting and, you know, a degree of full and free exchange of views and ideas … without fear or favour.* (Interview with Chair 4)

Generally, staff work towards their chair, reinforced by the increasingly pro-active role that chairs play in committee work compared to members. Clerks commented that this has increased since the election of chairs was introduced in 2010 (FWD 6.2.19, FWD 36.9.9), which the last chapter showed. So, officials need to be on hand to support their chair with writing speeches and giving briefings on topics in advance of not only committee activity, but of committee-*related* activity (Interview with Official 3). This led the Liaison Committee to call for an increase to resources (House of Commons Liaison Committee, 2012b), which was eventually granted in the 2015 parliament (House of Commons Commission, 2016, p. 17).

Some clerks are worried that the growing role of chair, and chair-clerk relation-ship, has affected their relationship to other members. One clerk said that MPs *'don't quite appreciate the role of the clerk and they see the clerk as maybe being the chair's creature'* (Interview with Official 3). Clerks see themselves as servants of the committee (and the House) as a whole, something made very clear throughout interviews and fieldwork observations. However, one clerk acknowledged that an equal level of service is not possible in practice: *'I'm working for them* [committee members] *as much as for the chair, in theory, but in practice that's not really how it works'* (Interview with Official 7). Clerks mentioned in interviews that they would like to work more closely with members, but accepted that this was made difficult due to the competing demands on an MP's time (Interview with Official 10; Interview with Official 4). The level of contact and involvement between members and chairs is so different on an everyday level that there are only limited opportunities for a closer relationship to develop with members (Interview with Official 7). As demonstrated in previous chapters, a chair is involved in almost all aspects of their committee's work; a committee member is usually (although not always) interested in only specific inquiries or projects. That said, this tension is rarely stress-tested because most MPs accept that chairs and clerks are likely to have a close working relationship (e.g., Interview with MP 17; Interview with Chair 7).

This discussion reveals that the typical role that staff play in supporting MPs goes far beyond the formal idea of providing procedural advice with which clerks are commonly associated. They play a key managerial role in order to sustain the work of a select committee and to push forward multiple inquiries; they are the bedrock for an inquiry's work. In order to make sure that staff perform this role effectively, they build significant skills in identifying the needs and wishes of members. They develop political antennae, something which is crucial in an environment where MPs disagree with one another on a regular basis and often in fervent terms. Without these antennae, committee work would be impossible because members would not be able to carry out inquiry work or support an inquiry's conclusions. In other words, clerks try to limit staff-driven aspects of their work to keep scrutiny member-driven. Part of this requires staff to act as amplifiers for members' interests, which has been demonstrated above through scoping inquiries according to members' interests, identifying and inviting witnesses from whom MPs want to hear, and drafting reports in a way that will build a sense of consensus. These are not easy tasks, and often throw up tensions in the everyday that staff have to negotiate.

This section has looked at some of the underlying everyday practices and tensions that staff have to negotiate. It has shown that inquiry support is often a balancing act between different committee interests; that giving advice to members requires political antennae, deftness and tact, as well as impartiality; and that ensuring effective working relationships between committee members, chairs and officials relies on being able to support MPs in a range of ways as amplifiers. These three tensions present perennial issues that staff face in supporting an individual group of MPs while simultaneously offering service to the institution of Parliament as a whole.

Concluding remarks

Clerks are hidden servants of accountability in the House of Commons. They exist to give unwavering support to select committees behind the scenes. The first section has, importantly, indicated the broad setting or situated agency in which clerks operate. This has revealed not only organisational complexity but some deep-rooted challenges to modernise Parliament as a workplace and safeguard those that work there. The second section of this chapter explored how staff themselves interpret their role, and identified a performance style of clerkliness. This is made up of three facets: being hidden, unparalleled service and passionate impartiality. In doing so, this has indicated that there are a number of everyday tensions that staff negotiate, which were explored in the third section. Staff exist both to serve Members of Parliament and to protect the reputation of the House of Commons. This is an underlying dilemma that is played out in the Palace of Westminster on a daily basis, in which staff have to use their beliefs and practices to adjudicate between service to a particular group of MPs and to the institution as a whole. Alongside formal roles that staff play, they also act as amplifiers for MPs' interests, develop astute political antennae, and manage relationships on committees to foster consensus.

This chapter has sought to open a perspective on scrutiny by a group of actors about whom we know very little from the academic literature. In part, it is a testament of clerks' success at 'being hidden' that has ensured staff are not centre-stage actors in the scrutiny process. However, I argue that we can learn a lot about accountability by looking at how officials support the process. So, this chapter has sought to open a debate about the role of clerks in ensuring effective scrutiny. I argue that officials play a pivotal role in calming the unpredictability of everyday life in Parliament through their permanent support to chairs and committee members that was highlighted in Chapter 3, building also on understanding of the wider 'clerkly culture', as examined by Emma Crewe (2017b).

Notes

1 In this book, the terms 'officials', 'clerks' and 'staff' are used interchangeably unless stated otherwise.
2 My fieldwork for this book took place in the 2010 parliament, before the organisational reforms instituted by the House of Commons from 2015 onwards took place, and also long before allegations of bullying came to light. My empirical findings therefore focus predominantly on the organisational complexity at the time, and how staff have navigated this.

6

Scenes of scrutiny

Immediately before a committee hearing with a permanent secretary, a specialist adviser turned to me and whispered: '*This is going to be a piece of theatre!*' (FWD 3.1.9). Her excited comment reinforced other fieldwork observations and responses by interviewees that indicate the performative element of committee hearings, in particular, but the extent to which theatre is a useful analogy to supplement analysis of scrutiny, more generally. Indeed, some have taken this even further, with one theatre company producing a play about a select committee's inquiry into the 2015 bankruptcy of Kids Company (Donmar Warehouse, 2017). While previous chapters have focused predominantly on the complexity and diversity of how actors interpret their committee roles, the remainder of this book shifts focus to the consequences of those interpretations on the conduct of scrutiny. In this chapter, specifically, I turn to the evidence-gathering processes of inquiries, including the most well-known or well-advertised aspect of committee work: committee hearings.

Committee hearings have received increasing attention in recent years, often with clips shared online, exchanges shown on TV news bulletins or dramatic images of witnesses printed in the press. However, while many instances of combative sessions have generated growing media coverage, these examples are arguably only the tip of a much bigger and deeper iceberg in terms of the work that committees undertake on a regular basis. This chapter therefore provides an insider account of how committees conduct scrutiny in three sections: first, I summarise the inquiry process and the role that evidence plays within this; second, I look at how committees prepare for committee hearings; and third, I explore how scrutiny is enacted. My argument in this chapter builds on the central theme of this book, namely that – in using a performative lens to analyse scrutiny – we can see that accountability is more than the abstract process of 'government by explanation' or an institutional relationship between government and legislature. Rather, scrutiny is produced through the actions of particular actors, and that production is shaped by their interpretations of scrutiny.

Conducting scrutiny

Select committee inquiries have many different steps, of which committee hearings are only one part. Over the course of my research, I identified 11 steps that led from an idea for an inquiry all the way through to a parliamentary debate on the findings of a committee's investigations. This chapter focuses mostly on the first half of an inquiry, i.e., the first steps, and we pick up on the remaining ones in the following chapter. For a summary of all steps, see Table 6.1.

Setting the agenda

Some interviewees believed that agenda-setting is the most important stage of any committee inquiry because it reveals the committee's priorities. Furthermore, the framing of an inquiry affects all other stages:

> *If we don't get things right at the beginning, if we don't identify what the key political choices that face the government are on any particular issue, we very often head off in the wrong direction and by the time you've taken the wrong oral evidence and asked the wrong questions, you can't get it back.* (Interview with Official 10)

This suggests that choosing an inquiry is important not only for focusing the priorities of committees but also because it practically affects the time that they can then go on to devote to key issues. This point reinforces something raised in earlier chapters: time is a much sought-after resource.

So, how are inquiries chosen? Normally, at the beginning of a parliament, clerks present the committee with a paper to outline options:

> *So anywhere between a dozen and three dozen, you know, potential lines of inquiry. So their job is to say to a committee, 'These are the things going on', 'These are the things you might want to inquiry into', 'These are the things that look interesting'.* (Interview with Official 12)

More generally, a chair explains:

> *Periodically, we have a session devoted to what inquiries shall we have. We'll bat them around and again at least 50% of the inquiries are suggested by other members of the committee.* (Interview with Chair 9)

He went on to summarise the current inquiries of his committee, listing individual members associated with them (which committee members confirmed in separate interviews). Through interviews and fieldwork observations, this approach seemed typical, with most committees choosing their inquiries based on informal and private discussions. There is, then, no formal or systematic approach, except through the Liaison Committee's 'core tasks'. However, as one official put it to me, when referring to MPs, '*nobody even knows what the core tasks*

Table 6.1 Inquiry steps and processes

Theme	Step	Description
Agenda-setting	(1) Inquiry idea and agreement	A committee will often begin with an informal discussion about ideas for inquiries, which are subsequently agreed by the committee.
	(2) Terms of reference	Committee staff will write draft terms to establish boundaries for the inquiry, which are then discussed, amended and agreed by the committee.
Evidence-gathering	(3) Written evidence	Terms of reference will be published along with an open call for evidence by the public (some groups and individuals may be invited to submit evidence).
	(4) Oral evidence	This stage is closed in that witnesses need to be invited to attend and give evidence to committees (see Chapter 7 for a discussion).
	(5) Committee visit	Some committees may choose to supplement their investigations with a committee visit, which can range from domestic visits to international expeditions.
Report-writing	(6) Heads of report	Once all evidence has been collected, staff analyse the material and identify key themes, which are then discussed by committee members and the chair.
	(7) Chair's first draft	With the heads of report in mind, staff will write a draft report that will then be considered by the chair, which will then be sent out to the committee members.
	(8) Report consideration	Members are invited to submit amendments that will be discussed informally and formally by the committee. Usually, committees seek to agree to a report unanimously at this point.
Policy-informing	(9) Publication of report	Once a report has been agreed, it will be published. Embargoed copies may be sent to witnesses, relevant civil servants/departments, and occasionally the media and other interested bodies.
	(10) Government response	The government is expected to respond to the committee's report within two months, particularly with regards to the committee's recommendations.
	(11) Parliamentary debate	This is an optional step, in which some committees may choose to debate the report on the floor of the House or at Westminster Hall.

are' (Interview with Official 8). Another clerk pointed out that his chair was not keen on being forced to undertake certain inquiries or evidence sessions because it would allow others (particularly the government) to put things on her agenda (Interview with Official 5). Based on fieldwork, core tasks were rarely mentioned by either staff or elected representatives in day-to-day work. This suggests that core tasks are a useful device to frame committee work generally and to give coherence to the system, but usually *post hoc*.

A range of factors might affect a committee's priorities and choices over inquiries. Most obviously and importantly, a committee will scrutinise relevant government policy, so significant reforms will affect the ability for committees to choose their own priorities. This is especially so if a policy is high on the political agenda. Since 2010, for instance, the Work and Pensions Committee has been preoccupied with flagship government policy to introduce and roll out Universal Credit (which combines a number of social security benefits), and the repercussions of this for other welfare issues (e.g., House of Commons Work and Pensions Committee, 2012, 2018). This has been an ongoing priority for the committee and stretches across three parliaments to date. So, for some committees, there are '*ready-made*' (Interview with Official 12) topics for inquiry.

That said, if something is high on the political agenda and also potentially divisive or partisan, then it may be less likely to be pursued, as these two chairs suggested:

> *We work best when we're concentrating on perhaps less ... exposed areas where there is a degree of consensus, like* [XX]. ... *These are all wonderfully interesting areas of our work where there is a lot of non-partisan discussion and disagreement but it's generally, I regard that as the meat and drink of the committee's work.* (Interview with Chair 4)

> *I did consciously avoid the areas of overt partisan debate on the floor of the House because at the end of the day this is a group of party politicians and they, they're interested in* [the committee's policy area], *and yes, they can develop their own view independent of their party, but if there's a high octane electorally significant debate going on, then that's much more difficult.* (Interview with Chair 10)

This is also something that I noticed through fieldwork observations, in which at least one possible inquiry was vetoed because it could have electoral implications (FWD 49.11.11). So, some partisan considerations do play a role in select committee work. This is not to say that committees consequently avoid contentious issues (Universal Credit is far from non-controversial); rather, the framing is crucial to avoid replicating the same debates as on the floor of the main chamber, particularly to build buy-in from across political parties.

Inquiry priorities are affected by other factors, too, with interviewees noting that recommendations from the public and media could play a role. Some committees ask the public for inquiry ideas, such as the Transport Committee (2012) and the Science and Technology Committee (UK Parliament, 2018). In many other cases, however, this process is informal. One chair recounted that in at least one case his committee investigated an issue as a result of a '*constituency experience*' (Interview with Chair 1), something that other interviewees suggested was common (and ties in with the idea of a 'constituency champion' raised in Chapter 3). Certain committees, such as the Home Affairs Committee (HAC) under the chairship of Keith Vaz, were also keen to shape public debate. But, rather than asking the public for inquiry suggestions, this committee conducted inquiries that would result in high-profile media coverage in order to draw attention to the HAC's work (White, 2015b, pp. 14–22). Another, more recent, example of this may be the Digital, Culture, Media and Sport inquiry into 'fake news' (House of Commons Digital, Culture, Media and Sport Committee, 2019).

In addition to outside forces, MPs themselves play a significant role: a lone wolf might want to cover something only tangentially relevant to the committee's remit, while a constituency champion will make a suggestion for an issue that's recently come up in her or his area. MPs' individual interests push scrutiny in different directions, as noted in Chapter 3. The approaches adopted by chairs are especially important in this regard. One official explained (off the record) that the agenda of their committee was set entirely by the chair. On my own committee, the chair was very robust in setting the agenda, too. On one occasion, for instance, a member raised a potential topic to which the chair responded that there was no time available, only to then list a number of topics that he himself wanted the committee to investigate further (FWD 10.3.9). On another occasion, the committee's future programme was agreed without comment from over half of members present (FWD 19.5.17). However, this is not the case on every committee, with one chair explaining:

> *The committee decides, not me, about future* [inquiries]. *I mean, I may make suggestions, the clerk makes suggestions,* [a policy stakeholder] *makes suggestions. We've always said to bodies, if you've got any ideas of what we should be looking at, you know, don't wait for us to call the inquiry and give evidence – tell us what we should be inquiring into! In the end it's our decision, nobody else's decision. It's a committee decision.* (Interview with Chair 7)

What this discussion emphasises is the possibly reactive nature of scrutiny in many cases, reinforcing Benton and Russell's (2013, p. 778) finding where only 8% of committee inquiries were 'agenda-setting'. Committees do not plan their scrutiny activities in a systematic fashion that lasts for a whole parliament (although the Defence Committee is a notable exception); rather, many inquiries can and do arise in response to either external forces or in response to the interests of those people that make up committees.

Once the broad thrust of an idea is agreed, it is often parliamentary officials who are asked to tie this down into a manageable inquiry through 'terms of reference'. This is not easy because, as one experienced clerk explained, inquiries need to be open enough to ensure flexibility but also narrow enough to address a specific policy issue (Interview with Official 10). It is only once evidence trickles into the committee that it becomes clear if it has made the right choices.

The role of evidence

Committees publish an open call for written evidence after they agree the terms of reference for the inquiry. Any member of the public and/or organisation may write to the committee about the topic and submit evidence as part of its investigations. This is a crucial way by which an individual, organisation or body of research may come to the notice of committee staff, who are the first to receive, look at and usually analyse written evidence. The amount of evidence received by committees varies hugely: some, such as the Work and Pensions Committee, can receive a lot of individual submissions because of the daily impact of certain government policies; others, such as the Political and Constitutional Affairs Committee, receive far less attention and receive fewer submissions.

Committees may supplement the formal evidence-gathering process with a committee visit or other public engagement activities. Between 2010 and 2015, the main period of study, committees have visited a range of places across the UK, which amounted to 640 field visits (based on data from sessional returns). This is often perceived as a useful way to engage the public with parliamentary work (e.g., Interview with MP 10). For example, in 2014, the Work and Pensions Committee visited Newcastle on the topic of Employment and Support Allowance, about which the chair said:

> We want to hear from people who have experience of making a new claim for Employment and Support Allowance or who have been through the incapacity benefit reassessment process. Their observations on how the system is working and, crucially, suggestions for how it can be improved, will help inform our ongoing inquiry. (UK Parliament, 2014)

The visit was subsequently quoted in the report as part of 'the claimant experience' (House of Commons Work and Pensions Committee, 2014a, paras 16–18), indicating the importance of experiential forms of knowledge in committee work and framing that emphasises implementation.

Committees regularly engage with the public in other ways beyond formal evidence-taking which inform their thinking. In 2015, the House of Commons Liaison Committee commissioned a report to give an overview of these activities, which included: inviting the public to suggest committee inquiries; using Twitter to solicit questions; and e-consultations, web forums and internet consultations to gather information from service users and stakeholders (House of Commons Liaison Committee, 2015). To give a specific example, one MP was proud of using online forums (in this case, Mumsnet) as part of the Business, Innovation and Skills Committee inquiry into *Women in the Workplace* (2013). More recently, the Health and Social Care Committee and Housing, Communities and Local Government Committee sponsored a citizens' assembly on social care to explore citizens' views on the topic, the findings of which were incorporated into their joint report (House of Commons Health and Social Care and Housing, Communities and Local Government Committees, 2018). Importantly, these are not about disseminating reports to the public or explaining how committees work; rather, they are about trying to get input from the public as part of committee inquiries. Although these examples illustrate some of the ways in which committees are changing their engagement with stakeholders and the public, research conducted by Matthew Flinders and colleagues also notes that the engagement is 'uneven' and has not been 'fully embedded' into the culture of Parliament (House of Commons Liaison Committee, 2015, para 91). In part, this may be because committees continue to depend on formal mechanisms to recognise 'evidence', which these forms of information-gathering are currently unable to replace.

Formal mechanisms of evidence include not only written submissions, but oral evidence, too. Fieldwork suggests that oral evidence is most likely to make an impact on scrutiny, and to shape committee behaviour – although, of course, written evidence, field visits and public engagement activities are important elements. Committee hearings are a site of direct and visible engagement between MPs and evidence. There are a number of reasons for this. First, it is the most high-profile form of participation in select committee inquiries, and so they are more likely to be picked up by the public, media or other stakeholders. In this way, it also means that this is the most likely medium by which the public see committee work. In fact, one senior official explained that select committees '*provide public access to the political process*' (Interview with Official 13). Committee hearings therefore have a wider symbolic purpose in embodying beliefs, values or policy positions (on symbolic representation in legislatures, see discussion by Cristina Leston-Bandeira, 2016). Second, hearings bring different claims to knowledge, scientific advice and evidence to life, with which written evidence cannot compare. So, committee chairs and members are more likely to attend evidence hearings than they are to read written submissions (Kenny *et al.*, 2017). Hearings allow MPs to actively engage with evidence when it is presented to them and to critically assess its value. Indeed, echoing a theme from Chapter 3, MPs also use these opportunities to build expertise about a policy area that they can use in other areas of their work (legislative scrutiny, debates in the main chamber, etc.). Third, while anyone can submit written evidence, oral evidence depends on invitations. So, committee hearings reveal to us who is invited to speak and to whom a committee is listening (Geddes, 2018a). None of this is to say that written evidence does not matter, but rather that committee hearings are a particular site of privileged access to influence a committee's inquiry. Thus, the remainder of this chapter delves into this aspect of the evidence-gathering process in more detail as the *stage* on which scrutiny plays out.

Scrutiny on the back stage

To repeat a quote from Chapter 3, an MP believed that committee meetings were a '*constant*' in an otherwise unpredictable and ever-changing world at Westminster (Interview with Chair 2). Committee meetings usually happen once a week, and these structure the organisation of committee work – both for MPs and for officials. For officials, in particular, weekly meetings are the deadline against which other work is set. Here, I explore this ebb and flow by taking a more detailed look at what leads up to these meetings, including witness invitations and attendance, the role of briefing papers as ever-evolving scripts, and MPs' preparation for scrutiny more generally.

Inviting witnesses

It is usually committee staff that write an initial list of potential witnesses, which is then discussed by the committee. These suggested lists are based on written evidence, colleagues (from the Committee Office, the House of Commons Library, the Parliamentary Office for Science and Technology, or further afield), specialist advisers and informal policy networks. Indeed, one senior official argues that it is part of the clerks' role to get '*stuck into the wider policy community in* [their] *particular area and encourag*[e] *them to contribute and finding expertise outside*' (Interview with Official 12). During my fieldwork, one clerk told a group at a Monday Seminar (see previous chapter) that knowing potential witnesses is very important to increase the chances of them agreeing to give evidence; calling at random is far less successful (FWD 41.10.14).

In any case, staff are guided by focus of the inquiry:

> *Some people select themselves because they have the knowledge that you want and they've done the research or analysis or they represent, you know, different client groups or whatever.* (Interview with Official 11)

Although this makes intuitive sense, there are strong constraints placed on staff in finding the witnesses that have '*the knowledge that you want*' (a phrase that itself needs unpacking – see below). First, officials are servants of their elected rulers, which means that the political direction from MPs matters. Fieldwork observations and interviews suggest that the extent to which MPs recommend witnesses varies, with many relying on officials to do the job for them (e.g., one member of staff: '*I knew that there are some organisations* [the chair] *just didn't like, so I'm not going to invite* [them]' (Interview with

Official 8). One MP explained that he would '*not very often*' suggest names so long as the committee hearings explored '*a range of views*' (Interview with MP 8). However, others do make suggestions, with one MP explaining that he would make suggestions '*both formally and informally*' and '*often significantly*' change the witness plans brought forward by staff (Interview with MP 1). Meanwhile, a clerk comments:

> *So, members will make suggestions. Very often they are straight from the usual suspects lists. I mean that's the biggest problem we have … there are a group of people who come often to give evidence and getting out beyond that group is a challenge.*

He went on to say that this is possibly accentuated by lobby groups who have become '*more crafty*' at getting their message in front of MPs, in order to subsequently be suggested for oral evidence (Interview with Official 10). On my committee, the chair would often set strategic priorities and review draft witness lists with officials (e.g., FWD 2.1.23); committee members themselves would have minimal involvement. The extent to which there are 'usual suspects' that persistently give evidence is not clear, although some findings do suggest that witness diversity is an issue in the House of Commons (Childs, 2016; Geddes, 2018a), which the Liaison Committee has recently sought to address (House of Commons Liaison Committee, 2018b).

A second, and related, consideration for staff is the need for political balance and/or breadth. MPs are acutely aware of the political nuances between different organisations that come to give evidence to committees, which staff pre-empt through diversity in witness lists:

> *You try and make sure you've got a balance of witnesses and sometimes that's, the committee have said, 'We want to hear from this person in particular', 'We want to hear from the Tax Payer's Alliance'. Sometimes you're doing it, you're pre-empting it, and I suppose that is staff influence, but this isn't me saying, 'I believe in the Tax Payer's Alliance, I think they are absolutely wonderful and we should have evidence from them'. It's me saying, 'We had this person, so now I need somebody who says the opposite'.* (Interview with Official 2)

This is a key point because it illustrates an overriding concern for the committee to ensure political balance over the course of an inquiry, irrespective of other concerns (such as the types of knowledge or advice received). The same interviewee explained: to '*balance*' a lot of academics that give oral evidence – who are '*generally seen as left-wing*' by MPs – she has suggested policy experts from centre-right think tanks to the committee at an upcoming session (Interview with Official 2). A similar point was also borne out in focus group discussions:

> **HC Librarian 1:** *… everybody was on one side, apart from* [Think Tank A], *who are bonkers. So, but you have to have them in because they're the only people on that side. And they're then given a disproportionate weight for what they do.*

Researcher 1: *A BBC problem.*
HC Librarian 1: *Yeah, exactly.*
HC Committee Clerk 3: *It's a big problem for us, that ... you've got everybody on one side of the argument because that's where the truth is, but you've got to give equal weight to the people who are on the wrong side of the argument.*

Committee staff, then, need to consider not only the ostensible quality of evidence (however this might be interpreted), but where it sits on the political spectrum. This clearly echoes themes from the previous chapter, in which officials believe in fairness to all sides. MPs themselves also prefer this:

> *If we think there's two big organisations ... that are going to say exactly the same, which they probably will, we'll just choose one of them and try and get somebody along to say something different.* (Interview with Chair 5)

This indicates that decisions about who should come before a committee is not necessarily led by attempts to get the best-available evidence, although this may well be a factor in considering diversity of views, but, rather, the political balance and nature of who can present evidence.

Reticent witnesses

Not all potential witnesses want to attend. In theory, availability for witnesses to attend committee hearings should not be a concern to Parliament; after all, committees have a statutory right to send for persons, papers and records, including an official summons for an individual to attend if necessary (HC SO Nos. 121–52, particularly HC SO No. 135). In practice, this happens rarely. Committees informally discuss attendance with potential witnesses, and only send invitations to them once they have informally agreed. Most relationships between committees and witnesses are constructive, so most witnesses are willing, some even enthusiastic, to attend. Those that decline do so for a variety of reasons, such as not being the appropriate expert in the field (FWD 8.2.16, FWD 41.10.16). For most witnesses that are asked to attend to impart information (e.g., academics, researchers, charity workers, etc.), being unable to attend is usually accepted.

However, some further witnesses may remain reticent to avoid scrutiny. On such occasions, committees usually rely on soft powers of persuasion. For example, during fieldwork, the office of a potential witness excused themselves on the grounds of being too busy. My clerk told me that I was being 'too nice', and that my invitations need to be more authoritative; a select committee hearing should not be dismissed so easily. In the end, the focus of the evidence session changed sufficiently that the witness was not required (FWD 14.4.46, FWD 21.5.27). If this issue had persisted, there are some means at the committee's disposal. One interviewee suggested the following: persuade the individual of the benefit of coming for themselves, i.e., that they can put their views on record; alternatively, indicate that refusal could end with a negative comment in the final report; or, even worse, the committee could issue a press notice to publicly embarrass the witness. This, however, presents '*a real danger*':

> *Do it once or twice, you look powerful and strong. Do it every week and you'll look like you've got no power and you can't, you're not influential because nobody wants to come and talk to you. So you don't want to look that way.* (Interview with Official 10)

High-profile witnesses, including Mike Ashley (founder of Sports Direct) and Sir Philip Green (former owner of BHS), attended committee hearings in 2016, despite previously declining. In both cases, the press headlines about their refusal to attend exerted enough pressure to persuade them to attend (Armstrong, 2016; Bury, 2016; Davies, 2016).

For other witnesses, this is not enough. Only a formal summons and the danger of being found in contempt of Parliament could convince a witness to attend. This happened in 2011, when Rupert and James Murdoch gave evidence to the Culture, Media and Sport Committee's (2012) inquiry into phone-hacking. What happens if a witness ignores a summons? In 2011, Irene Rosenfeld, CEO of Kraft Foods, declined to appear over an inquiry into the Cadbury's-Kraft merger; in 2018, both Mark Zuckerberg, CEO of Facebook, and Dominic Cummings, campaign director for Vote Leave, both declined to appear before the Digital, Culture, Media and Sport Committee during its inquiry into 'fake news'. Formally, these individuals could be found in contempt of Parliament, which means that they are subject to punishments that include being admonished by the Speaker of the House (not used since 1956–7), being fined by Parliament (not used since 1666) or being imprisoned (not used since 1880). All three punishments would risk reputational damage to the House of Commons and possibly a legal challenge under modern human rights principles (Gordon and Street, 2012; Joint Committee on Parliamentary Privilege, 2013; Natzler, 2017). In the first two cases (Rosenfeld and Zuckerberg), the individuals are beyond the UK's jurisdiction, so they are unlikely to be punished. The case of Cummings, however, raises an as yet ongoing and live issue for select committees: are their powers only for show?

Setting the stage

Although committees face problems in identifying and inviting witnesses, there are further dilemmas in organising committee hearings. One issue stems from the desire among committee members to extend the number of hearings as an inquiry is taking place, which means that '*there's pressure on the timetable*' (Interview with Official 3). One official explained that an inquiry where four evidence sessions were planned, '*ended up being 12 to fit people in because their* [i.e., MPs'] *ideas kept adding* (Interview with Official 2). This issue of time – an always scarce resource – is exacerbated further by the event-based nature of some committees, such as the Home Affairs Committee and Public Accounts Committee. What another clerk described as *'ambulance chasing'* (Interview with Official 11) was noticeable on my committee on occasion, with the chair asking for a one-off *'newsy'* evidence session to raise the committee profile (FWD 39.9.16). Consequently, inquiries are drawn up at short notice, and pre-planned sessions are moved to make room for urgent business. Alternatively, evidence sessions result in multiple witnesses facing questions at the same time, possibly even back-to-back meetings, to squeeze MPs' wishes into the timetables (MPs, meanwhile, complain that too many witnesses limits depth of questioning (Interview with MP 1; Interview with MP 8)). This affects the availability of witnesses to attend (Interview with MP 19; Interview with Official 8).

The unpredictability of everyday practices along the committee corridor takes its toll on witness diversity. As previous research has shown, committees draw more heavily from witnesses that have to travel the shortest distance, who have more resources at their disposal, and with fewer responsibilities such as child-care – i.e., those who are London-based, middle-class and male (Geddes, 2018a). For some officials, this has opened a debate about the extent to which legislatures should do more to widen access and be more proactive in promoting social diversity of witnesses and evidence (e.g., FWD 20.5.7, FWD 40.9.4). As noted earlier, this has been taken forward by the UK Parliament (Childs, 2016; House of Commons Liaison Committee, 2018b), as well as other legislatures (e.g., Bochel and Berthier, 2018).

Preparing the scripts

Evidence sessions are usually prefaced by a private meeting of the committee. It is here where the committee can discuss key issues related to the hearing, and it is often the time when the chair sets out strategic priorities for the hearing ahead and discuss possible lines of questioning. In all committees I observed, this was done thematically and with discussion from members (although interviewees alluded to alternative processes in which more dominant chairs directed proceedings). Almost always, questions come from a briefing paper, written by committee officials in advance of a hearing for committee members. The chair receives a heavily annotated copy in order to lead discussion. Briefings contain summaries of written evidence, overviews of witnesses, analysis of particular topics that committee members may wish to pursue, and suggested questions for members to ask witnesses. So, briefing papers are more than an administrative document alone; they are important for selecting, sorting and ordering knowledge and strategy (Freeman and Maybin, 2011).

To adopt the language of dramaturgy, briefings can be described – very loosely – as 'scripts' for hearings, by which committee members and chairs try to scrutinise the evidence put in front of them. In fact, one clerk explained that briefs normally have a neat *'narrative'* or *'story'* running through them, which builds up over the course of an inquiry (FWD 41.10.9). In any case, briefing papers bind all actors in the evidence-gathering process together. For chairs, briefings are a strategic structuring device. They divide the brief among their supporting cast (and usually take the part that interests them the most). Chairs will be keen that all themes of a brief are covered, and if not, are likely to ask follow-up questions (and as noted in Chapter 4, they can have different approaches to doing this). Meanwhile, committee members use the brief to familiarise themselves with topics. Specialists are likely to use it as a base, but do not necessarily stick to it; learners are more likely to be reliant on it. Themes or questions may be brought to life with constituency examples, as a constituency champion is likely to do. Lone wolves will ignore the brief; or pick a theme and run on a different riff. On the whole, MPs note that they use them, whether it is as an *'outline'* (Interview with MP 2), a *'basis to work from'* (Interview with MP 14) or as a *'crutch'* (Interview with MP 21), with one explaining that they *'heavily make use of* [them]' (Interview with MP 18).

The brief is a tangible example of 'passionate impartiality' at work (see previous chapter). Officials write briefing papers with all MPs in mind (a difficult task given the diversity of interests) and need to balance between giving enough information without overloading MPs (Interview with Official 11; FWD 26.6.18). During an evidence session, staff listen intently to the questions that are asked and the lines of inquiry picked by committee members. From this, officials will rethink the themes for future sessions. If briefing papers were not attuned to the wishes of MPs, they would not use them. And, indeed, they have alternatives – from parliamentary researchers, lobby groups and more – especially if the evidence session is high-profile (Interview with MP 20).

Importantly, it is not only the committee's MPs that receive briefing. Depending on witnesses, some may receive broad ideas about the nature of the session from committee officials. It is often to reassure them, as this clerk explains:

> We give them a kind of really broad brush description of what the session is going to be like and try to allay any nerves that they may have. I do that for witnesses now because there's a general nervousness amongst witnesses because all they see on television is [Chair A] and [Chair B] tearing shreds off of officials and that's quite counterproductive to the vast majority of select committee work, trying to get people to come and give evidence to us, I think. (Interview with Official 4)

Colleagues would do something similar on my committee (FWD 7.2.6). Clerks suggested that briefing is more detailed for smaller and under-resourced organisations (such as charities), while larger organisations will receive minimal information (FWD 41.10.25). Sessions that seek to hold witnesses to account, particularly ministers, receive no information.

This subsection highlights the importance of good preparation for good scrutiny. However, this only represents an element. Some sessions rely heavily on briefing material; others do not. Lines of questioning can come from briefing material or, equally likely, from a particular MP's interpretation of scrutiny. It is the combination of lots of little details that then go on to affect the hearing as a whole. This is also brought out from the wider preparatory work that goes into making a hearing. Once the stage is set, and the production is ready, it is time for scrutiny to play out on the front stage.

Scrutiny on the front stage

In July 2011, Rupert Murdoch gave evidence to the Culture, Media and Sport Committee about phone hacking. It was intense and, along with two other witnesses, lasted close to five hours. It was dramatically interrupted when an activist pulled a stunt by assaulting the owner of News International with a foam pie. In May 2013, Margaret Hodge, chair of the Public Accounts Committee, told representatives from Google (whose slogan is that it doesn't 'do evil'): 'I think that you do do evil, in that you use smoke and mirrors to avoid paying tax' (House of Commons Public Accounts Committee, 2013, Ev23 Q219). An even more adversarial committee hearing took place with Sir Philip Green in June 2016, including the memorable moment when the witness asked a committee member, Richard Fuller, to stop staring at him (House of Commons Work and Pensions Committee and Business, Innovation and Skills Committee, 2016, Q1786). In June 2018, Arron Banks, businessman and political backer of Leave.EU, was questioned by the Digital, Culture, Media and Sport Committee until he theatrically walked out, saying he did not wish to be late for a lunch appointment (House of Commons Digital, Culture, Media and Sport Committee, 2018).

All of these exchanges generated lots of media coverage and demonstrate the high-profile nature of certain scrutiny hearings with MPs. There are countless further examples. Committee hearings, such as those examples noted above, are easily construed as theatrical moments, language that even clerks themselves have used to describe these hearings (Mellows-Facer and Shaw, 2017). Thinking about scrutiny using this analogy of theatre and performance draws attention to the fact that accountability plays out not only in terms of the content of 'evidence' submitted to inquiries, but also through the *delivery* of scrutiny. The way that scrutiny is enacted has – as in the cases above – increased media coverage of committee work and thereby public awareness and debate on these issues. However, it is also important because scenes of scrutiny can influence (consciously or not) the behaviour of committees and witnesses. As Cheryl Schonhardt-Bailey (2017, p. 30) points out, 'subtle facial expressions, gestures, and other signals such as voice may provide important insights into not only the intentions of committee members but also the competence, trustworthiness, and credibility of the witnesses who are being held to account'. Taken in conjunction with earlier chapters that demonstrate the importance of interpretations of scrutiny in offering how MPs behave, committee hearings are powerful events in which exposure, sustained questioning and drama can help us to see how actors think, the way that politicians interact with evidence, and to see how people make sense of different ideas. I want to illustrate this with two vignettes from 2014: one from the Public Administration Select Committee (PASC), and another from the Work and Pensions Committee (WPC). Both sessions questioned ministers on the same morning, but the two performances were very different in space, speech and style.

Vignettes of scrutiny

On 11 June 2014, Francis Maude, then minister for the Cabinet Office, was asked to give evidence before PASC (2014b). The evidence session took place in a committee room in the Palace of Westminster and, though scheduled to begin at 9.30am, started at 9.50am. The committee wanted to make the minister wait. As the main minister that answers to PASC (making it a quasi-departmental, quasi-cross-cutting committee), the session focused not only on one of its inquiries regarding impartiality of the civil service, but additionally on other topics (regarding a late response to a report on the Advisory Committee on Business Appointments (ACOBA) and regarding the delay of the Chilcot Inquiry, something that featured in the news around that time: Graham, 2014; Wintour, 2014).

Although calm, the session arguably did not go well. Francis Maude's answers were designed to shut down discussion. Two (of many) examples:

Q482 Lindsay Roy: Is it your contention that the main fault for the delay lies within the Civil Service?
Mr Maude: No, I would not want to say that. I am not going to apportion blame. All of us should have moved more quickly on this, and I regret that we didn't.
Q483 Lindsay Roy: So what key lessons have you learned from this?
Mr Maude: To do things more quickly.
Q487 Paul Flynn: Isn't the likely explanation for the delay that everyone involved – civil servants and politicians – has a vested interest in keeping a watchdog like ACOBA continuing in its futile way without teeth or claws and with no powers to impose its views? Isn't it that we have got the establishment deciding not to act, sitting on their hands for 21 months to protect their prospects for retirement jobs?
Mr Maude: No.

More generally, the body language adopted by the minister, and his actions on occasion (tapping desk, looking around the room, long intakes of breath, etc.), indicate resistance or boredom to answering questions. The session was not helped by the approach or performance style taken by some members. Paul Flynn, in particular, adopted the role of 'lone wolf': an ardent anti-war campaigner, his questioning focused on the Chilcot Inquiry beyond the wishes of the chair; furthermore, his questions (i) were adversarial in tone, (ii) acted as disguised speeches, and (iii) were closed rather than open (particularly Q497, Q498, and Q499). In the end, the committee learned little from the minister.

By contrast, on the very same day and at the very same time, the Work and Pensions Committee questioned the minister of state for disabled people, Mike Penning, and three civil servants, on the operation of Employment and Support Allowance and Work Capability Assessments (House of Commons Work and Pensions Committee, 2014b). This session took place in a very different setting: the Grimond Room of Portcullis House, a modern room in a parliamentary building that opened in 2001. While the session with Francis Maude started over 20 minutes behind schedule, this one began on time and lasted much longer. I bring attention to this session because MPs adopted a range of styles, including a specialist or expert role (Debbie Abrahams drew on her record in public health research), constituency champion role (Sheila Gilmore identified constituency issues on two occasions), and absentees (in that Kwasi Kwarteng, although present, only asked one minor question, Q487). This session was also party-political, given the news coverage around welfare reforms (and especially regarding the role of Atos, a public service provider; BBC News, 2014a). For example, after Glenda Jackson described the need for specialist examiners as part of contractual agreements for a new public service provider to replace Atos, she asked (and then interrupted):

Q469 Glenda Jackson: How are you going to ensure – I presume this is going to be a requirement of the new contract – that these promises will, in fact, be met and monitored?

Mike Penning: Yes, it will be.

Q470 Glenda Jackson: How?

Mike Penning: If I can just explain…

Glenda Jackson: Good.

Mike Penning: I do not speak quite as fast as some of you.

Q471 Glenda Jackson: It is not a question of speed of word; it is a question of speed of thought, but please do go on.

Mike Penning: It may be, but if you are not willing to listen to the answer, it is a bit difficult.

Glenda Jackson: Well let us hear it.

Chair: Minister, the floor is yours.

Or more generally regarding welfare reforms:

> **Q418 Sheila Gilmore:** I am sure that organisations like Parkinson's will be very pleased to find that in June 2014, you are now discussing the question of whether these people are in the appropriate place, given that this is a matter that was raised, I think, with you when you first came into office – which is now a matter of some eight or nine months ago – with your predecessor, and with her predecessor.
>
> **Mike Penning:** And the predecessors before the last election as well.
>
> **Sheila Gilmore:** This has been specifically raised and not dealt with over the last few years…

Unsurprisingly, there were occasions when the government side felt that they needed to protect the minister, and so some committee members adopted the role of 'party helper' or safety net:

> **Q442 Graham Evans:** Can I just give an example to the Minister of a constituent who is paraplegic? The changes that this Government introduced have enabled her to get a job in my constituency working for the public authority, so there are examples other than those the ones my colleagues on this Committee have given, which always seem to give the negative rather than the positive. Some of the changes that have been put forward do help people into work.

And later:

> **Q479 Graham Evans:** In the evidence from Atos on Monday, they were saying that Dr Litchfield's recommendation regarding the introduction of the mental function champions was introduced in January and it had a positive effect. Whoever takes up the contracts in future, will those lessons be learned – that mental function champions can make a positive difference?
>
> **James Bolton:** Yes, absolutely. Mental function champions have been in place since July 2011; as you highlight, Dr Litchfield pointed to the very positive contribution they make, and that will form an integral part of the contract.
>
> **Graham Evans:** Thank you.

While this does not comprehensively evaluate the way this impacts the effectiveness of committee inquiries and reports, the key point of these two illustrative vignettes is to demonstrate the wider issue about how different conceptualisations of scrutiny and its enactment directly affect the way in which scrutiny processes play against one another and affect the overall evidence-gathering process. In other words, committee work is impacted in a direct, substantive way through actors' interpretations of the idea of scrutiny. It additionally raises issues about questioning techniques and training of MPs, echoing themes from Chapter 3 (see also Coghill *et al.*, 2008, 2012). Moreover, it raises questions more generally about relationships between committee members and performance 'teams'. This is something that we return to in Chapter 7, and it is sufficient to note here that: first, clearly good working relationships are necessary to prevent the persistence of partisan questioning, or, put more simply, everyone has their own role to play, but these roles must work in harmony; and, second, the role of chair is key in shaping working relationships between committee members, which also affects the approach that MPs take (see Chapter 4). These two points seek to show that roles develop not only through individual beliefs but through actions and practices of others.

Committee hearings are not just about the findings, the content and the final product for the report – they are moments of scrutiny in and of themselves. As one official put it, '*what makes inquiries effective more nowadays is managing them as a whole rather than seeing them as merely a process of feeding into a report*'. By this, he suggested that '*the effect*' of scrutiny '*had already happened, by the confrontation, by exposing, you know, the tax dodgers, public scorn or the home secretary to public scorn or whatever it is*' (Interview with Official 12). Evidence sessions are moments when the credibility of witnesses is assessed and judged by MPs, often with implications for public policy. This is most clearly the case in hearings with ministers, or witnesses who are directly being held to account for their (or their organisation's) actions and behaviour. It also, however, applies to witnesses that have been called to impart information and share their knowledge with the committee. I want to focus on this now.

The political performance of evidence

It is easy for evidence sessions that are supposed to be information-gathering exercises, i.e., those with academics or others that want to impart information, to stray into the political sphere. Over fieldwork, for example, one academic witness noted (to her surprise) that the hearing was '*very intense*' and '*very political*' despite the fact that she was trying to give the committee information (FWD 15.4.6). In my focus group with officials, they also noted this possibility. Giving the example of consumer protection, a clerk explained that when MPs ask for an academic witness to provide an overview of the topic, they:

> *Just attack them* [witnesses] *for all the deficiencies in the government's policies which are nothing to do with them and have a very tangential to do with the research that they've been doing recently ... you get this moment in the room, it happens a lot in oral evidence sessions, members take against a particular person, but also witnesses take against the members, and you suddenly have this breakdown.* (Focus Group, HC Committee Clerk 2)

This reinforces points made by the aforementioned research by Flinders and colleagues, in which witnesses indicated that questions by MPs can be much broader than the formal terms of reference, and also more political (House of Commons Liaison Committee, 2015, para 77 and paras 83–5). As a result, while committee chairs and MPs enact scrutiny, it is up to witnesses to perform evidence; they are part of the performance. This is something that interviewees have acknowledged:

> *There are people who you know are renowned experts but who are just crap witnesses. And there is an element of theatre to it, you know? … We had a seminar the other day, it wasn't oral evidence session, but we had a seminar and we had high hopes of two people who were just so enthusiastic on the phone you thought this is going to be brilliant, they're just going to blow the committee away. And it was so boring. And they were so uninspiring and they turned into these grey technocrats with nothing to say and you're like, 'Oh god!'* (Interview with Official 10)

He noted that this '*theatrical performance*' needed to have witnesses who were '*accessible and understandable to members*' (Interview with Official 10).

The performative element in evidence-giving was a recurring theme in the focus group with parliamentary officials. One clerk stated:

> *It's why who delivers it is important as well. Because if it's someone sitting there who is glib, persuasive, authoritative, they take that on board much better than a dusty old man, mumbling arcane symbols and stuff that they just go pfffff.* (Focus Group, HC Committee Clerk 1)

Not all witnesses are able to convey information in this way, while simultaneously trying to navigate the complex personal and political relationships between committee members and their priorities for scrutiny. As such, witnesses are performers, and asked to enact a particular kind of role. This requires applying the right social cues and etiquettes, as well as the right form of speech and tone of voice (i.e., performing with a voice that is deemed fit for giving evidence). As a wealth of previous research has shown, this is mediated by gender, ethnicity, education and class in multifaceted ways (e.g., Puwar, 2004; Crewe, 2015, p. 215; Rumbul, 2016; Rai and Spary, 2019).

This demonstrates that evidence sessions are not necessarily about absorbing scientific or other expert advice in a detached, rational manner, as idealised versions of scrutiny and evidence-based policy literatures postulate. Rather, hearings are framed politically to lead to particular outcomes, and are often affected by relationships and priorities of individual MPs on committees. As such, it is important not to underestimate the political nature of accountability and scrutiny hearings, nor that evidence can be used for other, often symbolic, purposes (e.g., Boswell, 2018, pp. 98–120; Russel, Turnpenny, and Rayner, 2013; Turnpenny, Russel, and Rayner, 2012). This is crucial because it indicates that committees' pursuit of consensus is not the result of deliberation and taking stock of all the evidence, but depends on more directly visible (and, indeed, invisible) political dynamics.

These insights from select committees reinforce a bigger picture about evidence in Parliament, as Emma Crewe (2017c) shows in her detailed analysis of the passage of a piece of legislation through Parliament, for example, or Louise Thompson (2015b, pp. 94–118) demonstrates with her analysis of evidence use in bill committees. Meanwhile, the only up-to-date report on the use of evidence in Parliament by the Parliamentary Office of Science and Technology (Kenny *et al.*, 2017) finds that research is in high demand, interpreted broadly and used in diverse ways. What all this research on evidence and Parliament so far suggests, including what I also found in this book, is that evidence-gathering processes and use of knowledge claims are complex, messy and, most importantly, political. Evidence and knowledge claims are mediated *through* politics. This echoes a much bigger literature on evidence-informed policy and practice (Boaz *et al.*, 2019).

Concluding remarks

To put knowledge claims and political decision-making into conversation is far from new and stretches back into political theory from as early as Plato's ideas of philosopher-kings. Making political decisions based on the best-available knowledge and evidence has always been intuitively appealing. This is also the point of the evidence-gathering process of select committees. However, as this chapter shows, this process is inherently complex and even messy given its political nature and involvement from 11 MPs that have different interpretations and ideas about scrutiny. Returning to the central theme of this book, it reminds us that scrutiny is pushed and pulled in diverse directions by those MPs, and plays out most visibly on the stage of a committee hearing. This chapter has demonstrated this by using the analogy of theatre to bring out different elements of the scrutiny process. Committee officials become stage directors and production managers. Sitting at the edge of the stage, they make and pass notes, analyse information and give procedural advice to keep the scene going. They also write briefing papers that can act as loose scripts for MPs. The chair of the committee will often take on the role as lead actor – and many others acknowledge her or him as that. They direct the questioning, select who speaks, and provide the priorities for the committee. They are central to the style and atmosphere of the hearing. Meanwhile, committee members act as a supporting cast. Each has their moment in the limelight in order to promote their own interpretations and priorities. And finally, witnesses themselves are caught up in this performance of scrutiny. In the middle of the stage, with all chairs and tables directed towards them, facing the chair, it is the witness and their evidence that is very much under the spotlight. In using this analogy, it reveals to us the importance of how scrutiny happens – not just the content of the evidence, the focus of the questions, or the recommendations in the final report. They are all necessarily shaped by the delivery of scrutiny.

This chapter also alludes to a more general question about scrutiny as a uniform or systematic process, and the extent to which evidence is diverse enough to ensure Parliament is able to effectively hold the executive to account. This has largely been an implicit theme. But it brings us to a key theme that has emerged from this book, and which I address directly in the next chapter: I want to suggest that talking of 'webs' of scrutiny is more appropriate than 'systematic' scrutiny.

7

Building webs of scrutiny

Networks and relationships are fundamental to understanding accountability. They are often neglected in quantitative analysis and difficult to ascertain from interviews or documentary analysis alone. Being embedded in the House of Commons, however, allows you to see and even experience those relationships. Over the course of my fieldwork, I noticed this. And I draw attention to networks and relationships here because of their influence in shaping scrutiny practices along the committee corridor and beyond. This forms the basis of this chapter. It shifts focus from the evidence-gathering process, and how MPs and officials interact with evidence, to how MPs interact with each other over the course of a select committee inquiry (and beyond). This is important because, after the evidence-gathering stage, MPs attempt to agree reports and recommendations. Traditionally, reports are agreed by unanimous cross-party support, i.e., consensus. This is interesting because our adversarial system of politics does not lend itself easily to agreement between different parties on a range of issues – especially given the growing divergence between the two main parties in recent years. Moreover, given the diversity of ways that MPs approach their role, their beliefs tend to push and pull scrutiny in different directions. So, this chapter aims to do two things: first, it asks how MPs are able to construct consensus in a select committee environment; and second, how committees contribute to the scrutiny landscape in Parliament.

In order to make sense of inquiry processes and the wider scrutiny landscape, this chapter delves into the depths of everyday life in the House of Commons. It is split into four sections. First, I examine the ways in which relationships matter to MPs and what factors affect them. Second, I broaden the scope to look at how relationships are built through everyday practices, the extent to which this creates committee norms and values, and how these processes and practices shape attitudes to consensus in a committee context. Third and finally, I turn to look at how committee relationships affect wider scrutiny networks. I argue that while scrutiny may well be a formal and systematic relationship between government and Parliament, it depends on everyday practices to produce 'webs' of scrutiny on which parliamentarians rely in their quest for accountability.

Consensus and the power of relationships

Interviewees widely shared the belief that one of the real positives of select committee work is the ability to overcome partisan considerations to establish cross-party agreement on issues of policy concern. For example, one chair noted that the *'added value of a select committee, really, is its cross-party nature'* (Interview with Chair 10). A committee member, similarly, noted that without cross-party consensus, you *'create a potential for a partisan minority'* and are consequently denied the label of *'the powerful all-party parliamentary ... select committee'* (Interview with MP 6). Another noted that those committees *'that split on party political lines are a waste of time'* because *'the government can ignore them'* (Interview with MP 21). Hannah White (2015c, pp. 23–4) explains why:

> Recommendations agreed by MPs from across the political spectrum cannot simply be dismissed as partisan. And, if a cross-party committee manages to come to agreement on an issue, that is often a good test of a politically-workable solution, to which the government should pay attention. ... Party political consensus is a powerful tool for impact.

Thus, consensus is a foundational element of committee work because this is a source of committee authority and legitimacy.

In order to achieve consensus, the personal attitudes and approaches of MPs is important. They suggested the importance of being able to *'leave party badges at the door'* (Interview with MP 22) or, as another put it, to tell the whips to *'sod off'* (Interview with MP 14). However, while this may well be true in theory, it is not entirely possible in practice. During fieldwork, my clerk would occasionally comment that MPs behave in a *'politician mode'* (FWD 20.5.12) and questioned whether they were able to think outside this mode (FWD 26.6.3). Another official:

> *They're political people and they have deeply held views about the world which aren't left at the door. ... Tory members of my committee were very partisan, Conservative, quite right-wing and their view was the free market should be left to it, in all sorts of areas, and any smack of regulation was wrong in principle. And the Labour people generally have the opposite view and I think ... it'd be naïve to think ... that as politicians they would suddenly just abandon that. That is their mindset.* (Interview with Official 5)

It was acknowledged by certain MPs: *'our viewpoint on an issue is covered by our view on, you know, the world rather than anything that's strictly party political'* (Interview with MP 18). These outlooks do shape committee work and, in particular, approaches to consensus. One clerk noted, for example, that the addition of a very left-wing MP to his committee, someone *'very assiduous and quite clear in his line'*, has *'ruffled a few feathers'* and possibly made the committee *'less consensual'* (Interview with Official 4). On my committee, too, MPs would bitterly disagree over a range of issues as a result of their diametrically opposing belief about the purpose of politics (FWD 15.4.1, FWD 16.4.28). The effects of different philosophical outlooks do not need to be negative, however, because – to give a final example – one official explained how two MPs who were on opposing wings of their respective parties (one being a right-wing Conservative MP and the other a left-wing Labour MP) got on very well because they, first, both had traditional ideas about their particular policy area but, second, found common ground over their Euroscepticism (Interview with Official 2; FWD 42.10.4). What this suggests is that wider attitudes to politics are factors that can and do explain committee behaviour.

The above brings out the importance of personal relationships, something that most MPs noted. For example:

> *Having a good personal relationships with members is very important insofar, shall we say, it acts as a way of restraining any sort of excesses in debate in committees, yeah, if you genuinely get on fairly well as a group of people.* (Interview with Chair 9)

> *If you're not collegiate, this doesn't work. This place doesn't work. … A lot of this place works on: you support your colleagues.* (Interview with MP 9)

> *The key component within the committees is actually having that degree of common working together and understand the respect for each other.* (Interview with MP 20)

> *They* [relationships] *are quite important that you feel some, kind of, comfortable with each other and there's sort of trust and it's, you know, it's all private.* (Interview with MP 18)

Relationships develop in a range of different ways, in which trust and respect are key. A number of MPs noted that leaking information is '*poisonous*' for committee relationships (Interview with MP 17), with one MP telling me (off the record) that they left a committee because of leaks.

While trust and respect are key markers for political relationships, most interviewees acknowledged another factor that shapes the ability for MPs to work together: their personalities. For example:

> *The committee's work depends very much on the personality of chairs. And we have brilliant chairs and we have disastrous chairs.* (Interview with MP 2)

> **MG:** *I've been trying to work out what drives the relationships in Parliament between MPs on committees.*
> **I:** *Oh, very complicated. Very personal. I mean … I suspect it's the leadership, it's the chairman* [sic] *that determines how a committee functions. The chairman – and I hope I am – is open and reasonable and places his trust or her trust in members of the committee and the staff …* (Interview with Chair 4)

> *Over the top of it* [political relationships]*, you have to also layer a healthy dose of personality. And some of them, no matter how ideologically barking they might be, are really*

loveable people who just get on with everybody and others have plenty of decent and intel-
ligent things to say but are such awfully horrible people to deal with that nobody likes
them … and so … you have to look at all of these other things. And it does contribute to,
you know, what makes a committee successful. (Interview with Official 10)

These quotes are illustrative not only of the wider argument that personalities affect the success of a committee, but also because they go to the heart of
explaining the way in which simple, everyday relationships and behaviour affect
scrutiny. To take a specific example, one chair noted his positive relationship to
the vice-chair of his committee, which was fostered through a shared interest in
football (although, as in politics, they support different teams) (Interview with
Chair 9). More generally, a committee member noted:

You can have friends in other political parties and people in your own party you barely
say hello to and that's the nature of the way this place is. So you have personal friendships
and you have political acquaintances. I have exceptionally good friends in the Liberal
Democrats as well as them being party colleagues. I have friends in the Conservative
Party and the Labour Party who I'm not politically in tune with at all. (Interview
with MP 15)

This feeds into a final and wider point about parliamentary friendships.
Although easily dismissed as non-political or unimportant, this can make
an impact, as Sarah Childs (2014) has shown with respect to women in the
Labour Party and their negotiation of the gendered nature of Parliament. In
terms of scrutiny practices, one MP saw past his colleagues' antagonistic behaviour (FWD 42.10.4) because of their friendship. Another noted that he joined
the committee because he was friends with the chair (Interview with MP 12),
which was echoed by a chair who said that '*the flavour of Labour members*' has
changed because '*people have encouraged their friends to come on the committee*'
(Interview with Chair 1). Friendship can have real effects in changing scrutiny
behaviour or, as the following quote shows, to overcome stereotypes of their
political adversaries:

I mean I'm really impressed with [MP A]. *I thought he was a, you know, a sort of*
Scottish fossil to start with, and worried where he's coming from, but he's really, really
… and he is also very supportive. He's always been loyal and supportive. (Interview
with Chair 4)

Friendships can act as ways to build greater solidarity and enhance the cross-party
scrutiny conducted by committees – indeed, it is dependent on this respect, trust
and support for one another.

Not all MPs agreed with this, with one saying that even if MPs build close
working relationships, they '*are still politicians and this is about power*' (Interview
with MP 16). In 2017, Labour MP Laura Pidcock attracted attention when she

said that she could never be friends with Conservative colleagues, something which was echoed more recently by the shadow chancellor, John McDonnell (Pavey, 2017; BBC News, 2018). This is a reminder that personalities, philosophical outlooks and political ideas are closely interwoven. These factors are key to understanding scrutiny, and will affect the ability of a committee to reach consensus. They play out in everyday practices, which I want to explore further now.

Committee cohesion

Relationships are shaped not only by the approach to scrutiny, philosophical outlooks and personalities of members – i.e., their individual beliefs – but also through daily interaction in the House of Commons, or the everyday practices of scrutiny. Some of these practices were explored in earlier chapters, but it is worth directly focusing on their manifestation here by: first, looking at how norms and values create unique committee 'traditions'; second, exploring the effects of changing membership on committee cohesion, norms and values; and third, how these factors lead to a committee's ability to build consensus.

Committee norms and values

One interviewee believed that 'norms of civility' govern not only select committee behaviour but all of Parliament (e.g., courtesies and conventions in the main chamber). He believed that these norms and values are all around Parliament and key factors in sustaining partnership and collaboration. Although he noted quite simple examples – politeness in opening and closing doors for one another, or passing water during meetings – these 'micro' practices foster an atmosphere of collegiality that overcomes the harsh realities of adversarial politics (Interview with MP 11). These are especially important in committee hearings, which one interviewee called 'a kind of dance which is imperceptible' (Interview with MP 16). Some of these norms of civility are broadly shared by committee members, such as a general agreement, or 'good manners', not to 'steal somebody else's thunder' (Interview with MP 15) nor 'wanting to pinch somebody else's question so they don't have anything credible to say' during an evidence session (Interview with MP 18). Another value, often used to carry committees over subjects where there is disagreement between members, is the use of humour, especially in private meetings (FWD 3.1.12). It means that members can discuss difficult subjects without letting this affect them personally and also keeping the committee cordial.

Beyond these 'norms of civility', each committee arguably has their own 'feel' to it (Interview with Official 2; FWD 29.7.8), which reinforces the committee's distinct tradition or webs of beliefs. Three quotidian examples suffice to make the point. First, on my committee, MPs would not generally interrupt one another during evidence sessions; on other committees, I noticed that there was a lot more free-flow or jumping in to ask follow-up questions (irrespective of whether the chair had asked the individual to come in or not). Second, the physical movement of members and staff. On some committees, members will not move from their seat during public meetings, instead passing notes to one another or sending quick emails through phones and tablets. In other committees, members freely moved to sit next to each other and discuss a point while a session with a witness is underway (I noticed this on the Treasury Committee, in particular). A third and final example, seating arrangements themselves. On some committees, members sit according to party line; in others, they do not. This may seem inconsequential, but the use of space has physical and symbolic effects. Physically, members from different parties may or may not be able to easily contact one another and talk directly to each other; symbolically, it reveals the extent to which a committee is committed to a cross-party process of undertaking scrutiny. One chair, for example, noted that he tries to make sure that the committee doesn't sit by party in order to '*act as one*' (Interview with Chair 6).

These three everyday behaviours are routine and quotidian, and, although they may appear mundane and insignificant, they matter in developing a relationship of trust, respect and sense of 'team' among the committee. As noted in other chapters, there is an active attempt, particularly by chairs, to '*hunt as a pack*':

> *I think it's really important that select committees hunt as a pack. … I think the most effective* [questioning] *is when you use the talents that different people have and I've also – to try and get the committee to gel – we had an away day. We only went across the river, but we still had an away day and that was to try and get them hunting and thinking together.* (Interview with Chair 5)

Another chair spoke of a '*common sense of moral purpose*' (Interview with Chair 6). Committee members are conscious of this too, with one member explaining the added benefit of training sessions for MPs:

> *I mean that's useful sometimes to … just to get to know each other a bit better because there's a danger of becoming quite competitive … in terms of, 'I'm going to get my say' and 'I've got this brilliant question I want to ask and I'm going to get it in regardless'.* (Interview with MP 3)

The extent of team spirit among the group and the wider committee traditions that underpin them has practical effects on scrutiny. For example, a number of MPs said that they would be far less willing to attend meetings without partnership among MPs (e.g., Interview with MP 1). It is worth quoting the following exchange from an interview with a newly appointed MP to a select committee that had comparatively low attendance over the 2010 parliament:

MG: *What were your expectations when you first joined?*

I: *Well, I thought we'd have a full committee for a start. I mean, I can't believe we only had four people there. I mean that really shocked me. … I don't know whether this happens with other select committees?*

MG: *As far as I know, some have higher attendance. I think it depends, though, on who the witnesses and…*

I: *Yeah, I don't think that's right. I mean, you know, there may be times when I can't attend the select committee. I've now got the idea in my head that you don't have to turn up – which is not a good thing. I personally think you should make every effort to attend every single session.* (Interview with MP 4)

This quote illustrates the importance of committee norms and values, not only in fostering a sense of common purpose, but also the role of socialisation. Although committees have always needed a level of cohesion (Arter, 2003), one MP believed that the level of cohesion that committees have developed in recent years and attributes this to the Wright reforms of 2010 (Interview with MP 7). This suggests – in line with Lord Norton's (1998) argument – that select committees are an important site for institutionalisation of the legislature. In any case, a committee needs a sense of belonging and ownership, and this culture is built up through everyday actions – including the basic act of attending evidence sessions. Otherwise, inquiries may lose attendance, have poorer preparation and questioning, or even break down in the consideration of reports altogether. It may also affect MPs' willingness to become members of committees in the first place.

The dilemma of changing membership

While one MP noted that he switched select committee because a vacancy had opened on a committee that was more relevant to his constituency, and another that he wanted to try something new, the bulk of changes to membership come as a result of frontbench reshuffles (of either or both the government and the opposition). The average length of membership between 2010 and 2015 was 32 months, or just over two and a half years (which varied between committees and members) (analysis based on sessional returns). This means that there is *'always a bit of movement'* (Interview with MP 3). One committee chair felt this to be *'extremely frustrating'* because it affected the political balance and descriptive representation of his committee, and required building relationships with new members all over again (his committee had comparatively high turnover) (Interview with Chair 1). Other chairs noted that this was *'quite a problem'* for similar reasons, additionally noting that you can lose talented members, especially if they have also gone through training sessions (Interview with Chair 5; Interview with Chair 9). Unsurprisingly, new members are more likely to adopt the role of 'learner' (see Chapter 3).

As a result of changing membership, new members join an established committee who could question existing practices. For example, one clerk pointed out that new members on his committee questioned a previously established understanding whereby members and the chair agreed that press notices and the media would be the chair's responsibility (Interview with Official 5). Although only one example, the wider point is that members' beliefs and practices could be '*completely at odds with the norms that that group has already established*', as this clerk recounts:

> *I've seen on a handful of occasions, members walk in, take no notice at all of the norms that the group has, and start to force divisions on reports and … it really upsets people because you have years of unanimity and consensus is blown away because some upstart's walked in and started, you know, voted on things when you've never had to vote on anything before.* (Interview with Official 10)

Put slightly differently, new members' ideas and beliefs affect the pre-existing web of beliefs of the committee. One MP believed that a period of high turnover was '*psychologically disruptive because you don't know who's going to be in the room when you walk in*' (Interview with MP 23).

Other interviewees, however, have also pointed out the positive aspects to changing membership. New members can offer fresh ideas, experience and purpose to committee work (e.g., Interview with MP 15; Interview with MP 18; Interview with Official 8). Nonetheless, the ability for this to work depends on the committee's ability to absorb changes through socialisation. One committee member developed an example of this from changes early in the 2010 parliament. He explains that, initially, newly appointed MPs saw their role in party political terms (having been elected for the first time at that general election), which led to '*really quite difficult scenes*' because '*there was a bloc effectively seeing itself as having a different job from either the chair or the other members*'. He went on, however, to say that '*that all quite surprisingly changed around and actually the committee as it is now is a very cohesive committee*'. He explained that this was because these members changed their understanding of their role:

> *This was going to be a committee report and that you were a member of a committee as opposed to a sort of visitor on behalf of a bloc and that your function was not remotely the same as you would expect it to be on the floor of the House, but no one said that – it was just kind of, it came to be.*

He explained that this happened because, first, the chair was '*very patient and inclusive*', who tried to '*include everybody in all the discussions*' and, second, other long-serving committee members were '*prepared to work together on that* [consensus] *and other people started to fall in behind them*' (Interview with MP 7). This example highlights the distinctive role of the chair, who will provide the consistency in approach and style over the course of their five-year tenure.

One clerk went further and suggested, more generally, that changing membership empowers the chair: '*I think it probably strengthens the chair in a sense that there's nobody else who can challenge her knowledge or expertise or background*' (Interview with Official 5). This is an important point, and returns us to a theme covered in Chapter 4, in that the chair drives forward not only the strategic priorities of the committee but also plays a key role in developing norms and values.

Taking changing membership into account with other themes raised in this section, it demonstrates that committee scrutiny is driven forward in many respects through everyday practices and committee traditions that develop over time. The argument of this chapter is that this affects the extent to which committees are able to construct consensus for their reports. I now want to turn my focus directly on this issue by picking up themes raised in the last chapter (which dealt with the first half of an inquiry, i.e., evidence-gathering) and combine it with insights here to explore how MPs construct consensus and agree reports (i.e., the second half of an inquiry process).

Constructing consensus

Consensus is not something that occurs only in the final stages of a committee's inquiry; it is constructed from the very beginning. For example, agenda-setting and choosing inquiries not only enables committees to set their strategic agenda but it is also the earliest opportunity for MPs to build a common purpose. The framing of inquiries is particularly important. Interviewees have explained that not replicating debates from the floor of the House of Commons is seen as a particular route to this. Alternatively, others point out that issues without a high profile (and therefore likely to be without a strong government view) are areas where committees can play an important role.

Agenda-setting is also about the ownership that committee members feel about their committee's work. This may involve some horse-trading or '*give-and-take*', as these two interviewees explained:

> *I think you want to have a lot of behind-the-scenes chat and negotiation with different members and some of them* [chairs] *are good at that, you know, being able to say, 'Well, look, you know, I know you don't much like this inquiry, but I'd be really keen if you could turn up, and we'll do your inquiry choice next'. A lot more give-and-take like that.* (Interview with Official 5)

> *There is a sort of culture that you don't … contradict aggressively because everyone gets their turn at it. So therefore you're not going to kill somebody's pet idea for an inquiry because it might be yours next week that you'll try at it. So there is a sort of give-and-take – which works, usually, but if somebody keeps saying, 'we must, we must' … that really irritates.* (Interview with Official 3)

The sense of ownership acts as an undercurrent that binds committees together, not only in inquiry choices but throughout the process, such as during evidence-gathering. As the above interviewee explained:

> If the chair constantly interrupted everyone's questions – I've seen that – drive the members to distraction. Or other members, you get a good riff of a question going and suddenly another member will just butt in in the middle of it and that ruins it. You can see them – absolutely seething. And if that's repeated, that's a problem. (Interview with Official 3)

This brings us directly to how evidence-gathering can shape consensus. Interviewees noted that public sessions are often 'pretty polite' (Interview with Chair 6), and depend on good personal dynamics or 'personal chemistry' because 'if you've got that basic goodwill, it's much easier to sort of rein somebody in or to accept in good humour that they need to shut up' (Interview with Chair 9). Personal chemistry or goodwill can be established in the margins of meetings, where members will chat and gossip, learn about one another, share ideas, make jokes and caricature each other – all things that I observed on my committee (FWD 2.1.2, FWD 3.1.12, FWD 52.12.3).

One of the most influential ways to build consensus is through committee visits. According to one MP, they 'pull people together' as part of a 'common experience' (Interview with MP 21). This is a widely shared view:

> The relationship on a select committee, I think, is crucial. … there will be occasions when you go away on visits. … So you're travelling with these people. You're going to the same briefing sessions. You are there as British MPs, you are not there as a Lib Dem MP. (Interview with MP 15)

> When you travel together and you go for dinner together the night before, then, you know … you start to learn about people's, their family and things like that. So you see them real and … you can sympathise with them and the difficulties with their childcare and the travel and the constituents, you know. So there is a lot that we do share and that … building of the relationship, I think, is really important. (Interview with Chair 5)

> Travel and intense period together tends to bring you together and create a sort of personal bond that … might not otherwise be there, that's very helpful, you know. (Interview with Chair 6)

Given that MPs are under time pressure almost all of the time, visits can be especially important because it is time spent together with minimal or no interruptions (although this makes it complicated to arrange visits in the first place). This does not mean that MPs will like each other more; it means that MPs have greater sense of respect for one another and understand their colleagues' approaches to scrutiny.

Additionally, a field visit can be pivotal for the work of the committee itself. One chair commented that 'visits confront people with the facts', and went on to give a specific example of an inquiry where a visit had *'significant influence'* on committee members' views. He gave another example:

> *There was a classic occasion when … my committee, we tried to, we were struggling to agree a report on a difficult issue and benefited greatly from being stuck in* [an] *airport for a long time because of fog and a great many disagreements were resolved in the time we had.* (Interview with Chair 1)

Thus, consensus is not something that happens after evidence is collected and analysed in some sort of dispassionate manner; the process itself, from the beginning, is important in terms of constructing consensus.

Once all the evidence for an inquiry has been collected, it usually falls to officials to write a draft report (*'you can't write by committee'*; Interview with Chair 3). This commonly follows a discussion by the committee of so-called 'heads of report' (quite literally: the section headings to be used for the draft report). For some committees, this is a detailed process in order to identify *'where the sticking points might be'* (Interview with Official 11). Other committees do not discuss it in detail, which suggests different norms have been established by the group. The draft report is written for the chair, who will identify *'pinch points'* (Interview with Chair 5).

The chair's draft report is discussed and agreed at 'report consideration'. This is pivotal for members because they will have a direct impact on the extent of consensus for a report. One MP stated:

> *You either respect or disrespect people at the end of that. People come out with their views. They compromise, don't compromise. They can articulate their views as they mean. Whatever. You get to know people in that process. It's a combination of outside the committee and inside the committee that does that.* (Interview with MP 21)

Committee members are likely to give an input into a draft report because it is the key and visible output from the scrutiny process – and all MPs' names are attached to it. Most will seek to do so by submitting amendments either formally or informally.

Committee members' amendments at report consideration can be informed by a range of things and it is at this stage that many dynamics of the previous sections and chapters come into play: different interpretations of scrutiny, personal relationships, and their political priorities – all of which are mediated by the chair's skills to build cross-party support. This was crystallised in report consideration of one of my committee's reports. In this case, the inquiry had failed to resonate with existing members and had lost momentum. In early discussion, in a meeting with staff, the chair accepted that the report would make minimal impact and so it should be *'slipped out'* (FWD 34.8.19). When the draft report was eventually written, the chair remained lukewarm (FWD 49.11.11). The inquiry topic had never been part of his core committee interests, while the original member that suggested the inquiry had left the committee. At report consideration itself, MPs gave their views. Two Labour members were opposed to it because the report accepts or condones too much privatisation. Others disagreed, including one Conservative MP who gave an extended example from his constituency (to which no one commented). At one point, the chair conceded that '*we've got to find consensus somewhere*', while the Liberal Democrat MP added that this was becoming too ideological and a bit of both – public ownership and privatisation – was the most sensible way forward. Two newer committee members did not make significant points because they were not part of the inquiry for large parts. Nonetheless, the discussion continued in a robust left-right, but good-natured, tussle. There was no partisan debate; instead committee members raised broad philosophical opposition to the thrust of the report depending on their left-wing or right-wing inclinations. The chair became exasperated towards the end and asked what the committee should do with the report. One MP muttered loudly, '*Give it a good burial*', to the chuckles of others (FWD 52.12.3). The report was never published.

What does this example reveal about consensus? There are two lessons. First, it highlights that 'ownership' is a key theme in select committee work. One chair explained that '*members must feel that the report is partly theirs*' (Interview with Chair 9), which was shared by other interviewees. This needs to be built over the course of the entire inquiry, through buy-in of questions and themes, for example. Without the chair or, as in the above case, a committee member driving forward an inquiry, it is known as 'orphaned'. Second, consensus does not mean a wholehearted agreement with everything in a report, nor necessarily that the report is based purely on the weight of the evidence. It is about MPs' ability to broker a deal between themselves on political priorities and issues. This requires a different focus for some inquiry reports. A key negotiating tactic for cross-party agreement is the wording of reports. Multiple interviewees explained how members would try to change '*little nuances*' to '*softening*' of the language without amending recommendations (Interview with MP 10). Others said that recommendations and conclusions could be excluded from the final report to get consensus (Interview with Chair 1), while clerks explained that some recommendations are significantly watered down. This is something I witnessed for another committee's report (although some amendments were eventually pushed to a vote; FWD 53.12.5).

This discussion subtly changes the meaning of consensus in a select committee context: committees are important sites for political discussion, and scientific advice and expert-led evidence is contested in political terms. So, taken in conjunction with the findings of the previous chapter, a consensual report is not based on evidence but by what is politically feasible, something that reinforces findings by others (Boswell, 2008; Crewe, 2017c). Committee inquiries remain inherently political (which should not surprise us, given the institutional environment).

Committees and the scrutiny landscape

A key theme of this chapter is the reliance on relationships between parliamentary actors to enact scrutiny. This happens in lots of ways that extend beyond an individual committee's inquiry or meeting space. In this section, I want to broaden the scope to look at the wider scrutiny landscape in the House of Commons and the part that committees play within that.

Rubbing shoulders on the parliamentary estate

Before an evidence-session begins, MPs will chat and gossip; afterwards, it is possible to overhear MPs and officials say things like, *'can I grab you for a moment?'*, to hold impromptu discussions and meetings (FWD 1.1.20, FWD 2.1.2, FWD 2.1.16, FWD 2.1.17). This doesn't just happen in a committee room. For example, my chair would often use opportunities of the division lobbies to meet with frontbench politicians (FWD 59.13.4, FWD 19.5.10, FWD 49.11.11, FWD 57.13.7). Other interviewees have also noted this phenomenon in the division lobbies, with one explaining that he *'had a meeting in the margins of a vote with two other members of the* [XX] *Committee where we decided on the morning's work and how we should take it forward'* (Interview with MP 6). This is one of the reasons why there has been so much resistance to changing how MPs vote; it is one of many informal opportunities for MPs to interact with each other, which is preciously guarded. This 'rubbing shoulders' happens across the parliamentary estate:

> *I … will bump into* [MP A] *when we're both buying coffee and I'll say, you know, 'What do you think of that? I think we ought to be doing more or less', or 'Why the hell are we doing this?' And we'll spend 15 minutes with a coffee at Portcullis just nattering about it. You know, that kind of thing.* (Interview with MP 6)

> *If we bump into each* [other], *we'll say, 'What did you think about what so-and-so said?' and 'Could you believe this?' or I might ask, I might say, 'I really want to get this witness in, is that something that you think that's a good idea?' or 'Would you support me in that?'* (Interview with MP 23)

One committee chair remarked that he would *'bump into* [committee members] *all the time'*, and would make sure that he used those opportunities to share concerns and discuss the committee's work in advance of meetings (Interview with Chair 4). It may not seem significant, but this raises interesting questions about the nature of space and spatial arrangements of the parliamentary estate (Norton, 2018) and, indeed, a wider debate about the plans to refurbish the Palace of Westminster (Flinders *et al.*, 2017; Meakin, 2019). The organisation of space – whether the design and layout of meeting rooms, debating chamber or the Palace as a whole – affects the everyday nature of scrutiny, and reforms could make a difference to this. One clerk captured this in his thoughts:

The changes in the geography of the estate have reduced the opportunities for us to come across Members. So Millbank used to be a shared space between Members and staff. So we were falling over them in the canteen and, you know, you were rubbing shoulders with them all. If you go back far enough, we were dining in the dining rooms in the evening because the House sat late and everybody was there and you were rubbing shoulders with them ... there was just more opportunity for those sorts of contacts to happen. (Interview with Official 10)

Meanwhile, some believe that co-location – where officials from different House authorities share an open-plan office – has fostered greater working together between staff, which may (in part) explain the rise of joint committees from 2015 onwards (Interview with Official 13; personal communication with former official, December 2018).

All of this suggests that scrutiny happens not merely through an inquiry, the publication of a report at its end and a government response two months after this. Rather, scrutiny is enacted across Parliament in big and small ways through everyday practices and behaviour, as this chapter has shown. This topic is also explored richly in Emma Crewe's (2005, 2015) anthropology of Parliament, as well as other research that has explored the impact of select committee activity. For example, Meg Russell and Daniel Gover (2017, pp. 205–33) examine select committee influence on the legislative process in great detail. They note that committees (from both the Commons and Lords) are mentioned more than 140 times per parliamentary bill (on average), with the Treasury Committee mentioned the most often overall. Furthermore, these mentions are by a variety of actors, including government frontbench, opposition frontbench, and backbenchers, to either defend or question government legislative policies. It suggests to us that committee reports do not simply sit on shelves; they are used for 'ammunition' in debates, as Russell and Gover (2017, p. 227) put it. Not only are select committee reports widely respected, but committee members themselves are too. In particular, chairs of committees are called earlier in House of Commons debates and they are often also attributed status and authority for their backgrounds (Russell and Gover, 2017, p. 218). This brings us to a wider issue and question about the relationships between chairs and committees.

Relationships between committees and their chairs

Formally, the Liaison Committee of the House of Commons is in place to oversee the activities of the departmental and cross-cutting scrutiny committees, and is made up of the chairs of these committees. In the past, this group has campaigned to make the committee system more effective through high-profile reports (e.g., *Shifting the Balance*, 2000b). However, the Liaison Committee has lacked leadership qualities, for at least two reasons. First, there is a structural problem in that the committee has more than 30 members. Second, each committee chair seeks to guard their own remit and terrain, making collaboration more difficult (although joint inquiries are addressing this to some extent) (White, 2015c). This may well have been an unintended consequence of the Wright reforms, with one official explaining that there is '*less team-player attitude of the elected chairs*' (Interview with Official 12). This is noticeable when the committee sits to question the prime minister, with no interaction between committee chairs; each has their own protected issue area (for analysis of prime ministers' appearances in front of the Liaison Committee, see research by Kelso *et al.*, 2016). The Liaison Committee is therefore not (nor was it designed to be) a cohesive whole that can act with one voice, even if the committee was designed to keep oversight of the scrutiny system as a whole through its 'core tasks'.

So, rather than any formal or institutionalised relationship between chairs, the wider scrutiny landscape along the committee corridor is governed by informal relationships. These are often characterised by the aforementioned competitive environment, especially between chairs. For example:

There's a certain amount of jostling for the limelight, you know, to be top committee ... yes, I mean it's a, and there's healthy competition and perhaps one or two chairs are too obviously competitive to get into the limelight. I hope I'm not one of them! [laughter]. (Interview with Chair 4)

Although one committee member called this '*childish*' (Interview with MP 18), it was a sentiment shared by other MPs. One member explains that committees have to '*tread quite carefully so as not to tread on another select committee's toes*' (Interview with MP 19). A chair used similar language: '*I think that we try and* [be] *quite sensitive to when they think we're treading on their toes*' (Interview with Chair 2). This was equally noted during my placement. On a couple of occasions, my committee's chair complained that another committee should get '*off our patch*' (FWD 52.12.3, FWD 57.12.7). Likewise, if my chair veered into the remit of another committee, officials would strongly encourage the chair to contact his respective counterpart (FWD 39.9.7). Indeed, where committees do encroach on another's work, it fell to the relevant chairs to resolve tension by agreeing boundaries (Interview with MP 1). Alternatively, committees could conduct joint inquiries, although they were often seen as '*cumbersome*' to organise (Interview with Chair 7) during fieldwork. Attitudes have changed since at least 2015, given the noticeable growth of joint inquiries (House of Commons Liaison Committee, 2018a).

Through informal relationships, committees establish a reputation against one another and, in doing so, a '*pecking order*' (Interview with Official 10). While on the whole this reflects government departments (especially the great offices of state: HM Treasury, Home Office, and Foreign and Commonwealth Office), the chair's personal standing often affects the informal hierarchy among committees and the extent to which committees are regarded as important in the House more generally. One clerk, for example, noted the shifting reputation of the Public Accounts Committee: seen as '*very senior*' before 1979, it '*lost a lot of its significance with departmental committees coming in*', but has been '*re-galvanised by a new and very active chair*' to do things that are '*interesting to the public*' (Interview with Official 4). It is perhaps unsurprising that the Public Accounts Committee is consequently seen as a competitor for many other committees. This informal standing matters because, as one MP pointed out, it serves as an indication of how seriously a committee should be taken by not only other committees and colleagues within the House, but more widely by the public and potential witnesses (Interview with MP 11), with possible wider implications for the effectiveness of committees (Monk, 2010). Perhaps most importantly, it re-emphasises the importance of informal relationships and practices, which play a key role in embedding scrutiny in the House of Commons.

What is the impact of all this committee activity? At the end of inquiries and following the publication of reports, committees await the government's response to them. Government has a duty to respond to reports within two months (although there are occasions when this does not happen). Research conducted by others shows that these reports and their recommendations can be highly influential. For example, Meghan Benton and Meg Russell (2013) found that around 40% of recommendations targeted at central government were implemented (of which, 55% were small-level, 31% were medium-level, and 14% were large-level). They also explain that committees are important for spotlighting issues, providing evidence, influencing debate, brokering agreements, acting as forums of accountability and public exposure, and generating 'anticipated reactions'. So, committees play a hugely important role in order for the House of Commons to fulfil its accountability function as a legislature, something which this book echoes.

Through parliamentarians' everyday practices, they weave webs. These 'webs' of scrutiny are built on relationships and networks: between chairs and committee members; between chairs of committees through the Liaison Committee and through their status and authority on the floor of the House; between MPs and policy stakeholders; between stakeholders and parliamentary staff, who nurture their knowledge of policy networks where possible; and, ultimately, between Parliament and public. In some policy areas, this may be densely developed and subject to significant, high-profile and effective interventions from committees; in others, the webs may be fragile and need to be nurtured further. Understood in this way, scrutiny is contingent on the beliefs, practices and traditions of a range of parliamentary and extra-parliamentary actors. This echoes a theme of 'court politics' that R. A. W. Rhodes has developed with colleagues (Rhodes, 2013; Rhodes and Tiernan, 2013, 2016). They argue that executive politics – i.e., the decision-making at the heart of government – can be understood through a 'court', which 'focuses attention on the contingencies, personalities and the ebb-and-flow of conflicts and negotiations between interdependent actors in the overlapping networks that constitute the core executive' (Rhodes and Tiernan, 2016, p. 340). As described above, scrutiny in the House of Commons works in a similar way, in which select committee members and chairs negotiate between each other both within and beyond individual committees, which in turn are affected by their personalities, philosophical outlooks, interpretations of scrutiny, and more.

The idea of a web of scrutiny arguably challenges conventional understandings of accountability in parliaments. Indeed, there are few theoretical frameworks through which accountability can be analysed, having been under-theorised (surprisingly) in parliamentary studies (Friedberg, 2011, pp. 525–6). In a US context, one influential theory is put forward by Mathew McCubbins and Thomas Schwartz (1984), who distinguish between 'police-patrol' and 'fire-alarm' models of oversight. The former of these is a centralised form of scrutiny, in which policy areas are 'patrolled' on a regular basis; the latter is a decentralised form of scrutiny, in which Congress intervenes in response to the sound of an 'alarm'. Their model has been identified and widely adopted (Balla and Deering, 2013), including in the UK (Flinders, 2008; Matthews and Flinders, 2015). It is certainly the case that, through systematic core tasks from the Liaison Committee and the existence of committees for every department, the idealised relationship of accountability is one that characterises 'police patrols'. However, findings for this book suggest that practices of committee members, chairs and officials do not chime with this idea of police patrols or fire alarms. Instead, a third approach focuses on the webs of scrutiny, as described here. This is the underlying conclusion from this chapter: we cannot understand scrutiny without examining the beliefs, practices and traditions of parliamentary actors involved in enacting scrutiny in the first place. So, accountability is more than an institutional arrangement to hold others to account, but a *practice* of doing parliamentary politics.

Concluding remarks

Scrutiny in the House of Commons, and especially along the committee corridor, is sustained by the everyday practices of MPs and officials. It relies on them to enact and entrench scrutiny. It is through those practices that committees build wider webs of scrutiny, which are pushed and pulled in lots of different directions by the priorities and beliefs that MPs hold, especially those of the chair. This chapter has sought to show this by clarifying why relationships matter. At this micro-level, it is clear that scrutiny of government is not affected only through formal, institutional relationships between the House of Commons and ministerial departments, but interpretations of scrutiny, philosophical outlooks, personalities of MPs and daily enactments of scrutiny. At a broader level, these practices give sustenance to norms and values that form within a committee. These, in turn, shape committee approaches but also, in a circular fashion, may help to institutionalise and socialise MPs into committee work.

Taking the analysis from this chapter one step further, it indicates that, although we may think of scrutiny as 'systematic' given that the select committee system has become a permanent and formal part of UK parliamentary politics, scrutiny processes in the House of Commons depend on 'webs' of scrutiny. The broad thrust of this chapter has not been an empirical analysis to evaluate the effectiveness of relationships, performances or committee cohesion, but to illustrate the importance of the everyday in the Palace of Westminster. In thinking about scrutiny as a web rather than as systematic, it focuses attention on the contingencies and ebb-and-flow of everyday scrutiny behaviour, as well as the personalities and relationships that make up committees. Scrutiny cannot be systematic if MPs choose to adopt the role of learner, push accountability to the margins as a lone wolf, or mask it by addressing grievances of their constituents. This does not mean scrutiny doesn't occur; rather, it highlights the effect of beliefs, practices and traditions. Scrutiny can still be very effective – the constituency champion may have uncovered a national problem; the lone wolf may push the minister, which others have failed to do; and the learner may become a subject expert. However, effectiveness is not guaranteed; it is contingent upon the webs of scrutiny that MPs and officials weave. This argument is central to understanding committees in the House of Commons.

8

Dramas at Westminster

Yelling across the floor of the House of Commons to ask a question of the prime minister over the shouts of boos is far from effective in holding government to account, yet it remains one of the most prevailing assumptions among the public (and some corners of academic research) that this is supposedly when Parliament is scrutinising the executive.[1] Meanwhile, daily enactments of scrutiny by select committee members are underappreciated and even neglected (although this is changing). In this book, I have sought to open up everyday life along the committee corridor of the Palace of Westminster and the scenes of scrutiny taking place in Portcullis House. I have explored individual beliefs, identified perform-ance styles and examined commonplace dilemmas of committee members, chairs and officials. In doing so, I have argued that 'scrutiny' is interpreted in many different ways by parliamentary actors, which affects the nature of the account-ability relationship between Parliament and government in many small, multifa-ceted and possibly unforeseen ways. In this conclusion, I want to revisit some of the central ideas of this book and establish some wider, cross-cutting themes that have emerged, including the impact of the Wright reforms, the diverse functions of committees, the wider scrutiny practices around Parliament and government, and the pressures on scrutiny today. I want to close this chapter, and this book, by reflecting more generally on the extent to which this study informs us of the wider place of politicians and Parliament in British politics.

Interpreting parliamentary scrutiny

At an abstract level, we would be forgiven to think that institutions or sites work as they are designed. In the select committee context, this would mean that MPs attend evidence sessions regularly and fully prepared; that MPs ask robust questions and follow-up evasive responses from witnesses; and that reports offer a balanced assessment of widely collected evidence. In textbooks, this is how committees are described; as small groups to investigate matters and hold gov-ernment to account.

This book has challenged assumptions that are made in good faith about the way that select committees work by beginning a study of the House of Commons from a different vantage point. In Chapter 2 of this book, I reflected on the established literature and perspectives of Parliament, and outlined a set of theoretical principles to studying parliaments from an interpretive perspective. This has been an important exercise for two reasons. First, studies of the UK House of Commons, specifically, and legislatures, generally, have not often engaged substantively with these sorts of debates. Traditionally, studies of Parliament adopt old or new institutionalist lenses without critical reflection as to whether this best reflects how we can make sense of institutional behaviour. So, this book provokes a wider question and debate about how we approach the study of representative institutions. Second, this book adopts an interpretive approach (developed prominently in UK executive politics by Mark Bevir and R. A. W. Rhodes) and applied it to a new arena using insights from a wider field of research (particularly dramaturgical approaches). This book sits alongside other research that has sought to supplement, even challenge, the old institutionalist studies of the past, such as the anthropological work of Emma Crewe (2005, 2015), the performative lens of Shirin M. Rai and colleagues (Rai and Johnson, 2014; Rai and Spary, 2019), or the constructivist approach from Cristina Leston-Bandeira (2012, 2016). These scholars have made significant inroads into a field that still has much untapped potential.

More generally, this book's emphasis on the power of ideas and interpretation stands on the shoulders of a growing interpretive field that is rich in its diversity regarding a vast array of topics from executive governance to street-level bureaucracy. I have used the opportunity of this research project to widen this field further by empirically exploring the meaning of 'scrutiny', and it is here that the main empirical contribution lies. MPs of all colours and attitudes have interpreted select committee work in such diverse and interesting ways that my original research topic and questions – on the House of Commons' scrutiny of public or arm's-length bodies – fundamentally changed (I explore this a little further in the Annex). Instead, I lingered on the question of how political actors interpret and perform their role on select committees. For this study, I identified six performance styles in Chapter 3 that MPs might adopt: specialists, lone wolves, constituency champions, party helpers, learners and absentees. These are not fixed roles or types that MPs take on throughout their career, but flexible styles that they adopt depending on the type of committee hearing or inquiry in which they are participating, or the broader political agenda of the day. This list is far from exhaustive. The performance styles outlined here are illustrative rather than definitive. I focused on these because they were the most prominent in my observations and, based on interviews and transcriptions of committee hearings, seem to be the most commonly adopted roles. The attempt here is, once again, to provoke a debate about how we can understand scrutiny behaviour. This book provides suggestions and ideas; it is not comprehensive or definitive.

In the fourth chapter, the focus shifted to how a select number of MPs interpret their leadership role as chairs of committees (in addition to their approaches to scrutiny generally). MPs and officials' reflections indicate that being a chair is a 'House role', which has arguably been strengthened since the Wright reforms of 2010 took place (more on these reforms below). I argue that chairs adopt leadership positions along a spectrum: at one end are committee catalysts, who are committee-orientated and usually seek to make policy contributions; at the other end, we find committee chieftains, who are leadership-orientated and usually seek to influence wider public debates. These two extremes are crude caricatures, designed to highlight characteristics that chairs may adopt. The extremes are more easily identifiable and therefore more often referenced, although the majority of chairs arguably adopt different characteristics of both, and change emphasis depending on the type of evidence session and witness in front of them. Given the continued prevalence of Parliament in the media in recent years – especially since the general election of 2017 returned a minority government to the House of Commons – it will be interesting to see how the role of chair continues to develop. We have already seen the dominant positions of Margaret Hodge and Keith Vaz in the 2010 parliament; meanwhile, since 2017, a number of previous frontbench and high-profile politicians won elections to become chairs of committees, including Yvette Cooper for the Home Affairs Committee and Nicky Morgan for the Treasury Committee, not to mention the high-profile interventions of Hilary Benn and the Exiting the EU Committee in the Brexit process. This chapter is a marker of the importance to study parliamentary leadership, and therefore opens many further questions that the book has not explored. Although there are exceptions (Kelso, 2016), the study of parliamentary leadership is one of many examples of the untapped potential of studying MPs' behaviour in the House of Commons – and deserves to be studied much further.

MPs are the stars of the show. Yet they rely on what I call the 'hidden servants' of accountability: parliamentary officials and supporting staff. I draw attention to this under-researched group in Chapter 5. Here, the chapter focuses on clerks' ability to remain hidden from view, while they nonetheless offer unparalleled service to MPs and bear a commitment to passionate impartiality. These three facets weave together to form a wider tradition of 'clerkliness'. It informs clerks' ability to navigate a perennial dilemma that most officials face in their day-to-day lives, in which MPs' practices and behaviour rub up and against parliamentary conventions, protocols and procedures. This overarching issue deserves much more attention from research, and is something which is especially timely given recent debates about the role of the clerk of the House of Commons (Geddes and Meakin, 2018) and wider reforms taking place in how the House authorities are structured (Cox, 2018; House of Commons Commission, 2018), both of which were briefly discussed in Chapter 5. Other recent events have also drawn attention to clerks. For example, in January 2019, the Speaker of the House allegedly overruled advice from clerks (Swinford, 2019). Meanwhile, another clerk was accused of 'plotting' with backbench MPs to upend government control of House business (Shipman, 2019b). Both cases came to light as a result of Brexit, showing us once again what the many diverse challenges the referendum decision to leave the European Union has brought to the UK's political institutions.

Combined, these three chapters on committee members, chairs and officials suggest that scrutiny is contested and actors inevitably push and pull accountability in different directions. Notably, this tells us that we cannot only look to the output of select committee reports to understand the effectiveness of committees to hold the executive to account or to improve and enhance government policy. Committee reports are the culmination of a range of preceding processes, including agenda-setting, evidence-gathering and report-writing. This was explored in the final two empirical chapters. In Chapter 6, I focused particularly on the evidence-gathering practices of the House of Commons committees. It reveals to us the diverse issues that committees must confront in gathering evidence for their investigations, whether it is the diversity of their witnesses (Geddes, 2018a), the ability to persuade reticent witnesses to appear, or how the framing of terms of reference affects inquiry processes. Most importantly, it emphasises the way in which knowledge claims are mediated through politics and the specific meaning of 'evidence' in a committee setting. Although this has been a major theme of research on the relationship between evidence and policymaking (e.g., Cairney, 2015), it has not been addressed in significant detail when it comes to parliamentary settings (exceptions include Crewe, 2017c; Goodwin, 2015; Kenny *et al.*, 2017). This chapter therefore opens a multitude of questions about the role of different knowledge claims in select committees, specifically, and the UK Parliament, more generally.

The final chapter, Chapter 7, turned to how MPs interact with one another to build scrutiny. It looked at the relationships within and beyond committees, which are fundamental to understanding wider scrutiny practices, with a particular focus on how MPs develop cross-party, consensual working relationships in order to ensure committee cohesion. This is crucial because much of the policy impact of select committees hinges on their ability to demonstrate feasible, cross-party recommendations that the government cannot easily ignore. The chapter also begins to draw out some of the wider consequences of individual beliefs and everyday practices on the scrutiny landscape within the House of Commons. For example, this book highlights that committees play a much bigger role in scrutinising the executive than we ordinarily assume – as the above two factors have already demonstrated. It raises a wider concern or question about how we approach the study of 'accountability', 'scrutiny', 'parliamentary control' or 'over-sight'. The concept of accountability has been widely adopted and studied in relation to public administration and policy, and refers to a plethora of processes, ideas, concepts and values. This diversity has often made it difficult to study because, first, the academic literature on the topic is disconnected and, second, most scholars produce specific definitions for their particular purposes (Lewis, O'Flynn, and Sullivan, 2014). Mark Bovens (2010) groups these into two: as virtue (i.e., as a normative concept to evaluate the behaviour of public actors) and as mechanism (i.e., as an institutional arrangement to hold others to account). This book sits squarely within the second of these. Furthermore, it challenges the idea raised by others that we can understand scrutiny through 'police-patrol' and 'fire-alarm' models (McCubbins and Schwartz, 1984). Instead, the chapter has shown that scrutiny is enacted as part of contingent webs of beliefs among a range of parliamentary actors with different priorities, values or approaches.

In sum, this book therefore argues that we can understand scrutiny in the House of Commons only by examining the beliefs of MPs and officials, how they enact those beliefs through everyday practices and performances, and what affects their priorities in the wider web of beliefs or traditions of parliamentary politics. In thinking about accountability in this way, the book has also brought to the surface some wider themes in approaching scrutiny in Parliament. I want to highlight some of these before placing the book's conclusions in a wider context.

Themes in studying select committees

I want to highlight three themes that cut across this book: the Wright reforms; the functions of committees; and the pressures of scrutiny.

Wright reforms

This book did not focus exclusively on the impact of the Wright reforms on select committees in 2009–10 (House of Commons Reform Committee, 2009). However, the timeframe and focus of this study made it impossible not to con-sider their impact – especially given that there are not many detailed studies of the reforms or their consequences (but see Bates et al., 2017; O'Brien, 2012; Russell, 2011). Although it is easy to exaggerate the influence of the Wright reforms, they have arguably affected committees in at least three ways. First, election of chairs by the whole House and election of committee members through party groups meant that parliamentary actors view committees with 'renewed authority and zest' (Flynn, 2012, p. 74). Chairs themselves have therefore changed how they approach scrutiny, which has arguably made them more dominant in scrutiny processes. This interpretation of a changing role of committees may not dem-onstrate tangible or concrete increases in policy influence, but it does indicate that committees are regarded as more important by elected representatives. In other words, the beliefs around committees have changed, which in and of themselves are important for changing the behaviour of MPs. Although no interviews were conducted with ministers or civil servants, this may also have the effect of ensuring that frontbench colleagues pay closer attention to committee investigations and their findings. This has been demonstrated by others with data from before the Wright reforms (Hawes, 1992; Russell and Gover, 2017). Moreover, there is some research suggesting that the media are also paying more attention to select committees. The extent to which this is true requires more detailed analysis, but initial conclusions from some researchers (Dunleavy and Muir, 2013), and anecdotally over fieldwork and other data, would suggest an impact. Further research would be needed to explore how the changing standing of committees has affected policy-making.

Second, and related to the above, the changing perception surrounding committees has placed greater demands on them as mechanisms to hold the executive to account. This has worked in various ways. Most obviously, it has changed some committees' approaches to inquiries. Some investigations are only tangentially related to government policy, for instance, which makes it difficult for committees to have a real policy impact. A specific example of this would be committee hearings with Sir Philip Green in 2016 into the collapse of BHS (House of Commons Work and Pensions Committee and House of Commons Business, Innovation and Skills Committee, 2016). Although these evidence sessions received widespread media coverage, there was little obvious connection between select committee scrutiny and government policy. It suggests that committees are broadening their accountability role to include wider issues of public concern or 'extra-governmental conduct' (Mellows-Facer and Shaw, 2017), raising wider questions about committees' role (see below). Another example of this may be the Digital, Culture, Media and Sport Committee's (2019) inquiry into fake news.

Given the broadening of the role and the increased exposure of committee work, some MPs – chairs in particular – are putting more of their time and energy into this part of their role. This consequently raises the issue as to whether committees are adequately resourced (House of Commons Liaison Committee, 2012a) or if existing resources are efficiently deployed. Findings from this project indicate that a blanket increase in resources is not a panacea because of the many other dilemmas that members, chairs and officials face. However, much more consideration must be made to ensure training and skill development for MPs, especially with regard to their questioning skills of witnesses in committee hearings (although most MPs remain resistant and even ignorant to making use of training opportunities that committees already provide).

A third and final factor that has come to the fore as a result of the Wright reforms is the nature of relationships within, between and beyond committees.

Among MPs, this has two elements. On the one hand, there is a growing sense in which committees see themselves as part of a *'cohesive whole'* (Interview with MP 7) and therefore develop stronger bonds of trust and respect. This was explored in Chapter 7, and feeds into a wider point about committee cohesion and institutionalisation. On the other hand, the relationship of accountability has changed between chairs and members, where the former are now less likely to see themselves accountable to their committee than in the past. This has strengthened the leadership role of chairs (Chapter 4). A closely related factor to relationships between MPs is the relationships between MPs and witnesses, which seem to have evolved in recent years. Perhaps this stems from greater media attention, but interviewees have noted that evidence sessions have become more high-profile and combative than in the past (for a case study, see Felicity Matthews and Matthew Flinders' (2015) exploration of the scrutiny of public appointments). While some general issues regarding evidence practices were the focus of Chapter 6, such as persuading reticent witnesses to give evidence, there are many further unanswered questions about the conduct of witnesses and MPs, the appropriate powers of committees over witnesses, and the extent to which scenes of scrutiny affect accountability in Parliament more generally (and echoes issues about MPs' questioning techniques and skills).

In sum, the Wright reforms have been most important – for the purposes of this study – in changing relationships between: MPs and chairs, committees and main chamber, MPs and witnesses, and committees and the media. There are still many issues over the effect of the Wright reforms that deserve attention, of course, including the medium- and long-term impact of the reforms on gender (Goodwin *et al.*, 2019; O'Brien, 2012), MPs' engagement with committees and committee work (Bates *et al.*, 2017), and their policy impact (Benton and Russell, 2013). Finally, the Wright reforms are also unfinished. Not only do questions about a House Business Committee remain, but there is the specific issue of how chairships are allocated to parties, to which there are no easy answers.

Function of committees

The previous section has already implied that the roles and functions of committees are evolving. One of the cross-cutting findings from this book is not only that perceptions around scrutiny are important, but that committees have roles that go beyond their accountability role. They serve multiple functions both within the House of Commons and beyond. Within the House, committees are a way to give members and chairs a structure to their everyday parliamentary lives and can act as a training ground for newly elected MPs (perhaps even older ones, or those that are returning from the frontbenches). Not only do they offer ways for MPs to learn about policy area, but they are also spaces in which MPs practise scrutiny activities and engage in debates with one another. For some

MPs, committee hearings are a way to rehearse questions or test lines of inquiry that they would be able to pursue in other spaces, including debates on the floor of the House or in Westminster Hall. All of this also suggests that committees are key sites for socialisation (Rush and Giddings, 2011) and institutionalisation (Norton, 1998). In this sense, it is clear that the reforms of the 1960s and 1970s have fulfilled their aims.

In relation to the above, select committees also function as an information-gathering tool. As Christina Boswell (2018, pp. 98–120) has shown in her research on the Home Affairs Committee, committee scrutiny often involves asking for more information in order to inform the House and wider public debate. So, committees gather evidence for inquiries but, importantly, also for the House to use. Committees hold evidence sessions to put information in the public domain as well as to scrutinise the executive, even if that evidence doesn't lead to a final report. Indeed, traditional interpretations of accountability often emphasises the *explanatory* way in which it works by providing answers or information, not necessarily forcing government to take action. Thinking about scrutiny in this way, it broadens the horizon of a committee as not only a method of holding government to account but as an information-gathering tool for Parliament. It does so in a very different way to briefings or research notes by the House of Commons Library or the Parliamentary Office for Science and Technology, but it performs this role nonetheless. And as a result, as Russell and Gover (2017) have shown with respect to the legislative process, committees can be used for other parliamentary work. It means, once again, that the evidence base for committees should be a hugely important consideration. There is an understandable tension here between 'policy learning' and 'scrutiny'. Some MPs may adopt the role of learner when they should be holding a minister to account, or conversely attack an academic as a lone wolf when they should be adopting a style of learning to extract information. This means that committees must be very clear to develop their overall strategies to ensure effective scrutiny.

Beyond the House of Commons, as noted previously, committees have gained more media attention and coverage. This is likely to increase if chairs continue to adopt a House-role and speak on behalf of policy areas more openly. However, I also want to emphasise that this attention has an impact on public understanding of, and engagement with, committees. In Chapter 6, and through other research (Geddes, 2018a), I have indicated the important role that committees have in linking Parliament to the public. The relationship between Parliament and the public has been studied by a range of other authors in expert ways (House of Commons Liaison Committee, 2015; Leston-Bandeira, 2013), and so I want to only briefly touch on this theme by emphasising the opportunities that arise as a result of public involvement with select committee inquiries. The standing of parliaments among the public has declined considerably in recent years. The House of Commons, as one of the foundational institutions of representative democracy, must try to re-engage people with politics. One way to do this is to encourage further engagement between the public and MPs through select committees, whether it means taking evidence from a more socially diverse group of people, making greater use of field trips and visits, or taking part in experiments such as deliberative democracy. This role for committees and the link to the public has often been overlooked because it is not a core select committee function – i.e., to hold government to account. However, as one senior official remarked to me, select committees 'provide public access to the political process' (Interview with Official 13). So, given the broadening role and profile of committees, this is one (even if small) way to address public disaffection in politics.

Scrutiny under pressure

An issue that has been noted both explicitly and implicitly throughout empirical chapters of this book is the issue of time pressure and multiple loyalties. This has been noticeable throughout interviews and observation. During fieldwork, it was evidenced that MPs worked hard and faced a range of tasks to ensure that they fulfilled their role as elected representatives. This book has not comprehensively assessed the range of roles that constitute being an MP, but focused on a small aspect of their role. This alone suggested multiple demands on committee members and chairs, with at least three effects. First, scrutiny under pressure empowers the chair because, although committee members may attend meetings regularly and prepare for them where possible, the chair is prepared for every session and immersed in their policy area, while members focus more specifically on only a smaller proportion of select committee work. Furthermore, chairs are more likely to remain in their position over the duration of a parliament (or longer), while the average length of service for committee members is around two and a half years. This reinforces the chair's ability to set the agenda and, consequently, enhances their power vis-à-vis committee members.

Second, multiple loyalties create a short-termist and occasionally last-minute framework in which scrutiny occurs. MPs are placed in a reactive position that gives staff little time to write scoping notes or organise committee activities. As Chapter 6 and other research (Geddes, 2018a) has sought to show, this affects evidence and the spectrum of witnesses that give evidence to committees. It additionally raises questions about the quality of inquiries more generally (which goes beyond the scope of this book). In particular, certain committees must consider the extent to which their reactive, short-termist approach enhances or hinders effective scrutiny. Findings from this research project indicate that the positive effects of paying attention to the media cycle may be outweighed by other factors, including their ability to adequately explore issues, ensure social diversity in evidence-gathering, and the depth of analysis of evidence (which is often politically coloured).

Third, multiple loyalties and time pressures weaken the ability for MPs to build effective relationships with one another. Chapter 7's focus on relationships emphasised the importance of these networks, particularly to ensure cross-party support for inquiries and building consensus. As members face competing demands on their time, their ability to devote time to getting to know each other and ensure cross-party working is under pressure (especially because contentious inquiries would require significant time for members to resolve their differences). This possibly raises the question as to whether committees are conducting too many inquiries and over-stretching their capabilities (which arises often in response to media coverage of issues that committees, including mine, wanted to tap into). In addition to the effect on MPs, parliamentary officials are also under pressure to navigate these complex loyalties.

What does all of this tell us? It suggests that select committees have changed considerably since 2010 in lots of (unintended) ways. It also suggests that committees have a wide-ranging effect on the scrutiny landscape and play a range of roles. And finally, this book has revealed some pressures that exist on scrutiny. These are symptomatic of wider challenges that MPs face in enacting their role, and on Parliament's place in British politics. I want to turn to this closing theme now.

Parliament's place in British politics today

Not only is scrutiny under pressure, as the last subsection highlighted, but so are MPs in general. For example, it has long been acknowledged that MPs' constituency service has increased dramatically over the preceding decades (Gay, 2005; Korris, 2011). Although MPs have privileged this part of their role, they are carrying it out in the wider context of a decline in trust in MPs, with only 19% of the public believing that politicians would tell the truth (Ipsos MORI, 2018). As established in the introductory chapter, the context in which MPs undertake their role is increasingly challenging, in which people are generally voting less and voting in less predictable ways. At the same time, the political environment has become more polarised and MPs have become subject to increased abuse (James et al., 2016). This wider political and cultural context has direct effects on MPs' mental health and wellbeing (Flinders et al., 2018) and, as the above has shown, affects the capacity for MPs to fulfil their core functions effectively. This raises very important, and arguably urgent, questions about the role of MPs and politicians. For example, is it right that MPs privilege constituency casework over and above their legislative and scrutiny roles in Parliament? This is a debate about what we want our national politicians to do in Parliament. This book has shown the effects of the multiple pressures on MPs: in terms of time, it challenges their commitments to scrutiny and their ability to learn how to effectively question witnesses; in terms of their loyalties, it explains why 'party helpers' and 'constituency champions' are performance styles used in scrutiny settings.

Given the importance of everyday practices in Parliament, this book raises further interesting questions about the future of Parliament in the context of changing public debates. Parliament faces many challenges and I highlight only three here. First, and most obviously, UK politics is engulfed in a wide-ranging debate about its future in Europe after the referendum on membership of the EU. This, in conjunction with the 2017 general election result, has sparked many constitutional questions and debates. These challenges have put many parliamentary procedures and processes under the spotlight, including its ability to scrutinise the executive (and many examples of this were highlighted in the introductory chapter). This book has demonstrated the importance of building webs of scrutiny to strengthen Parliament's role *vis-à-vis* government, and these lessons need to be heeded in order for the House of Commons to effectively hold government to account on this issue. Second, Parliament faces a challenge over its own physical infrastructure. Restoration and renewal over the Palace of Westminster will span many years and requires vast sums of money. This book has highlighted the importance of space, which directly affects the performance of politics. As Westminster is the main stage for British politics, this project will affect everyday practices of parliamentarians in many and unpredictable ways that deserve closer attention. And third, Parliament faces a challenge over the decline of trust in politics by the public. There are no easy answers here. This book has sought to open up the everyday world of parliamentarians, albeit in a small way, in order to foster further public understanding of how MPs conduct their work. It is hoped that with greater public understanding of politics, we can, in part, combat public disaffection with politicians and be in a position to sympathise with the challenges that MPs face. However, that is not all. This book has highlighted small ways that may enable Parliament to stem the tide of growing distrust, including greater use of committee visits (to allow a wider range of people being involved in parliamentary processes) and ensuring more diverse evidence (to show that Parliament is listening to all corners of the United Kingdom).

This book does not aim to be a conclusive, comprehensive or definitive study of Parliament, or even select committees. Rather, the aim of this book has been to open a debate and to provoke: about how we study parliaments; about how we understand the relationship between Parliament and government; and about the place of Parliament in UK politics. In this sense, the book makes a *theoretical* contribution by arguing for the importance of beliefs, values, desires, practices, traditions and dilemmas in studying political phenomena; a number of *empirical* contributions on select committee scrutiny that have been summarised in this chapter and explored in depth in previous ones; and a number of *normative* contributions about supporting the place of Parliament in UK politics and the role that politicians play within that. There are a range of further questions that

I do not answer in this book – they are dotted around the margins of papers and previous drafts of this book, as well as in fieldwork notes and on others' published work. These questions are about deepening our understanding of scrutiny practices further; the influence of interpretation on government policy; the nascent development of parliamentary leadership (by chairs and others alike); the extent of performance styles in other parliamentary settings; the role of evidence in representative institutions, and more. In other words, this book and research project asks many more questions rather than conclusively offering answers to problems. This was always the aim: I did not write this book in order to end my study of parliaments, but to begin it.

Note

1 That is not to say that Prime Minister's Questions does not have other functions (Bevan and John, 2016; Lovenduski, 2014).

Annex

Methodological reflections

When I began my research on Parliament, it was highly unusual to use observation as a method to study it. However, over the years of completing this research project and writing up the findings for this book, things have changed in this research area – with a great deal of research on many more aspects of the UK Parliament, as well as greater openness to study the institution in different ways. Nonetheless, studying legislatures using insights from ethnography remains unusual across political science. So, I want to reflect on my methodology for the benefit of those that might be unfamiliar to this type of research. In order to do this, I sketch out some themes and issues that qualitative researchers face, including the position of the researcher and the research environment; the difficulties around gaining entry and access to the site under study; the issues around truth and bias in research interviews; and how principles of research methods rub up against actually *doing* it. In covering these themes, I draw on insights from challenges I faced personally. However, in doing so, I hope to clarify the benefits of studying parliaments using ethnographic insights and to suggest that this can be done by others.

Adopting a different vantage point

As noted in Chapter 2, observation allows the researcher access to everyday practices in ways that other methods can often miss, such as interviews or documents. This is a fundamental advantage to the approach, in which the researcher is able to immerse herself or himself into the relationships, structures, cultures, traditions and practices of the institutions being studied. In this way, I was able to see parliamentary politics play out from a different vantage point. It allows you to see things happening in real time and how people react to events and to each other. What interviewees might have missed out or thought to be routine and self-evident can be observed and stressed, such as unknown or informal power dynamics.

Adopting this method often requires a commitment to inductive, as opposed to deductive, research. In other words, it is far less fruitful to use observation merely to test theories, hypotheses or concepts, nor is it always easy to stick to research designs. Instead, research is guided by what participants tell you, what you can see from their interactions, or how the surroundings might (or might not) shape behaviour. This requires scholars to follow their intellectual curiosities. For traditional political scientists, this might ring alarm bells: the data will be partial and subjective. This view, however, implies that there is an 'objective' reality out there, waiting for us to study it in a detached manner. However, as I have laid out in Chapter 2 by adopting an anti-foundationalist viewpoint, this is impossible.

Researchers make decisions about their research all the time, especially with regards to what is perceived as important to study, what interests them in their research, and what is more likely to gain funding in an increasingly competitive and marketised system of higher education. Being open about this does not diminish our research, but strengthens it. Emma Crewe (2017a) explains how her interest and previous research on feminist projects sharpened her focus on issues relating to gender in Parliament, for example. In my own case, I was always interested in how MPs think, and what they believe they are contributing to democratic politics. It took shape in this specific project on scrutiny and so I pushed this further in interviews where I could, and ended with this book. Being aware of the fact that our interactions with research unavoidably shape it in some way ensures that we are more reflexive about it.

This demonstrates that researchers play a key role in all types of research, which is arguably accentuated in inductive fieldwork. It raises the question about the position of the researcher – not only in terms of their priorities for research, but actually carrying it out. Mike Crang and Ian Cook (2007, p. 9), both experienced ethnographers, believe that 'research is an embodied activity that draws in our whole physical person, along with all its inescapable identities'. Ethnographic research involves relationships developed between people of similar and/or different cultures, classes, genders, sexualities, (dis)abilities, generations, nationalities, skin colours, faiths and/or other identities. A key point is that research on everyday practices and social (political) relationships is made out of everyday practices and social relations, too. This can shape the researcher's environment as much as it shapes those with whom the researcher engages. Participants can behave in terms of what they believe is expected of them; some might try to limit normatively 'deviant' behaviour; others stress practices that they deem to be normatively 'good', while still others might react to the researcher's dress or accent. There were countless examples of this during fieldwork. For instance, the chair of my committee pointed at me one time and said that I could get the tea because I was 'the intern' (FWD 2.1.22). This was particularly instructive about power dynamics at play in Westminster. To give a more general example, it was interesting to see the location that interviewees chose. Some clearly intended to impress by bringing me into MP-only areas or Pugin-decorated tea rooms; others chose their offices; many preferred the atrium of Portcullis House. Being aware of this is important because they are clues to help us understand the nature of relationships, beliefs and values. They pervade all social interaction, which flows naturally out of Erving Goffman's (1990) ideas that social behaviour is 'performed' in all social life. As such, not only do MPs perform their roles as representatives and clerks as the guardians of procedure, but I myself performed the role of researcher. Once again, traditional political scientists might believe that this is 'contamination' of data, when it was actually important and even useful to see how MPs and officials reacted to me.

Entry and access

Going into the field has been cited by academics as one of the most difficult aspects of engaging in ethnographic research (Hunter, 1995; Moeran, 2009). This is especially true of political elites, which are, by their very definition, exclusive social groups with high entry barriers. Traditional ethnographic research has normally been conducted where the power dynamics are very different: with the researcher often (but not always) studying a less powerful group. Studying elites, who hold significant power, can be different. Political elites keep their cards close to their chests, for this is imperative to their political survival within a highly adversarial political culture such as the UK where different factions and groupings out-compete one another. This means that trust is a central concern for the research and participants: for the researcher, she or he needs participants to tell the truth; for participants, they need to know that researchers will not twist or exploit what they say or do in private.

Trust ensures a difference between 'entry' and 'access', i.e., you can be in an organisation but the data you want to collect is still out of reach. Hugh Gusterson (1995), for example, in his study on scientists working on nuclear weapons, described personnel as 'polite' and 'friendly', but who were also 'profoundly unhelpful' (p. 191). He had gained *entry* to the field, but not *access* to the right information. Furthermore, and more generally, access cannot be taken for granted; it is constantly renegotiated depending on the trust you have built up and the changing dynamics of the political environment. The powerful can refuse interviews, deny access, delay publication and declare documents confidential – even retroactively. This is an ever-present danger and one that I did not face thanks to the support of the House of Commons Committee Office (and Scrutiny Unit in particular). Indeed, as with most anthropologies (Fetterman, 2010, pp. 36–7), I gained access through a personal contact (my research supervisor and the Scrutiny Unit), and snowballed beyond this to build high-trust relationships.

Truth and bias

Interviewees are under no obligation to tell us the truth or to be dispassionate and objective about their views. Actors will consciously or unconsciously exaggerate their own role, or their memories could fail them to recount events. This means that we must be cautious in interviews. However, that does not mean that they should be discarded. As Rhodes and colleagues (2007b, p. 221) point out:

> All of us during our everyday lives develop skills in interpreting what others mean when they speak to us. Thus, we judge whether someone is lying by many verbal and body cues. We do not leave such skills at the door of the interview room. Every interview involves such judgements.

This point suggests that interviews are a two-way process and interaction, which reminds us also that it is not possible to access the beliefs of political actors in some neutral way. Interviews require good rapport, without which questions can fall flat, answers will be generic and uninformative, and discussion more generally will be brief. As Jody Miller and Barry Glassner (2004, pp. 141–2) point out:

> Meaning is not merely elicited by apt questioning, nor simply transported through respondent replies; it is actively and communicatively assembled in the interview encounter. Respondents are not so much repositories of knowledge – treasuries of information awaiting excavation – as they are constructors of knowledge in association with interviews. Interviews are collaborative accomplishments, involving participants in meaning-making work in the process.

They describe interviews as an 'interpersonal drama with a developing plot' (p. 149), which directly speaks to Goffman's idea, developed in Chapter 2, that social interactions are a performance. Interviews are not an exchange of words or information alone, but also involve physical gestures, silences, use and tone of voice, and laughter. These are all things that the interviewer needs to consider. Indeed, we are part of this drama in that we choose to wear certain types of clothes, try to appear disarming, always arrive on time to give a perception of reliability and punctuality, ask questions in a particular way to elicit the responses we want, and so on (Morris, 2009).

All of this depends on the types of interviews that researchers pursue. My own were semi-structured. They are balancing acts. They can be more like conversations at times, with a certain give-and-take and unpredictability. That is both an advantage and a danger of interviews. I did not start this project with much experience in interviews, and so I had to learn my lessons a hard way. Some proved more useful than others because we established the right rapport and the interviewee was interested in reflecting on her or his role; others were brisk, with interviewees distracted or too busy to engage with me.

From principles to practice

Turning to the process of undertaking fieldwork itself, this was arguably the single biggest challenge of this research project – yet also its biggest reward. It was exhausting because it was much more than simply studying select committees away from a desk. I had moved to a new city, began a new job, did not have a familiar network of friends around me, moved into a house with people I did not know, and had much of my family living in different cities and countries. At the same time, I was trying to study towards my first research project through observation, interviews and analysis of texts, while keeping up with trends in the academic literature (including attending conferences). These social effects were significant, and need to be acknowledged because they did make an impact. I made mistakes, I was slow to grasp some of the demands of the research placement and, indeed, felt foolish on occasions. For example, I was unable to complete tasks on time for my clerk because I was trying to observe my surroundings as well as undertake given responsibilities, which must have frustrated the committee team (FWD 12.3.17); another time, there was an awkward situation in which the chair of my committee asked my advice on an inquiry, yet I was completely unable to offer any thoughts because all my notes were about the committee itself and not about the inquiry (FWD 2.1.25). My chair did not ask my opinion on a committee matter again. Self-doubt over my research was noted throughout my fieldwork diary (e.g., FWD 38.9.36, FWD 38.9.40, FWD 39.9.24, FWD 42.10.23, FWD 51.12.27, FWD 52.12.1, FWD 53.12.16). Nonetheless, I fitted in very quickly (after only a few days, a member of staff introduced me as having worked for the committee for a couple of weeks; FWD 6.2.10). I was lucky in that I started working for my committee six days before another member of staff joined. This meant that there was someone else there who was also naturally inquisitive about the way that the select committee worked and asked a lot of questions (FWD 6.2.22).

I took notes in a variety of ways, which, over time, became my fieldwork diary. This was a personal and confidential journal, and not accessible to anyone other than myself (and shall remain so indefinitely). There are four comments that I would like to make about this, regarding process, content, style and status. First, the process. I wrote rough notes using pen and paper at the time of the events or closely afterwards, and then wrote these into a journal at weekends. Within two months of the placement, notes were typed up to make it easier to read and search for ideas. Second, the content. The FWD contains observations from a range of things that happened in Parliament (and also references to things outside). It contains discussions with staff and MPs, summaries of meetings, and summaries of my interviews. It summarised what I did each day and observations of what others did (in terms of performance styles, space and speech). The vast majority of the content is ordinary behaviour that would be banal – even indecipherable – to anyone except myself. Third, the style. The diary is written as an entirely confessional account, in the first person, in which I observe and reflect personally on the research process and my general everyday life. Any persons mentioned have been made anonymous through a code. Every paragraph was numbered for citation purposes. Fourth, the status. As the book's empirical chapters show, I draw on the journal throughout my time in Westminster. Where possible, I have sought approval from the Committee Office to make direct references to the FWD, but approval was not sought if the issue had been corroborated by interviewees and/or written records, refers to information already in the public domain, relates to details that are judged sufficiently minor, or has been published previously/elsewhere.

Ultimately, the fieldwork was the most fascinating part of doing this research. My research placement has been immensely valuable with far-reaching effects for this academic project on select committees. Working for the Committee Office confirmed the principle that simply 'being there' (Rhodes *et al.*, 2007a) is crucial to understanding a subject matter, place or community. I was immersed in the everyday life of people that inhabited an imposing, grand palace. I could have completed this project without ever setting foot in the Palace of Westminster. Would I really have understood their lives if I had not been there for a sustained period of time? On a daily basis, I was squeezed on the Victoria Line with a thousand other commuters at 7am; I ate lunch in the Palace next to (occasionally with) clerks of the House; caught up with friends in the Sports and Social Bar; rubbed shoulders with frontbench and backbench MPs as I rushed from meeting to meeting; and attended a range of events in the evenings where I had the opportunity to listen to (and meet) prominent parliamentarians – often by chance. Indeed, these chance meetings gave them the opportunity to share their points of view, experiences and expertise – some of whom I would not have met in any other way. Working for the Committee Office offered a wealth of other practical opportunities: I was close to the parliamentary estate, which meant that I could listen and observe evidence sessions and proceedings as I needed; I was given a parliamentary email address that hugely increased my chances of positive replies when requesting interviews with MPs and clerks; and, with my pass, I could be flexible for MPs' diaries and meet them in most places and at most times convenient to them. All of these things helped me to break down conventional access barriers that many academics face. These barriers could otherwise have prevented me from undertaking this project.

Aside from these practical opportunities, I was able to gain remarkable insights into the way that politics worked at the heart of British political life. I learnt how select committees operate, MPs' interpretations of their role, and committees' unwritten rules or 'norms' of behaviour. All of this has made a positive impact on the way that I look at Parliament and embedded new points of view for my study that I would not have thought about otherwise. For that, I'm extremely grateful to the Economic and Social Research Council and the White Rose Doctoral Training Centre for making the funds available, and to the Committee Office in the House of Commons for making the time and resources available (especially the Scrutiny Unit and the committee for which I worked). Without this opportunity, this book would be poorer and my understanding of British political culture more basic.

Final thoughts

Undertaking research using ethnographic insights is time- and resource-intensive, tiring and unpredictable. But it is hugely rewarding. This research project took on a life of its own as a result of fieldwork. It was exciting to see ideas and theories of the British state being lived out along the corridors of the Palace of Westminster, and to see how MPs sought to challenge or abide by the rules. Without fieldwork, I would not have bumped into MPs planning a rebellion in the corner of a corridor; I would not have had the chance to participate in debates with parliamentary staff over the right course of action to enhance a committee's investigations; I would not have been able to see all the different work involved to write a briefing paper and how MPs chose to take up the suggested questions I wrote (or use the idea of the question and amend it in their own ways). It was telling that I did not want to leave at the end of my research placement. Of course, there were problems, shortcomings and challenges with this research. But, once I embarked on this journey, it was infectious. It was easily the most interesting part of the research project: simply being there.

References

Abélès, M. (2000). *Un ethnologue à l'Assemblée*. Paris: Odile Jacob.

Albrow, B. (2018). *Stale Carrots, Illusory Sticks and Feeble Whips? Institution Reform, Social Change and the House of Commons Whips' Office: 1994–2018*. Unpublished MA Thesis, University College London, London.

Allen, P. (2018). *The Political Class: Why It Matters Who Our Politicians Are*. Oxford: Oxford University Press.

Andeweg, R. (1997). Role specialisation or role switching? Dutch MPs between electorate and executive. *The Journal of Legislative Studies*, *3*(1), 110–27. doi:10.1080/13572339708420502.

Andeweg, R. (2014). Roles in legislatures. In S. Martin, T. Saalfeld, and K. Strøm (Eds), *The Oxford Handbook of Legislative Studies* (pp. 267–85). Oxford: Oxford University Press.

Armitage, F. (2012). From elite control to democratic competition: Procedural reform and cultural change in UK House of Commons Speakership elections. *British Politics*, *7*(2), 135–62. doi:10.1057/bp. 2012.4.

Armstrong, A. (2016, 17 May). Mike Ashley agrees to appear before MPs. *The Daily Telegraph*. Retrieved 26 June 2019 from www.telegraph.co.uk/business/2016/05/16/exclusive-mike-ashley-agrees-to-appear-before-mps/

Arter, D. (2003). Committee cohesion and the 'corporate dimension' of parliamentary committees: A comparative analysis. *The Journal of Legislative Studies*, *9*(4), 73–87. doi:10.1080/1357233042000306263.

Aylett, P. J. (2015). *Thirty Years of Reform: House of Commons Select Committees, 1960–1990*. Doctoral Thesis, Queen Mary, University of London, London.

Balla, S. J., and Deering, C. J. (2013). Police patrols and fire alarms: An empirical examination of the legislative preference for oversight. *Congress & the Presidency*, *40*(1), 27–40. doi:10.1080/07343469.2012.748853.

Bates, S., Goodwin, M., and McKay, S. (2017). Do UK MPs engage more with select committees since the Wright reforms? An interrupted time series analysis, 1979–2016. *Parliamentary Affairs*, *70*(4), 780–800. doi:10.1093/pa/gsx007.

Bates, S. R., Kerr, P., Byrne, C., and Stanley, L. (2014). Questions to the Prime Minister: A comparative study of PMQs from Thatcher to Cameron. *Parliamentary Affairs*, *67*(2), 253–80. doi:10.1093/pa/gss044.

BBC News (2014a, 27 March). Fit-to-work tests: Atos contract to end. *BBC News*. Retrieved 26 June 2019 from www.bbc.co.uk/news/uk-26766345

BBC News (2014b, 8 December). Tory MP apologises for playing Candy Crush during committee. *BBC News*. Retrieved 26 June 2019 from www.bbc.co.uk/news/uk-politics-30375609

BBC News (2018, 21 November). 'I can't forgive Tories' – John McDonnell. *BBC News*. Retrieved 26 June 2019 from www.bbc.com/news/av/uk-politics-46296769/john-mcdonnell-i-can-t-forgive-tories

Bell, S. (2011). 'Do we really need a new "constructivist institutionalism" to explain institutional change?' *British Journal of Political Science*, *41*(4), 883–906. doi:10.1017/S0007123411000147.

Bennett, O. (2017, 23 August). Amber Rudd to be hauled before MPs after Home Office wrongly threatens to deport EU nationals. *Huffington Post*. Retrieved 26 June 2019 from www.huffingtonpost.co.uk/entry/eu-nationals-deport-amber-rudd_uk_599da0c6e4b0d97c4000a263

Benton, M., and Russell, M. (2013). Assessing the impact of parliamentary oversight committees: The select committees in the British House of Commons. *Parliamentary Affairs*, *66*(4), 772–97. doi:10.1093/pa/gss009.

Bercow, J. (2010, September). Speech to the Centre for Parliamentary Studies. Retrieved 26 June 2019 from www.parliament.uk/business/commons/the-speaker/speeches/speeches/speech-to-the-centre-for-parliamentary-studies/

Bercow, J. (2015, March). *A House Rebuilt? Progress, Governance and an Agenda Towards 2020*. Speech to the Hansard Society, London.

Besly, N., Goldsmith, T., Rogers, R., and Walters, R. (2018). *How Parliament Works* (8th edition). London: Routledge.

Bevan, S., and John, P. (2016). Policy representation by party leaders and followers: What drives UK Prime Minister's Questions? *Government and Opposition*, *51*(1), 59–83. doi:10.1017/gov.2015.16.

Bevir, M. (1999). *The Logic of the History of Ideas*. Cambridge: Cambridge University Press.

Bevir, M. (2006). 'How narratives explain'. In D. Yanow and P. Schwartz-Seah (Eds), *Interpretation and Method: Empirical Research Methods and the Interpretive Turn* (pp. 281–90). Armonk, NY: M. E. Sharpe.

Bevir, M. (2010). *Democratic Governance*. Princeton, NJ: Princeton University Press.

Bevir, M., and Blakely, J. (2018). *Interpretive Social Science: An Anti-naturalist Approach*. Oxford: Oxford University Press.

Bevir, M., and Rhodes, R. A. W. (2003). *Interpreting British Governance*. London: Routledge.

Bevir, M., and Rhodes, R. A. W. (2006). *Governance Stories*. London: Routledge.

Bevir, M., and Rhodes, R. A. W. (2008). Authors' response: Politics as cultural practice. *Political Studies Review*, *6*(2), 170–7. doi:10.1111/j.1478–9302.2008.00150.x.

Bevir, M., and Rhodes, R. A. W. (2010). *The State as Cultural Practice*. Oxford: Oxford University Press.

Bevir, M., and Rhodes, R. A. W. (2012). Interpretivism and the analysis of traditions and practices. *Critical Policy Studies*, *6*(2), 201–8. doi:10.1080/19460171.2012.689739.

Bevir, M., and Rhodes, R. A. W. (Eds) (2016). *Routledge Handbook of Interpretive Political Science*. London: Routledge.

Blomgren, M., and Rozenberg, O. (Eds) (2012). *Parliamentary Roles in Modern Legislatures*. London: Routledge.

Boaz, A., Davies, H., Fraser, A., and Nutley, S. (Eds) (2019). *What Works Now? Evidence Informed Policy and Practice*. Bristol: Bristol University Press.

Bochel, H., and Berthier, A. (2018). *Committee Witnesses: Gender and Representation* (No. SB 18–16). Edinburgh: Scottish Parliament Information Centre.

Bochel, P. H., Defty, D. A., and Kirkpatrick, J. (2014). *Watching the Watchers: Parliament and the Intelligence Services*. Basingstoke: Palgrave Macmillan.

Boswell, C. (2008). The political functions of expert knowledge: Knowledge and legitimation in European Union immigration policy. *Journal of European Public Policy, 15*(4), 471–88. doi:10.1080/13501760801996634.

Boswell, C. (2018). *Manufacturing Political Trust: Targets and Performance Measurement in Public Policy*. Cambridge: Cambridge University Press.

Boswell, J., Corbett, J., Dommett, K., Jennings, W., Flinders, M., Rhodes, R. A. W., and Wood, M. (2018). State of the field: What can political ethnography tell us about anti-politics and democratic disaffection?. *European Journal of Political Research*. doi:10.1111/1475–6765.12270.

Bovens, M. (2010). Two concepts of accountability: Accountability as a virtue and as a mechanism. *West European Politics, 33*(5), 946–67. doi:10.1080/01402382.2010.486119.

Brazier, A., and Fox, R. (2011). Reviewing select committee tasks and modes of operation. *Parliamentary Affairs, 64*(2), 354–69. doi:10.1093/pa/gsr007.

Brichzin, J., Krichewsky, D., Ringel, L., and Schank, J. (Eds) (2018). *Soziologie der Parlamente: Neue Wege der politischen Institutionforschung*. Wiesbaden: Springer VS.

Bull, P. (2003). *The Microanalysis of Political Communication: Claptrap and Ambiguity*. London: Routledge.

Bury, R. (2016, 11 March). Sports Direct's Mike Ashley hits out at 'antagonistic' MPs. *The Daily Telegraph*. Retrieved 26 June 2019 from www.telegraph.co.uk/business/2016/03/11/sports-directs-mike-ashley-hits-out-at-antagonistic-mps/

Cabinet Office (2015). *Ministerial Code*. London: HM Government.

Cairney, P. (2015). *The Politics of Evidence-Based Policy Making*. London: Palgrave Pivot.

Campbell, R., and Lovenduski, J. (2015). What should MPs do? Public and parliamentarians' views compared. *Parliamentary Affairs, 68*(4), 690–708. doi:10.1093/pa/gsu020.

Childs, S. (2004). A feminised style of politics? Women MPs in the House of Commons. *The British Journal of Politics & International Relations, 6*(1), 3–19. doi:10.1111/j.1467–856X.2004.00124.x.

Childs, S. (2014). Negotiating gendered institutions: Women's parliamentary friendships at Westminster. In S. M. Rai and R. Johnson (Eds), *Democracy in Practice: Ceremony and Ritual in Parliament*. Basingstoke: Palgrave Macmillan.

Childs, S. (2016). *The Good Parliament*. Bristol: University of Bristol.

Clarke, N., Jennings, W., Moss, J., and Stoker, G. (2018). *The Good Politician: Folk Theories, Political Interaction, and the Rise of Anti-Politics*. Cambridge: Cambridge University Press.

Coates, S. (2014, 18 August). Bercow's choice of Australian clerk 'is an embarrassment to the Queen'. *The Times*. Retrieved 26 June 2019 from www.thetimes.co.uk/article/bercows-choice-of-australian-clerk-is-an-embarrassment-to-the-queen-h72fgc587vv

Coghill, K., Holland, P., Donohue, R., Rozzoli, K., and Grant, G. (2008). Professional development programmes for Members of Parliament. *Parliamentary Affairs*, *61*(1), 73–98. doi:10.1093/pa/gsm051.

Coghill, K., Lewis, C., and Steinack, K. (2012). How should elected members learn parliamentary skills: An overview. *Parliamentary Affairs*, *65*(3), 505–19. doi:10.1093/pa/gss031.

Cooper, Y. (2018, November 21). Retrieved 26 June 2019 from https://twitter.com/YvetteCooperMP/status/1065298208304373760

Cowley, P. (2002). *Revolts and Rebellions: Parliamentary Voting Under Blair.* London: Politico's Publishing Ltd.

Cowley, P. (2005). *The Rebels: How Blair Mislaid His Majority.* London: Politico's Publishing Ltd.

Cox, L. (2018). *The Bullying and Harassment of House of Commons Staff: Independent Inquiry Report.* London: House of Commons.

Crang, M., and Cook, I. (2007). *Doing Ethnographies.* London: Sage Publications.

Crewe, E. (2005). *Lords of Parliament: Manners, Rituals and Politics.* Manchester: Manchester University Press.

Crewe, E. (2015). *The House of Commons: An Anthropology of MPs at Work.* London: Bloomsbury Academic.

Crewe, E. (2017a). Ethnography of Parliament: Finding culture and politics entangled in the Commons and the Lords. *Parliamentary Affairs*, *70*(1), 155–72. doi:10.1093/pa/gsw012.

Crewe, E. (2017b). Magi or Mandarins? Contemporary clerkly culture. In P. Evans (Ed.), *Essays on the History of Parliamentary Procedure: In Honour of Thomas Erskine May* (pp. 45–65). Oxford: Hart Publishing.

Crewe, E. (2017c). Reading the runes: Conflict, culture and "evidence" in law-making in the UK. *Redescription: Political Thought, Conceptual History and Feminist Theory*, *20*(1), 32–48. doi:0.7227/R.20.1.3.

Crewe, E., and Müller, M. G. (Eds) (2006). *Rituals in Parliaments: Political, Anthropological, and Historical Perspectives on Europe and the United States.* Frankfurt am Main: Peter Lang Publishing.

Crick, B. (1965). The prospects for parliamentary reform. *The Political Quarterly*, *36*(3), 333–46. doi:10.1111/j.1467–923X.1965.tb01110.x.

Crick, B. (1968). *The Reform of Parliament* (2nd edition). London: Weidenfeld and Nicholson.

Cumbo, J. (2017, 23 August). MPs probe university sector's £12.6bn pensions deficit. *Financial Times*. Retrieved 26 June 2019 from www.ft.com/content/de32c5f0-865f-11e7-8bb1-5ba57d47eff7

D'Arcy, M. (2011, 28 July). Time to salute the post-2010 election Parliament. *BBC News*. Retrieved 26 June 2019 from www.bbc.com/news/uk-politics-14330865

Davies, P. W. (1992, 9 July). Tories oust critic as chairman of health committee. *The Independent*, p. 2.

Davies, R. (2016, 2 May). Select committee chief lashes out at Sir Philip Green over BHS sale. *The Guardian*. Retrieved 26 June 2019 from www.theguardian.com/business/2016/may/02/iain-wright-mp-attacks-sir-philip-green-bhs-sale

Department for Chamber and Committee Services (2015). *Guide for Select Committee Members*. London: HMSO.

Dickinson, N. (2018). Advice giving and party loyalty: An informational model for the socialisation process of new British MPs. *Parliamentary Affairs*, 71(2), 343–64. doi:10.1093/pa/gsx035.

Donmar Warehouse. (2017, June). COMMITTEE… (A NEW MUSICAL). Retrieved 26 June 2019 from www.donmarwarehouse.com/production/196/committee/

Drewry, G. (Ed.) (1985). *The New Select Committees: A Study of the 1979 Reforms*. Oxford: Clarendon Press.

Dunleavy, P., and Muir, D. (2013, 18 July). Parliament bounces back – how select committees have become a power in the land. *Democratic Audit UK*. Retrieved 26 June 2019 from www.democraticaudit.com/?p=1106

Durose, C. (2009). Front-line workers and 'local knowledge': Neighbourhood stories in contemporary UK local governance. *Public Administration*, 87(1), 35–49. doi:10.1111/j.1467–9299.2008.01737.x.

Ercan, S. A., and Gagnon, J.-P. (2014). The crisis of democracy: Which crisis? Which democracy? *Democratic Theory*, 1(2), 1–10. doi:10.3167/dt.2014.010201.

European Commission (2018). *Standard Barometer 89* (Eurobarometer). Brussels: European Commission.

Executive Committee (2016). *Director General's Review: The Final Report*. London: HMSO.

Fetterman, D. M. (2010). *Ethnography: Step-by-Step* (3rd edition). London: Sage Publications.

Finlayson, A. (2007). From beliefs to arguments: Interpretive methodology and rhetorical political analysis. *The British Journal of Politics & International Relations*, 9(4), 545–63. doi:10.1111/j.1467–856X.2007.00269.x.

Finlayson, A., and Martin, J. (2008). 'It ain't what you say…': British political studies and the analysis of speech and rhetoric. *British Politics*, 3(4), 445–64. https://doi.org/10.1057/bp. 2008.21

Fisher, L. (2015). The Growing Power and Autonomy of House of Commons Select Committees: Causes and Effects. *The Political Quarterly*, 86(3), 419–426. doi:10.1111/1467–923X.12190.

Fitzgerald, S. (2015). *Spectators in the Field of Politics*. Basingstoke: Palgrave Macmillan.

Flinders, M. (2002). Shifting the balance? Parliament, the executive and the British constitution. *Political Studies*, 50(1), 23–42. doi:10.1111/1467–9248.00357

Flinders, M. (2004). MPs and icebergs: Parliament and delegated governance. *Parliamentary Affairs*, 57(4), 767–84. doi:10.1093/pa/gsh060.

Flinders, M. (2007). Analysing reform: The House of Commons, 2001–5. *Political Studies*, 55(1), 174–200. doi:10.1111/j.1467–9248.2007.00648.x.

Flinders, M. (2008). *Delegated Governance and the British State: Walking without Order*. Oxford: Oxford University Press.

Flinders, M. (2009). Constitutional anomie: Patterns of democracy and 'the governance of Britain'. *Government and Opposition*, 44(4), 385–411. doi:10.1111/j.1477–7053.2009.01294.x.

Flinders, M. (2012). The demonisation of politicians: Moral panics, folk devils and MPs' expenses. *Contemporary Politics*, 18(1), 1–17. doi:10.1080/13569775.2012.651263.

Flinders, M., Cotter, L.-M., Kelso, A., and Meakin, A. (2017). The politics of parliamentary restoration and renewal: Decisions, discretion, democracy. *Parliamentary Affairs.* doi:10.1093/pa/gsx012.

Flinders, M., and Kelso, A. (2011). Mind the gap: Political analysis, public expectations and the parliamentary decline thesis. *The British Journal of Politics & International Relations, 13*(2), 249–68. doi:10.1111/j.1467–856X.2010.00434.x.

Flinders, M., Weinberg, A., Weinberg, J., Geddes, M., and Kwiatkowski, R. (2018). Governing under pressure? The mental wellbeing of politicians. *Parliamentary Affairs.* doi:10.1093/pa/gsy046.

Flynn, P. (2012). *How To Be An MP.* London: Biteback.

Foa, R. S., and Mounk, Y. (2016). The danger of deconsolidation: The democratic disconnect. *Journal of Democracy, 27*(3), 5–17. doi:10.1353/jod.2016.0049.

Foster, D. H. (2015). Going 'where angels fear to tread': How effective was the Backbench Business Committee in the 2010–2012 parliamentary session? *Parliamentary Affairs, 68*(1), 116–34. doi:10.1093/pa/gst008.

Freeman, R., and Maybin, J. (2011). Documents, practices and policy. *Evidence & Policy, 7*(2), 155–70. doi:10.1332/174426411X579207.

Friedberg, C. (2011). From a top-down to a bottom-up approach to legislative oversight. *The Journal of Legislative Studies, 17*(4), 525–44. doi:10.1080/13572334.2011.617554.

Gains, F. (2009). Narratives and dilemmas of local bureaucratic elites: Whitehall at the coal face? *Public Administration, 87*(1), 50–64. doi:10.1111/j.1467–9299.2008.01741.x.

Gamble, A. (1990). Theories of British politics. *Political Studies, 38*(3), 404–20. doi:10.1111/j.1467–9248.1990.tb01078.x.

Gay, O. (2005). MPs go back to their constituencies. *The Political Quarterly, 76*(1), 57–66. doi:10.1111/j.1467–923X.2005.00656.x.

Gay, O. (2017). Slumber and success: The House of Commons Library after May. In P. Evans (Ed.), *Essays on the History of Parliamentary Procedure: In Honour of Thomas Erskine May* (pp. 33–43). Oxford: Hart Publishing.

Geddes, M. (2018a). Committee hearings of the UK Parliament: Who gives evidence and does this matter? *Parliamentary Affairs, 71*(2), 283–304. doi:10.1093/pa/gsx026.

Geddes, M. (2018b). The explanatory potential of "dilemmas": Bridging practices and power to understand political change in interpretive political science. *Political Studies Review, 17*(3), 239–54. doi:10.1177/1478929918795342.

Geddes, M., Dommett, K., and Prosser, B. (2018). A recipe for impact? Exploring knowledge requirements in the UK Parliament and beyond. *Evidence & Policy, 14*(2), 259–76. doi:10.1332/174426417X14945838375115.

Geddes, M., and Meakin, A. (2018). *Explaining Change in Parliaments: Dilemmas of Managerial Reform in the UK House of Commons.* Presented at the Political Studies Association Annual Conference, Cardiff, 26–28 March.

Geddes, M., and Rhodes, R. A. W. (2018). Towards an interpretive parliamentary studies. In J. Brichzin, D. Krichewsky, L. Ringel, and J. Schank (Eds), *The Sociology of Parliaments.* Wiesbaden: Springer VS.

Glynos, J., and Howarth, D. (2008). Structure, agency and power in political analysis: Beyond contextualised self-interpretations. *Political Studies Review, 6*(2), 155–69. doi:10.1111/j.1478–9302.2008.00149.x.

Goffman, E. (1990). *The Presentation of Self in Everyday Life* (new edition). London: Penguin.

Goodwin, M. (2015). Political science? Does scientific training predict UK MPs voting behaviour? *Parliamentary Affairs*, *68*(2), 371–92. doi:10.1093/pa/gst011.

Goodwin, M., Bates, S., and McKay, S. (2019). Electing to do women's work? Gendered divisions of labour in UK select committees, 1979–2016. Under review.

Gordon, R., and Street, A. (2012). *Select Committees and Coercive Powers: Clarity or Confusion?* London: The Constitution Society.

Graham, G. (2014, 5 May). Stop delaying publishing the Chilcot inquiry, says Cameron. *The Daily Telegraph*, p. 6.

Gray, J. (2015, 3 November). What is an MP for? Retrieved 26 June 2019 from www.politicshome.com/news/uk/social-affairs/politics/house/60356/james-gray-what-mp

Griffiths, S., and Leach, R. (2018). *British Politics* (3rd edition). Basingstoke: Palgrave Macmillan.

Grube, D. (2014). Administrative learning or political blaming? Public servants, parliamentary committees and the drama of public accountability. *Australian Journal of Political Science*, *49*(2), 221–36. doi:10.1080/10361146.2014.880402.

Gusterson, H. (1995). Exploding anthropology's canon in the world of the bomb: Ethnographic writing on militarism. In R. Hertz and J. B. Imber (Eds), *Studying Elites Using Qualitative Methods* (pp. 187–205). London: Sage Publications.

Hagelund, C., and Goddard, J. (2015). *How to Run a Country: A Parliament of Lawmakers*. London: REFORM.

Hajer, M. (2009). *Authoritative Governance: Policy Making in the Age of Mediatization*. Oxford: Oxford University Press.

Hall, M. (2011). *Political Traditions and UK Politics*. Basingstoke: Palgrave Macmillan.

Hansard Society (2000). *Commission on the Scrutiny Role of Parliament*. London: Hansard Society.

Hansard Society (2001). *The Challenge for Parliament: Making Government Accountable*. London: Hansard Society.

Hansard Society (2017). *Audit of Political Engagement 14: The 2017 Report*. London: Hansard Society.

Hardman, I. (2018). *Why We Get the Wrong Politicians*. London: Atlantic Books.

Hawes, D. (1992). Parliamentary select committees: Some case studies in contingent influence. *Policy & Politics*, *20*(3), 227–36. doi:10.1332/030557392782718715.

Hawes, D. (1993). *Power on the Back Benches? The Growth of Select Committee Influence*. Bristol: SAUS Publications.

Hay, C. (2002). *Political Analysis: A Critical Introduction*. Basingstoke: Palgrave Macmillan.

Hay, C. (Ed.) (2010). *New Directions in Political Science*. Basingstoke: Palgrave Macmillan.

Hazarika, A., and Hamilton, T. (2018). *Punch and Judy Politics: An Insiders' Guide to Prime Minister's Questions*. London: Biteback Publishing.

Hazell, R., Chalmers, M., and Russell, M. (2012). Pre-appointment scrutiny hearings in the British House of Commons: All bark, or some bite? *The Journal of Legislative Studies*, *18*(2), 222–41. doi:10.1080/13572334.2012.673066.

Heurtin, J.-P. (2003). The circle of discussion and the semicircle of criticism. In B. Latour and P. Weibel (Eds), *Making Things Public: Atmospheres of Democracy* (pp. 754–79). Cambridge, MA: MIT Press.

Hindmoor, A., Larkin, P., and Kennon, A. (2009). Assessing the influence of select committees in the UK: The Education and Skills Committee, 1997–2005. *The Journal of Legislative Studies*, *15*(1), 71–89. doi:10.1080/13572330802666844.

House of Commons Business, Innovation and Skills Committee (2013). *Women in the Workplace* (No. HC 342). London: HMSO.

House of Commons Commission (2016). *38th Report of the Commission* (No. HC 788). London: HMSO.

House of Commons Commission (2018). *Annual Report and Accounts 2017–18* (No. HC 1381). London: House of Commons.

House of Commons Culture, Media and Sport Committee (2012). *News International and Phone-hacking* (No. HC 903-I). London: HMSO.

House of Commons Digital, Culture, Media and Sport Committee (2018). *Oral Evidence: Disinformation and 'Fake News'* (Oral Evidence No. HC 363). London: HMSO.

House of Commons Digital, Culture, Media and Sport Committee (2019). *Disinformation and 'Fake News': Final Report* (Eighth Report of Session 2017–19 No. HC 1791). London: HMSO.

House of Commons Governance Committee (2014a). *House of Commons Governance* (Report of Session 2014–15 No. HC 692). London: HMSO.

House of Commons Governance Committee (2014b). *Oral Evidence: House of Commons Governance, 02 Dec 2014* (No. HC 692). London: HMSO.

House of Commons Health and Social Care and Housing, Communities and Local Government Committees (2018). *Long-term funding of adult social care* (No. HC 768). London: HMSO.

House of Commons Liaison Committee (1985). *The Select Committee System* (First Report of Session 1984–85 No. HC 363). London: HMSO.

House of Commons Liaison Committee (2000a). *Independence or Control? The Government's Reply to the Committee's First Report of Session 1999–2000* (Second Report of Session 1999–2000 No. HC 748). London: HMSO.

House of Commons Liaison Committee (2000b). *Shifting the Balance: Select Committees and the Executive* (First Report of Session 1999–2000 No. HC 300). London: HMSO.

House of Commons Liaison Committee (2012a). *Select Committee Effectiveness, Resources and Powers* (Second Report of Session 2012–13 No. HC 697). London: HMSO.

House of Commons Liaison Committee (2012b). *Select Committee Effectiveness, Resources and Powers: Volume II, Additional Written Evidence* (Second Report of Session 2012–13 No. HC 697). London: HMSO.

House of Commons Liaison Committee (2015). *Building Public Engagement: Options for Developing Select Committee Outreach* (First Special Report of Session 2015–16 No. HC 470). London: HMSO.

House of Commons Liaison Committee (2018a). *Changing Committee Practice and Procedure: Enhancing Effective Working* (No. HC 922). London: HMSO.

House of Commons Liaison Committee (2018b). *Witness Gender Diversity* (Second Report of Session 2017–19 No. HC 1033). London: HMSO.

House of Commons Management Board (2014). *Corporate Business Plan 2014/15 to 2016/17*. London: HMSO.

House of Commons Political and Constitutional Reform Committee (2013). *Revisiting Rebuilding the House: The Impact of the Wright Reforms* (Third Report of Session 2013–14 No. HC 82). London: HMSO.

House of Commons Procedure Committee (1965). *Fourth Report from the Select Committee on Procedure* (Fourth Report of Session 1964–65 No. HC 303). London: HMSO.

House of Commons Procedure Committee (1978). *First Report from the Select Committee on Procedure* (First Report of Session 1977–78 No. HC 588). London: HMSO.

House of Commons Public Accounts Committee (2011). *HM Revenue and Customs 2010–11 Accounts: tax disputes* (Sixty-First Report of Session 2010–12 No. HC 1531). London: HMSO.

House of Commons Public Accounts Committee (2013). *Tax Avoidance-Google* (No. HC 112). London: HMSO.

House of Commons Public Administration Select Committee (2014a). *Oral Evidence: Accountability of Quangos and Public Bodies* (Oral Evidence No. HC 110). London: HMSO.

House of Commons Public Administration Select Committee (2014b). *Oral Evidence: Civil Service Impartiality and Referendums* (Oral Evidence No. HC 111). London: HMSO.

House of Commons Reform Committee (2009). *Rebuilding the House* (First Report of Session 2008–09 No. HC 1117). London: HMSO.

House of Commons Transport Committee (2012). *Future Programme: Autumn and Winter 2012–13* (No. HC 591). London: HMSO.

House of Commons Work and Pensions Committee (2012). *Universal Credit Implementation: Meeting the Needs of Vulnerable Claimants* (No. HC 576). London: HMSO.

House of Commons Work and Pensions Committee (2014a). *Employment and Support Allowance and Work Capability Assessments* (First Report of Session 2014–15 No. HC 302). London: HMSO.

House of Commons Work and Pensions Committee (2014b). *Oral Evidence: Employment and Support Allowance and Work Capability Assessments* (Oral Evidence No. HC 302). London: HMSO.

House of Commons Work and Pensions Committee (2018). *Universal Credit: childcare* (No. HC 1771). London: HMSO.

House of Commons Work and Pensions Committee and Business, Innovation and Skills Committee (2016). *Oral Evidence: The Pension Protection Fund and Pensions Regulator* (No. HC 55). London: HMSO.

House of Commons Work and Pensions Committee, and House of Commons Business, Innovation and Skills Committee (2016). *BHS* (First Report of Session 2016 (WPC) and Fourth Report of Session 2016–17 (BIS) No. HC 54). London: HMSO.

Hunter, A. (1995). Local knowledge and local power: Notes on the ethnography of local community elite. In R. Hertz and J. B. Imber (Eds), *Studying Elites Using Qualitative Methods* (pp. 151–170). London: Sage Publications.

Hutton, M. (2017). Where did it all go right? Developments in select committees, 1913–1960. In P. Evans (Ed.), *Essays on the History of Parliamentary Procedure: In Honour of Thomas Erskine May* (pp. 251–67). Oxford: Hart Publishing.

Independent Parliamentary Standards Authority (2019). MPs' pay and pensions. Retrieved 9 July 2019 from www.theipsa.org.uk/mp-costs/mps-pay-and-pensions/

Inglehart, R. F. (2016). How much should we worry? *Journal of Democracy, 27*(3), 18–23. doi:10.1353/jod.2016.0053.

International Institute for Democracy and Electoral Assistance (2016). *Voter Turnout Trends Around the World*. Stockholm: International Institute for Democracy and Electoral Assistance.

Ipsos MORI. (2018). *Ipsos MORI Veracity Index 2018*. London: Ipsos MORI.

James, D. V., Farnham, F. R., Sukhwal, S., Jones, K., Carlisle, J., and Henley, S. (2016). Aggressive/intrusive behaviours, harassment and stalking of members of the United Kingdom parliament: A prevalence study and cross-national comparison. *The Journal of Forensic Psychiatry & Psychology, 27*(2), 177–97. doi:10.1080/14789949.2015.1124908.

Jogerst, M. (1993). *Reform in the House of Commons: The Select Committee System*. Lexington, Kentucky: University Press of Kentucky.

Johnson, N. (1988). Departmental select committees. In M. Ryle and P. Richards (Eds), *The Commons Under Scrutiny* (pp. 157–85). London: Routledge.

Joint Committee on Parliamentary Privilege (2013). *Parliamentary Privilege* (No. HL Paper 30, HC 100). London: HMSO.

Judge, D. (1993). *The Parliamentary State*. London: Sage.

Judge, D. (2014). *Democratic Incongruities: Representative Democracy in Britain* (2014 edition). Basingstoke: Palgrave Macmillan.

Judge, D., and Leston-Bandeira, C. (2018). The institutional representation of Parliament. *Political Studies, 66*(1), 154–72. doi:10.1177/0032321717706901.

Jupp, P. (2006). *The Governing of Britain, 1688–1848: The Executive, Parliament and the People*. London: Routledge.

Kalitowski, S. (2009). Parliament for the people? Public knowledge, interest and perceptions of the Westminster Parliament. *Parliamentary Affairs, 62*(2), 350–63. doi:10.1093/pa/gsp001.

Kam, C. J. (2009). *Party Discipline and Parliamentary Politics*. Cambridge: Cambridge University Press.

Kellermann, M. (2014). Do oversight responsibilities encourage legislative specialization? Evidence from the British House of Commons. Presented at the Annual Meeting of the Midwest Political Science Association, Chicago, 26 June.

Kelso, A. (2003). 'Where were the massed ranks of parliamentary reformers?' 'Attitudinal' and 'contextual' approaches to parliamentary reform. *The Journal of Legislative Studies, 9*(1), 57–76. doi:10.1080/13523270300660004.

Kelso, A. (2009). *Parliamentary Reform at Westminster*. Manchester: Manchester University Press.

Kelso, A. (2016). Political leadership in Parliament: The role of select committee chairs in the UK House of Commons. *Politics and Governance, 4*(2), 115–26. doi:10.17645/pag.v4i2.573.

Kelso, A., Bennister, M., and Larkin, P. (2016). The shifting landscape of prime ministerial accountability to parliament: An analysis of Liaison Committee scrutiny sessions. *The British Journal of Politics and International Relations*, *18*(3), 740–54. doi:10.1177/1369148116633438.

Kenny, C., Rose, D., Hobbs, A., Tyler, C., and Blackstock, J. (2017). *The Role of Research in the UK Parliament: Vol. 1*. London: Parliamentary Office of Science and Technology.

Kidd, P. (2019, 16 January). Rebellion delivers biggest government defeat by a distance. *The Times*, p. 9.

King, A. (1974). *British Members of Parliament: A Self-portrait*. London: Macmillan.

King, A. (1976). Modes of executive-legislative relations: Great Britain, France, and West Germany. *Legislative Studies Quarterly*, *1*(1), 11–36. doi:10.2307/439626.

King, A., and Crewe, I. (2013). *The Blunders of Our Governments*. London: Oneworld Publications.

Korris, M. (2011). *A Year in the Life: From Member of Public to Member of Parliament*. London: Hansard Society.

Krook, M., and Mackay, F. (Eds). (2010). *Gender, Politics and Institutions: Towards a Feminist Institutionalism*. Basingstoke: Palgrave Macmillan.

Kubala, M. (2011). Select committees in the House of Commons and the media. *Parliamentary Affairs*, *64*(4), 694–713. doi:10.1093/pa/gsr014.

Kuhn, T. S. (2012). *The Structure of Scientific Revolutions: 50th Anniversary Edition*. Chicago: University of Chicago Press.

Latour, B. (1999). *Pandora's Hope: An Essay on the Reality of Science Studies*. Cambridge, MA: Harvard University Press.

Leston-Bandeira, C. (2012). Parliaments' endless pursuit of trust: Re-focusing on symbolic representation. *The Journal of Legislative Studies*, *18*(3–4), 514–26. doi:10.1080/13572334.2012.706059.

Leston-Bandeira, C. (Ed.) (2013). *Parliaments and Citizens*. London: Routledge.

Leston-Bandeira, C. (2016). Why symbolic representation frames parliamentary public engagement. *The British Journal of Politics and International Relations*, *18*(2), 498–516. doi:10.1177/1369148115615029.

Lewis, J. M., O'Flynn, J., and Sullivan, H. (2014). Accountability: To whom, in relation to what, and why? *Australian Journal of Public Administration*, *73*(4), 401–7. doi:10.1111/1467–8500.12104.

Lijphart, A. (2012). *Patterns of Democracy: Government Forms and Performance in Thirty-six Countries* (2nd revised edition). New Haven: Yale University Press.

Lilleker, D. G. (2003). Interviewing the political elite: Navigating a potential minefield. *Politics*, *23*(3), 207–14. doi:10.1111/1467–9256.00198.

Loewenberg, G. (2011). *On Legislatures: The Puzzle of Representation*. London: Paradigm Publishers.

Longino, H. E. (1990). *Science as Social Knowledge: Values and Objectivity in Scientific Inquiry*. Princeton, NJ: Princeton University Press.

Lovenduski, J. (2014). Prime Minister's Questions as political ritual at Westminster. In S. M. Rai and R. Johnson (Eds), *Democracy in Practice: Ceremony and Ritual in Parliament* (pp. 132–62). Basingstoke: Palgrave Macmillan.

Mair, P. (2013). *Ruling the Void: The Hollowing Out of Western Democracy*. London: Verso Books.

March, J. G., and Olsen, J. P. (1984). The new institutionalism: Organizational factors in political life. *The American Political Science Review*, *78*(3), 734–49. doi:10.2307/1961840.

Matthews, F., and Flinders, M. (2015). The watchdogs of 'Washminster' – parliamentary scrutiny of executive patronage in the UK. *Commonwealth & Comparative Politics*, *53*(2), 153–76. doi:10.1080/14662043.2015.1013295.

Mattson, I., and Strøm, K. (1995). Parliamentary committees. In H. Döring (Ed.), *Parliaments and Majority Rule in Western Europe* (pp. 249–307). Frankfurt: Campus Verlag.

McAnulla, S. (2006). Challenging the new interpretivist approach: Towards a critical realist alternative. *British Politics*, *1*(1), 113–38. doi:10.1057/palgrave.bp. 4200013.

McCubbins, M., and Schwartz, T. (1984). Congressional oversight overlooked: Police patrols versus fire alarms. *American Journal of Political Science*, *28*(1), 165–79. doi:10.2307/2110792.

McTernan, J. (2016, July 25). Parliament's fury at Philip Green is just grandstanding from powerless MPs. *The Telegraph*. Retrieved 26 June 2019 from www.telegraph.co.uk/news/2016/07/25/so-what-if-mps-are-furious-with-philip-green-theres-nothing-they/

Meakin, A. (2019). *Understanding Parliamentary Governance: Using the Multiple Streams Framework and Historical Institutionalism to analyse the Restoration and Renewal of the Palace of Westminster*. Presented at the Political Studies Association International Annual Conference, Nottingham, 10–12 April.

Mellows-Facer, A., and Shaw, C. (2017, 5 June). Lessons for new select committees from the BHS inquiry. *Hansard Society*. Retrieved 26 June 2019 from www.hansardsociety. org.uk/blog/lessons-for-new-select-committees-from-the-bhs-inquiry

Mezey, M. L. (1979). *Comparative Legislatures*. Durham, NC: Duke University Press.

Miller, J., and Glassner, B. (2004). The 'inside' and the 'outside': Finding realities in interviews. In D. Silverman (Ed.), *Qualitative Research: Theory, Method and Practice* (2nd revised edition). London: Sage Publications.

Moeran, B. (2009). From participant observation to observant participation. In S. Ybema, D. Yanow, H. Wels, and F. Kamsteeg (Eds), *Organizational Ethnography: Studying the Complexities of Everyday Life* (pp. 139–55). London: Sage Publications.

Monk, D. (2010). A framework for evaluating the performance of committees in Westminster parliaments. *The Journal of Legislative Studies*, *16*(1), 1–13. doi:10.1080/13572330903541904.

Moran, M. (2017). *Politics and Governance in the UK* (3rd edition). Basingstoke: Palgrave Macmillan.

Morris, Z. S. (2009). The truth about interviewing elites. *Politics*, *29*(3), 209–17. doi:10.1111/j.1467–9256.2009.01357.x.

Mouffe, C. (2005). *The Return of the Political*. London: Verso Books.

Mulholland, G. (2014, 26 June). Mulholland demands apology from NHS England over their attempts to thwart accountability over bungled children's heart review decisions. Retrieved 26 June 2019 from http://gregmulholland.org/en/article/2014/0857930/mulholland-demands-apology-from-nhs-england-over-their-attempts-to-thwart-accountability-over-bungled-children-s-heart-review-decisions

Natzler, D. (2017). *Powers and Select Committees: The Extent and Enforcement of the Powers of the House in Relation to Select Committees and Contempts*. London: House of Commons Committee of Privileges. Retrieved 26 June 2019 from http://data.parliament.uk/writtenevidence/committeeevidence.svc/evidencedocument/committee-of-privileges/select-committees-and-contempts/written/79204.pdf

Norris, P. (1997). The puzzle of constituency service. *The Journal of Legislative Studies*, *3*(2), 29–49. doi:10.1080/13572339708420508.

Norton, P. (1998). Nascent institutionalisation: Committees in the British Parliament. In L. D. Longley and R. H. Davidson (Eds), *The New Roles of Parliamentary Committees* (pp. 143–62). London: Frank Cass.

Norton, P. (2000). Reforming Parliament in the United Kingdom: The report of the commission to strengthen parliament. *The Journal of Legislative Studies*, *6*(3), 1–14. doi:10.1080/13572330008420628.

Norton, P. (2001). Playing by the rules: The constraining hand of parliamentary procedure. *The Journal of Legislative Studies*, *7*(3), 13–33. doi:10.1080/714003882.

Norton, P. (2017). Speaking for Parliament. *Parliamentary Affairs*, *70*(2), 191–206. doi:10.1093/pa/gsw031.

Norton, P. (2018). Power behind the scenes: The importance of informal space in legislatures. *Parliamentary Affairs*, *72*(2), 245–66. doi:10.1093/pa/gsy018.

O'Brien, D. Z. (2012). Gender and select committee elections in the British House of Commons. *Politics & Gender*, *8*(2), 178–204. doi:10.1017/S1743923X12000153.

Olsen, J. P. (2013). The institutional basis of democratic accountability. *West European Politics*, *36*(3), 447–73. doi:10.1080/01402382.2012.753704.

Pavey, H. (2017, 23 August). New Labour MP says she won't 'hang out' with 'enemy' female Tory MPs. Retrieved 26 June 2019 from www.standard.co.uk/news/uk/new-labour-mp-says-she-will-not-hang-out-with-female-tory-mps-because-they-are-the-enemy-a3618456.html

Peters, B. G. (2011). Institutionalism. In M. Flinders, A. Gamble, C. Hay, and M. Kenny (Eds), *The Oxford Handbook of British Politics* (pp. 57–74). Oxford: Oxford University Press.

Plunkett, J. (2013, 5 November). Paxman: Brand was right over public's disgust at 'tawdry pretences' of politics. *The Guardian*. Retrieved 26 June 2019 from www.theguardian.com/media/2013/nov/05/paxman-politics-russell-brand-voting

Polsby, N. (1975). Legislatures. In F. Greenstein and N. Polsby (Eds), *Handbook of Political Science* (Vol. 5). Reading: Addison-Wesley Press.

Power, G. (2007). The politics of parliamentary reform: Lessons from the House of Commons (2001–2005). *Parliamentary Affairs*, *60*(3), 492–509. doi:10.1093/pa/gsm029.

Puwar, N. (2004). *Space Invaders: Race, Gender and Bodies Out of Place*. Oxford: Berg Publishers.

Puwar, N. (2010). The archi-texture of Parliament: Flaneur as method in Westminster. *The Journal of Legislative Studies*, *16*(3), 298–312. doi:10.1080/13572334.2010.498099.

Rai, S. M. (2015). Political performance: A framework for analysing democratic politics. *Political Studies*, *63*(5), 1179–97. doi:10.1111/1467-9248.12154.

Rai, S. M., and Johnson, R. (Eds) (2014). *Democracy in Practice: Ceremony and Ritual in Parliament* (2014 edition). Basingstoke: Palgrave Macmillan.

Rai, S. M., and Reinelt, J. (Eds) (2015). *The Grammar of Politics and Performance*. London: Routledge.

Rai, S. M., and Spary, C. (2019). *Performing Representation: Women Members in the Indian Parliament*. Oxford: Oxford University Press.

Rhodes, R. A. W. (2011). *Everyday Life in British Government*. Oxford: Oxford University Press.

Rhodes, R. A. W. (2013). From prime-ministerial leadership to court politics. In P. Strangio, P. 't Hart, and J. Walter (Eds), *Understanding Prime-Ministerial Performance: Comparative Perspectives* (pp. 318–31). Oxford: Oxford University Press.

Rhodes, R. A. W., 't Hart, P., and Noordegraaf, M. (2007a). Being there. In R. A. W. Rhodes, P. 't Hart, and M. Noordegraaf (Eds), *Observing Government Elites: Up Close and Personal* (pp. 1–17). Basingstoke: Palgrave Macmillan.

Rhodes, R. A. W., 't Hart, P., and Noordegraaf, M. (2007b). So what? The benefits and pitfalls of being there. In R. A. W. Rhodes, P. 't Hart, and M. Noordegraaf (Eds), *Observing Government Elites: Up Close and Personal* (pp. 206–33). Basingstoke: Palgrave Macmillan.

Rhodes, R. A. W., and Tiernan, A. (2013). *From Core Executive to Court Politics: From a Bucket of Rice to a Bowl of Jelly*. Presented at the Political Studies Association International Annual Conference, Cardiff, UK.

Rhodes, R. A. W., and Tiernan, A. (2016). Court politics in a federal polity. *Australian Journal of Political Science, 51*(2), 338–54. doi:10.1080/10361146.2015.1127890.

Richards, P. (2017, July 12). Retrieved 26 June 2019 from https://twitter.com/Labourpaul/status/885091691249770496

Rumbul, R. (2016). Gender inequality in democratic participation: Examining oral evidence to the National Assembly for Wales. *Politics, 36*(1), 63–78. doi:10.1111/1467-9256.12101.

Rush, M. (2001). *The Role of the Member of Parliament Since 1868: From Gentlemen to Players*. Oxford: Oxford University Press.

Rush, M., and Giddings, P. (2011). *Parliamentary Socialisation: Learning the Ropes or Determining Behaviour?*. Basingstoke: Palgrave Macmillan.

Russel, D., Turnpenny, J., and Rayner, T. (2013). Reining in the executive? Delegation, evidence, and parliamentary influence on environmental public policy. *Environment and Planning C: Government and Policy, 31*(4), 619–32. doi:10.1068/c11330.

Russell, M. (2011). 'Never allow a crisis go to waste': The Wright Committee reforms to strengthen the House of Commons. *Parliamentary Affairs, 64*(4), 612–33. doi:10.1093/pa/gsr026.

Russell, M. (2013). *The Contemporary House of Lords: Westminster Bicameralism Revived*. Oxford: Oxford University Press.

Russell, M., and Gover, D. (2017). *Legislation at Westminster: Parliamentary Actors and Influence in the Making of British Law*. Oxford: Oxford University Press.

Ryle, M. (1965). Committees of the House of Commons. *The Political Quarterly, 36*(3), 295–308. doi:10.1111/j.1467-923X.1965.tb01107.x.

Ryle, M., and Richards, P. (Eds) (1988). *The Commons Under Scrutiny*. London: Routledge.

Ryle, M. T. (1981). The legislative staff of the British House of Commons. *Legislative Studies Quarterly, 6*(4), 497–519. doi:10.2307/439382.

Saalfeld, T. (2003). The United Kingdom: Still a single 'chain of command'? The hollowing out of the Westminster model. In K. Strøm, W. Müller, and T. Bergman

(Eds), *Delegation and Accountability in Parliamentary Democracies* (new edition, pp. 620–48). Oxford: Oxford University Press.

Schmauk, T. E. (1890). *The Voice in Speech and Song: A View of the Human Voice for Speakers and Singers and All Who Love the Arts of Speech and Song.* New York: John B. Alden.

Schmidt, V. A. (2008). Discursive institutionalism: The explanatory power of ideas and discourse. *Annual Review of Political Science, 11*(1), 303–26. doi:10.1146/annurev. polisci.11.060606.135342.

Schöne, H. (2010). *Alltag im Parlament.* Baden-Baden: Nomos.

Schöne, H. (2018). Makro – Mikro – Makro: Über Konjunkturen der Parlamentsforschung, den Beitrag der Soziologie und das Potenzial mikroanalytischer Perspektiven. In J. Brichzin, D. Krichewsky, L. Ringel, and J. Schank (Eds), *Soziologie der Parlamente: Neue Wege der politischen Institutionenforschung* (pp. 35–59). Wiesbaden: Springer VS.

Schonhardt-Bailey, C. (2017). Nonverbal contention and contempt in UK parliamentary oversight hearings on fiscal and monetary policy. *Politics and the Life Sciences, 36*(1), 27–46. doi:10.1017/pls.2017.7.

Scully, R., and Farrell, D. M. (2003). MEPs as representatives: Individual and institutional roles. *JCMS: Journal of Common Market Studies, 41*(2), 269–88. doi:10.1111/1468-5965.00422.

Searing, D. (1994). *Westminster's World: Understanding Political Roles.* Cambridge, MA: Harvard University Press.

Seldon, A. (1996). Elite interviews. In B. Brivati, J. Buxton, and A. Seldon (Eds.), *The Contemporary History Handbook.* Manchester: Manchester University Press.

Shipman, T. (2019a, 13 January). 'A very British coup' revealed: Commons plot to seize control from May. *The Sunday Times*, pp. 1, 2.

Shipman, T. (2019b, 20 January). Theresa May in Brexit meltdown. *The Sunday Times*. Retrieved 26 June 2019 from www.thetimes.co.uk/article/may-in-meltdown-h60z6nx8c

Smith, M. J. (2008). Re-centring British government: Beliefs, traditions and dilemmas in political science. *Political Studies Review, 6*(2), 143–54. doi:10.1111/j.1478–9302.2008.00148.x.

Strøm, K. (1997). Rules, reasons and routines: Legislative roles in parliamentary democracies. *The Journal of Legislative Studies, 3*(1), 155–74. doi:10.1080/13572339708420504.

Swinford, S. (2019, 9 January). How 'livid' John Bercow's unprecedented Brexit intervention paves way for constitutional crisis. *The Telegraph*. Retrieved 26 June 2019 from www.telegraph.co.uk/politics/2019/01/09/revealed-livid-john-bercow-overruled-commons-clerks-helped-hand/

Thompson, L. (2015a). Debunking the myths of bill committees in the British House of Commons. *Politics, 36*(1), 36–48. doi:10.1111/1467–9256.12094.

Thompson, L. (2015b). *Making British Law: Committees in Action.* Basingstoke: Palgrave Macmillan.

Tomkins, A. (2009). Constitutionalism. In M. Flinders, A. Gamble, and M. Kenny (Eds), *The Oxford Handbook of British Politics* (pp. 239–61). Oxford: Oxford University Press.

Treanor, J. (2017, 31 July). Nicky Morgan requests assessment of City's readiness for hard Brexit. *The Guardian*. Retrieved 26 June 2019 from www.theguardian.com/politics/2017/aug/01/nicky-morgan-assessment-citys-readiness-hard-brexit

Turner, P. V. (1982). *From Ritual to Theatre: The Human Seriousness of Play*. New York: PAJ Publications.

Turnpenny, J., Russel, D., and Rayner, T. (2012). The complexity of evidence for sustainable development policy: analysing the boundary work of the UK Parliamentary Environmental Audit Committee. *Transactions of the Institute of British Geographers*, *38*(4), 586–98. doi:10.1111/j.1475-5661.2012.00549.x.

Tyrie, A. (2015). *The Poodle Bites Back: Select Committees and the Revival of Parliament*. London: Centre for Policy Studies.

UK Parliament (2014, 13 May). Committee holds public meeting in Newcastle – news from Parliament. Retrieved 26 June 2019 from www.parliament.uk/business/committees/committees-a-z/commons-select/work-and-pensions-committee/news/public-meeting/

UK Parliament (2018, 12 November). Committee calls for ideas from the public – news from Parliament. Retrieved 26 June 2019 from www.parliament.uk/business/committees/committees-a-z/commons-select/science-and-technology-committee/news-parliament-2017/my-science-inquiry-launch-17–19/

VanHeerde-Hudson, J. (Ed.) (2014). *The Political Costs of the 2009 British MPs' Expenses Scandal*. Basingstoke: Palgrave Macmillan.

Vincent, D. (1999). *The Culture of Secrecy: Britain, 1832–1998*. Oxford: Oxford University Press.

Wagenaar, H. (2012). Dwellers on the threshold of practice: The interpretivism of Bevir and Rhodes. *Critical Policy Studies*, *6*(1), 85–99. doi:10.1080/19460171.2012.659890.

Walker, C. (2017, 12 July). Retrieved 26 June 2019 from https://twitter.com/_c_walker/status/885115841246900225

Walkland, S. (1960). The House of Commons and the estimates, 1960. *Parliamentary Affairs*, *13*, 477–88.

Walkland, S. (1976). The politics of parliamentary reform. *Parliamentary Affairs*, *29*(2), 190–200. doi:10.1093/pa.a054142.

Ward, I. (2004). *The English Constitution: Myth and Realities*. Oxford: Hart Publishing.

Weinberg, A. (2014). Should the job of national politician carry a government health warning? The impact of psychological strain on politicians. In *The Psychology of Politicians* (pp. 123–42). Cambridge: Cambridge University Press.

Weinberg, A. (2015). A longitudinal study of the impact of changes in the job and the expenses scandal on UK national politicians' experiences of work, stress and the home–work interface. *Parliamentary Affairs*, *68*(2), 248–71. doi:10.1093/pa/gst013.

Weinberg, A., and Cooper, C. (2003). Stress among national politicians elected to Parliament for the first time. *Stress and Health*, *19*(2), 111–17. doi:10.1002/smi.965.

Weinberg, J. (2018). *The Personal Side of Politics: A Study of Basic Human Values in the UK Parliament*. Doctoral Thesis, University of Sheffield, Sheffield.

White, H. (2015a). *Parliamentary Scrutiny of Government*. London: Institute for Government.

White, H. (2015b). *Select Committees Under Scrutiny: Case Studies from the 2010–15 Parliament*. London: Institute for Government.

White, H. (2015c). *Select Committees Under Scrutiny: The Impact of Parliamentary Committee Inquiries on Government*. London: Institute for Government.

White, H. (2016, 25 April). Select committees fill the scrutiny vacuum created by a divided opposition. *The Times*. Retrieved 26 June 2019 from www.thetimes.co.uk/redbox/topic/commons-conflict/select-committees-fill-the-scrutiny-vacuum-created-by-an-divided-opposition

Williams, O. (2018, 6 August). Meet the Tory backbencher taking on Mark Zuckerberg. Retrieved 26 June 2019 from www.newstatesman.com/science-tech/2018/08/meet-tory-backbencher-taking-mark-zuckerberg

Wintour, P. (2014, May 17). Cameron hopes Chilcot report will be out by end of the year. *The Guardian*, p. 8.

Wiseman, H. (1966). *Parliament and the Executive: An Analysis with Readings*. London: Routledge.

Wright, O. (2018, December 5). May to reveal full legal advice after vote of contempt. *The Times*, pp. 8, 9.

Wright, T. (2010). What are MPs for? *The Political Quarterly*, *81*(3), 298–308. doi:10.1111/j.1467–923X.2010.02100.x.

Yanow, D. (2004). Translating local knowledge at organizational peripheries. *British Journal of Management*, *15*(S1), S9–S25. doi:10.1111/j.1467–8551.2004.t01–1-00403.x.

Yong, B. (2018). The governance of Parliament. In A. Horne and G. Drewry (Eds), *Parliament and the Law* (2nd edition). Oxford: Hart Publishing.

Young Legal Aid Lawyers. (2012). *Nowhere Else to Turn: The Impact of Legal Aid Cuts on MPs' Ability to Help Their Constituents*. London: Young Legal Aid Lawyers.

Index

EU authorised representative for GPSR:
Easy Access System Europe, Mustamäe tee 50,
10621 Tallinn, Estonia
gpsr.requests@easproject.com

www.ingramcontent.com/pod-product-compliance
Lightning Source LLC
Chambersburg PA
CBHW052007270326
41929CB00015B/2828